BY JOHN SANFORD

NOVELS AND OTHER FICTION

The Water Wheel (1933)
The Old Man's Place (1935)
Seventy Times Seven (1939)
The People from Heaven (1943)
A Man Without Shoes (1951, 1982)
The Land That Touches Mine (1953)
Every Island Fled Away (1964)
The $300 Man (1967)
Adirondack Stories (1976)

INTERPRETATIONS OF AMERICAN HISTORY

A More Goodly Country (1975)
View from This Wilderness (1977)
To Feed Their Hopes (1980)
The Winters of That Country (1984)

LETTERS

William Carlos Williams/John Sanford: A Correspondence (1984)

AUTOBIOGRAPHY

The Color of the Air: Scenes from the Life of an American Jew,
    Volume 1 (1985)
The Waters of Darkness: Scenes from the Life of an American Jew,
    Volume 2 (1986)
A Very Good Land to Fall With: Scenes from the Life of an American
    Jew, Volume 3 (1987)
A Walk in the Fire: Scenes from the Life of an American Jew, Volume 4
    (1989)
The Season, It Was Winter: Scenes from the Life of an American Jew,
    Volume 5 (forthcoming)

JOHN SANFORD

A WALK IN THE FIRE

SCENES FROM THE LIFE OF AN AMERICAN JEW

VOLUME 4

BLACK SPARROW PRESS ■ SANTA ROSA ■ 1989

LIBRARY OF CONGRESS CATALOGING IN PUBLICATION DATA

Sanford, John B., 1904-
    A walk in the fire / John Sanford.
        p.   cm. — (Scenes from the life of an American Jew ; v. 4)
    ISBN 0-87685-758-6. — ISBN 0-87685-757-8 (pbk.) — ISBN
0-87685-759-4 (cloth signed)
    1. Sanford, John B., 1904-   —Biography. 2. Novelists,
American—20th century—Biography.   3. Jews—United States—Social
life and customs. I. Title. II. Series: Sanford, John B., 1904-
Scenes from the life of an American Jew ; v. 4.
PS3537.A694Z464   1985   vol. 4
813'.52 s—dc19
[813'.52]   89-847
[B]   CIP

to her father and mother
Henry Albert and Decky Wells Smith
for my beloved Maggie

A NOTE ON THE INSERTS

Each of the three preceding volumes of this Autobiography has contained excerpts from the author's commentaries on American history; the same practice has been followed in this volume. Here as there, the pieces are meant to convey a sense of the political climate in which the central character lives — "the color of the air."

J. S.

Contents

A Walk in the Fire:
Scenes from the Life of an American Jew
Volume 4

SCENE 1

GODS OF ANOTHER OLYMPUS (Summer of 1945)

> *They were very great indeed.*
> —a physicist at Los Alamos, N. Mex.

The air is purer at seven thousand feet,
rarer, and you see more clearly there,
    a longer way,
and if you're one of the great,
you see further than the far sierra
    of the Sangre de Cristos:
you see into the space beyond them,
where the mountains of the mind are ranged—
    and these, please remember,
were very great indeed.

    True, they didn't look like much, that oddly-dressed handful standing on
those steps in rising rows: they might've been a photograph grown older on
a wall, a ball-team, a class with thinning hair or none at all. But whatever
their appearance, however queer they may have seemed in their get-up of a
younger year, they could boast of this—they could compel the very clouds,
they could make the atom give up the ghost.

    The chairs they held were ivy-wound, their heads were crowned with laurel.
They knew all that was known of the composition of substances and their
transformations, and they knew as well the phenomena of the inorganic world,
the most fundamental of these motion, which embraced the fields of heat and
light, of sound and radiation, and therefore of the structure of matter—and
they had the equation for even more ($E = mc^2$, a wildhaired Jew had found);
they had the key to the ultimate door.

They throve there at that altitude
amid the scrub oak and the piñon
    near the timber-line.
They knew no shortness of breath,
nor did their skin turn blue
for want of oxygen in the blood.
Au contraire, they functioned perfectly
in the rarefied air of the mesa,
and being there to make a thingamaree,

a toy to kill with, so they did,
giving it this name:
    Little Boy.

It promised to be just the ticket for the place they took it to, a desert called
the Journey of Death, a *bolson,* which is to say a sink of white sand and gyp-
sum twenty miles wide and a hundred long, and in a dry lake at the bottom,
they rigged a tower with their *Kinderspiel* and blew the jimcrank up. The
blast was heard in Albuquerque half the state away, and it was seen there
too—seen!—by a blind girl, who cried *What was that?* No one replied: she
was never told

that the light inside her head
had been generated by an explosion
that freed gas and heat at high speed
and with godalmighty force;
none of those great ones ever said
that what she'd seen without sight
was bright too on Mars and Venus;
        they never informed her
of the bizarre behavior of animals,
crazed horses, speechless birds,
dogs that shivered as if freezing
though mercury stood at 100°;
they never described to her
the quarter-mile crater in the sand,
she was never given to understand
that, white once, it was green now,
a quarter-mile bowl of emerald glass.

The great were otherwise engaged. They were snake-dancing through the
alleys and streets of their camp, they were singing, cheering, slapping backs,
they were seeing and saying what none would ever remember, and some were
smoking who'd never smoked before—and then they shook more hands, or
the same ones twice, and they sang and spoke to vacant rooms and waltzed
alone as if they were paired. But for *What was that?*, they had no replies as,
under the sky's new hues, they made their way (in protective shoes) to where
a heap of ash lay in a green glass bowl.

And now the camera shows them again, posed as before in the same or
similar misfit clothes—but this time they stand in vitrified sand and stare at
a few skeins of steel that protrude from the desert floor. And long, until the
print fades away, will they stay where they are, beside those remains, and
you'll not know, for none will say, what thoughts his mind contains. Had

anyone heard what the blind girl said, and was he saying it himself in his
head—or are they all, as they gaze at the fused green sand, thinking of the
glaze they mean to put on Japan . . . ?

Are they thinking of the new sun
due to rise for the little yellow people,
the one that, inscribed with dirty jokes,
would explode over Dr. Shima's hospital
and vaporize all life in its kill-radius
                of a mile,
none, though, with a smile
at the killing humor
of the scribbled ribaldry?

> Mr. Hashimoto, who was at
> the Itsukaishi station four
> miles away from the city,
> said *I saw a huge cloud,*
> *and on both sides beauti-*
> *ful smaller clouds spread*
> *out like a golden screen.*

And are they thinking of other beauties
that awaited his arrival:
the charred streetcars and their cargoes
of charcoal passengers;
the River Motoyasu and its bridges
of rigid bodies,
                like pontoons;
of shadows burned into concrete
and kimono patterns printed on skin
                by the heat?

> *I have never seen anything*
> *so magnificent,* Mr. Hashi-
> moto said.

Or were they thinking of the long silence
that would follow the shatteration,
the stillness of the all-around world,
where there were soundless screams,
                where birds were mute,
or they sang and no one heard them?

That beautiful cloud! Mr.
Hashimoto said. *Its beauty
defies description.*

Thinking, were they, of the dead-squid stink
of the stunned and dazzled survivors,
their clothes burnt into their bodies,
their ears and noses cooked away,
their flesh hanging like loose wallpaper,
their teeth melted, and the fillings too,
thinking of Mrs. Kaneko, who,

> digging in the ruins for
> her son, found bones that
> were still steaming and
> knew they were his because
> among them lay his belt-
> buckle?

The great among their own ruins,
were they thinking of these coming things,
were they who could see so clearly
back to the bang at the Beginning
seeing three weeks hence to the End,
seeing not the lovely clouds of Mr. Hashimoto,

> *clear-cut in the clear blue
> sky,* he said, *and neither
> red nor yellow,*

but this,
the blood in uterine discharges,
the blood in piss and spit
and (by some) in sixty shits a day?
They who could see so far,
could they see the near three weeks away?
Could they see the clouds
that Mr. Hashimoto missed,
the flies that would hatch
in a hundred thousand broiled lives,
and finally, could they guess
what the bombardier would say
when the shock waves hit the *Enola Gay:*

> *The sons-of-bitches are
> shooting at us!*

SCENE 2

LITTLE BOY BLUES (August 1945)

"What made you pick me?" you said.
And he said, "I read *The People From Heaven*."

You'd seen him often, at parties, at meetings, at Musso & Frank's—Tom English, his name was—but you couldn't recall that you'd ever spoken to him beyond a hail-fellow on your way to speak to someone else. He was a composer, and he ran mostly with his kind, but you were acquainted with his work, which you admired, and whenever you heard it, the word *troubadour* came to mind. It was one your mother had used, and with it came her pretty image of the strolling singer of the Middle Ages. Now, though, you knew what lay behind it: if not the verray parfit knight of old, he lived at least in gentil fashion, and if castle halls had never known him, his music from without reached within the walls—and its theme was Revolution.

English was a strange one to be bent on overturning the order. His pillared home bespoke barracoons; he wore pince-nez ribboned to his hand-sewn lapel; and his coat-sleeves unbuttoned at the cuff as for a show of lace and lawn. And yet he wrote no gavottes or minuets, no tunes for the assignation and the hunt: his songs were of the ill-used and the outworn and the no-spikka peoples, the poor devils that the rich devils passed by. He was a strange one, that English, and never stranger than when he proposed an association—you to write the lyrics and he the music for a work to be based on the atomic bomb.

"*The People From Heaven*?" you said. "Our Downtown friends didn't think that book—how did they put it?—*came off*."
"What did they object to?" English said.
"They claim it calls for an impossible revolution." *Revolution*, you thought. "But that's what *you* do."
"That's what led me to you."
"I'm answered. Count me in."
"I like to work from a title—it keeps the aim in mind. What do you think of *Hell On Earth*?"
And you said, "What do you think of *Little Boy Blues* . . . ?"

§

19

You never asked and you were never told how he managed to arrange a meeting with three physicists from the University of California, one of them known to you by name and the other two not. All you've retained of the encounter is a single impression, a frame of film caught by the shutter of your mind. Dimly you see a room somewhere and brightly the one face you recognize, as if it alone were in full light, but no sound-track comes with it, and it does not speak.

But from wherever it was that you met with those three, you remember coming away with a feeling of fear, as if you were a child again and had gone too near the hidden force, the forbidden room. It may have been their fear too that you took along, though you understood nothing of what they'd done to the world you'd known—they'd shown it the end! You couldn't, therefore, share in the White Sands excitement of listening to the time-signals—*minus twenty minutes ... minus fifteen*—you couldn't, when the count reached *minus forty-five seconds*, forget to breathe. . . .

and then they opened the door, and the brightest, the most blinding light was seen, as though the sun had risen only six miles away, and with that dawn came a flood of sound that drowned the world, and a cloud evolving from the fire to a height of forty thousand feet, a great bouquet in gorgeous hues

§

"What did English want to see you about?" Maggie said.

"He has an idea that's a natural," you said. "A song, a cantata, a blues— about the atomic bomb."

"It *is* a good idea, but where do you fit in?"

"I'm to write the lyrics."

"Doesn't he usually do that himself?"

"He read *The People From Heaven*, he said, and it caught his eye."

"It caught mine. *Which do you choose, we said, Heaven or hell?*"

"Every now and then, you come out with one of my lines. What do you do—memorize them?"

"Not that I'm aware of. They just stay in mind."

"That's a high compliment."

"I'm complimenting myself. I knew you could write from *The Water Wheel* on. I was years ahead of Tom English."

"It would be a fine thing, a song about the bomb."

"How was it left?"

"I told him I was his man."

"Good," Maggie said.

§

Your desk faced a window that gave on a neighbor's lemon grove. The small and orderly trees, the blossoms in season, the fruit that hung like ornaments, all these drew the eye, and in the converging rows, in those outside distances, you'd sometimes find what you'd been seeking in your mind. But on the day you began to work on the lyrics for *Little Boy Blues,* you found nothing in the room or out of it that you could use to your purpose—conveying what happened a few hundred feet above a name on a map of Japan.

Japan, you thought, but when you tried to call up what you knew of it, all that came was illustration—pictures of people, things, places as alien now as they'd always been, an album of the strange. You were not even sure of the country's shape: a curving reef, you thought it, a thousand miles long and somewhere east of Asia. How, then, were you to write of what fell from the sky that day, how tell of the great bird that flew in from Tinian to drop its great exploding turd on—what was it called?—Hiroshima?

In the HAR to HUR volume of your Encyclopedia, only a paragraph was given to the city, but in its sixteen lines lay all you'd need for your lyrics. It was on a plain, you read, near the southern end of Honshu, and it was hemmed in by hills from which there was a view of the bay and Itaku-Shima, known to all of Japan as the Isle of Light. A shrined and sacred site, it was, and none dwelt there save the priests who tended the temple of the goddesses of the sea. Between the isle and the city, there rose from the waters of the bay a red torii, and upon it perched the fowls that sang to the deities at the break of day. . . .

daybreak came that morning with the Enola Gay, *and it was such a dawn as those priests and fowls had never seen—nor did any who saw it see again, for they were stricken blind as by the light of a stupendous rising sun. It lit the isle as none had done before, and in days to come, there would be sorrow for those priests, who so venerated the place that they would not till its soil, and there would be mourning for the fowls, whose very song was ash, and the goddesses, who would not have wished to outlive the wrong*

Little Boy Blues, you thought. . . .

§

Telephoning to ask for a conference, English named a meeting-place that was neither a restaurant nor a streetcorner, and neither his home nor yours: his choice for the encounter was the part of Griffith Park where a few old-style railway cars and locomotives were maintained for exhibition. The relics, as brightly painted as the day they'd left the shops, had been transported from the Southern Pacific yards to a short section of track buffered at either end. Waiting for English to arrive, you stood beside the drive-wheels of a freight engine, and you tried to put yourself back to its heyday on the road, but it was dead iron now, rolling-stock that would roll no more. . . .

"This country ought to have more songs about its railroads," English was saying.

He too was gazing at the engine, taking in its tall stack and its small drivers. Otherwise proportional, it seemed to have been stunted, and you found yourself thinking of Lautrec.

"We have ballads about lumberjacks and cowboys," English said, "and we have jailhouse songs and hobo songs and sailor songs, but except for 'John Henry' . . . Was there ever a real John Henry, do you think?"

"Was there ever a real Achilles?" you said. "It doesn't matter. It's the Homers that count."

He indicated the silvered connecting-rods, the sandbox, the steam dome, saying, "This is a Consolidation, a 2-8-0—four sets of drivers and a pair of wheels for the front truck. Every type of engine gets its name from the wheel-arrangement."

"I've ridden in the cabs, Tom. I bummed across the country once."

And he said, "A man named Ed Doty came to see me yesterday."

"The Malibu commissar."

"What do you think of him?"

"Oh, I can stay in the same room with him—if it's well-ventilated."

"He doesn't like you either."

"He doesn't like any writers later than Beaumont and Fletcher."

"He said he'd heard we were working together."

"And . . . ?"

"He said you weren't the best choice for the job."

Standing uncoupled behind the Consolidation was a passenger car with wooden siding. Its open ends, overhung by the roof, wore scowls that were fixed on another century.

"Did he?" you said.

"According to him, you're hard to get along with."

"Everyone is. But what's the rest of it?"

"In his opinion, you're not good enough."

"What about *your* opinion?"

"I didn't agree with him."

"That should've ended it."

"Should've, maybe," English said. "But he let the air out of the thing. All of a sudden, it went flat."

"No harm done, Tom," you said. "I'll write about the bomb some other day,* and nobody will interfere. But keep this in mind: as long as there are socialists like Ed Doty, capitalism is safe."

§

"All your life," Maggie said, "you've expected too much of people."

"The Dotys are full of spite—I know that. But why doesn't a good cause make them better?"

"Maybe people can't be better. Maybe they'll always be what they are."

"If that's true, we landed on a damn poor planet. We've improved everything on it but ourselves. We can fly now, but we're still the same sons-of-bitches that once had gills."

"You say you know people now, but tomorrow you'll make the same mistakes you made today. The world you put your trust in isn't here."

"Where is it, then?" you said. "If we can *think* a good one, why can't we make it?"

"Because we're dealing with a very low order of animal. . . ."

§

A few days later. when you heard Maggie's car in the driveway, you went out of doors to greet her.

"The people you go with," she said. "My people call them trash."

And you said, "That's a hello with cold teeth."

"He came to my office today. What gall!"

"Who came?"

"That Ed Doty."

"What the hell did he want?"

"He's on the lot, writing a film for Sam Zimbalist, and in he bounces big as life and twice as natural, and he says, 'Maggie dear, why do the Dotys see so little of the Sanfords?' "

"And what did Mrs. Sanford say?"

"I said, 'Don't sit down, Ed. Don't even let go of the doorknob. Just think of this as you go: You're trash!' "

"You've never used that word."

" 'You're trash!' I said, and away he went."

---

* And you did, but not until 1975.

SCENE 3

NIGHT-FLIGHT TO A FUNERAL (August 1945)

Your Uncle Harris had died on a Thursday morning, and orthodox custom required that he be buried before sundown on the morrow, when the Sabbath would begin. Your father, unable to make the journey to New York, had asked you to take his place (*Julian,* he'd said, *no better man than Harris ever lived*), and to honor him as well as the dead, you'd done his bidding.

It was nearly dusk when your plane took off, and within moments the light-mass of the City of the Angels had shattered, into clusters at first, and then to lone gleams that were merely imperfections in the dark, and finally to starless space that ended fifteen thousand feet below. In a come-and-go of thoughts, one was dominant, that you were the prisoner of *g,* and more than once you wondered how long you'd take to fall three miles at 32 feet per second per second. You'd never flown before, and your mind turned to such things.

At times, though, it fixed on travel's end, on the man your father esteemed, a brother-in-law in fact but prized even more than a brother of the blood. He'd married your father's sister Sarah half a century before, and time had not diminished him, nor death (*no better man, Julian, no better ever lived*). Looking out at your reflection, you were also looking in at yourself, and you remembered how you used to observe your uncle, trying to light on the qualities you might have missed, and you remembered too that for long you could make out nothing behind his inexpressive, his unimpassioned face: a house with drawn blinds, you'd think, and the word *cold* would come to mind. There'd be a day, though, when the blinds would be raised—and they'd be your own, not his—and you'd see what your father had always seen, a purity of nature that time did not impair, as if it were proof against the wear and tear of age.

You thought back to a call you'd paid him at a hospital, where he'd undergone surgery. For some days, it'd been touch and go, but one afternoon, when visiting was at last permitted, you'd looked in on him during the course of a walk. What you'd intended was a family courtesy, that and no more, and your stay had been brief (had you stood, you wondered, or taken a seat?), and with you as you went away was your name as he'd spoken it—*Julan,* he'd said, instead of *Julian*—and you've never been certain whether that wasn't why you returned on another day, and soon again on another—

and not merely for a moment hat in hand at the bedside, but for hours, hours on end, as if you couldn't get enough of him.

How he'd talked those hours away! You'd never have known him, he said, no, nor would your *treue* Aunt Sarah or your *grossartig* father, were it not for a rare and fateful circumstance, and the circumstance was this. Having performed certain labors for a merchant in an outlying village, he'd come home to Kovno, the possessor, to the wonderment of all, of a Gladstone bag. To his own wonderment also, it may be remarked, for he'd let the merchant's daughter (*ach, Julan, eine Schöne!*) beguile him into accepting the Gladstone bag (as good as new) in lieu of rouble wages. Now, a Gladstone bag, he said, was of as little use to him as an iron anchor, for he had no intention of traveling, yet travel he must or reveal his shame — and to keep hidden the *Schande* of being gulled by a girl, he could only pack the Gladstone bag and take ship for the American States, a *Klage* on Columbus!*

And there'd been more, and it poured from him during your calls, now made daily, and always he seemed to be awaiting your arrival, as if you'd been chosen to hear his elegy. But what did he mourn?, you wondered — his lot had fallen in pleasant places — or was it only the flight of time he lamented, the clock that never stopped? Listening as if in a spell to the tale of his life, you failed to realize that it was being told in a language you'd never before heard, in artless rhythms and phrasing, so simple, you thought, that you could reproduce it at will. You were wrong, alas: some of the narrative was recoverable, but the naive poetry never. . . .

And now, turning again to the window, you saw a few crisscross lines of light that petered out in blackness, and someone said Amarillo. . . .

§

At your uncle's funeral, you did as you thought your father would've done: you sat with the widow through the chapel services, you rode at her side to Queens, and you gave her your arm for the walk from the car to the grave. At seventy-five, she'd worn life thin, and for what little was left, she seemed now to care not at all. As the casket was lowered, she let it go without a tear, as though it were her own that she was watching in the year to come, or the next but one.

The cemetery, called Bayside, was an extension of the older Acacia, and there, within sight from where you stood, was a plot surrounded by a

---

* The story is told in its entirety in *A More Goodly Country*, 1975.

cast-iron fence. A few yards long and a few yards wide, and representing the only permanent settlement your family had made in America, it was held in mortmain by your grandparents Sinai and Rachel Shapiro, by an unnamed still-born, and by a stranger to the line, your mother, buried there in the summer of 1914. Only one other time had you set foot on that ground, at the unveiling of her headstone in the following year, when someone told you to place a pebble on the plinth in token of a rite that no one explained.

As you gazed from one grave-site to the other, your mind replayed a scene that thirty years had rung down on. You saw a pile of fill-dirt, sand-tan and lifeless, covered in part by a mat of green raffia, and around it in black stood a circle of the bereaved, among them you, and you saw, from here at Bayside and there at Acacia, a pine box descend from view, and then you heard shovels scrape and shovelfuls fall, resonant at first and then with no sound at all. The worst moment came when you made a move to help the workmen, when you sought to join in the game, but your father stopped you, brought you back, and the crowd, you remember, wept. . . .

Your uncle's funeral was over, and your Aunt Sarah was saying, "Come, Julian. Take me now to see my father and mother, *zelig,* and your mother too."
You didn't want to go, but you went.

§

The manuscript of *A Man Without Shoes* had been sent on ahead of you to Henry Volkening, your agent, through whom it had reached editor John Woodburn at Harcourt Brace. Soon after your arrival in New York, you were summoned to his office.

He did not rise to greet you as you entered, nor did he offer you a hand. Instead, he flicked the thick binder lying before him, saying, "Tell me something. Just what the hell is this screed supposed to be?"
"You haven't asked me to sit," you said, and you sat.
Again he indicated the manuscript, and he said, "What is this — the latest version of the Manifesto?"
"It's a novel. Not the one I promised you. Not the one I started to write. But it's a novel, and don't ever think it ain't." You smiled at the use of your father-in-law's phrase.
"To me, it's 1073 pages calling for a revolution."
"Well, me and Tom Paine. . . ."
His gesture swept the window. "But for Christ's sake," he said, "there's no revolutionary situation out there!"
"There always is."

"You think so? Take a look at the street. All those people seem to be going about their business."

"Sure, because they don't know they're being plucked."

"And you're the lad to wise 'em up, is that it?"

"Somebody has to," you said. "And that's what I do in the book: it says the reason for the poor is the rich. Why should that make you sore?"

"It isn't true!"

"*I* think it is, and I have the right to say it."

"Without a doubt, but you can't say it here."

"Where's that free press I hear so much about?"

He slapped the manuscript, saying, "Why don't you ask these Reds you write about—Mig DeLuca, Tootsie Powell? They'll tell you where it is."

You drew the manuscript from under his hand, and rising with it, you gave him a half-salute.

He said, "I'm authorized to say we'll take the book if you get rid of the politics."

"By whom?"

"The editor-in-chief."

"Tell him I'll be thinking of him next time I wipe my ass."

As you turned to the door, he said, "You're making a mistake."

"Me and Paine," you said. "And all we want is to see things change."

And you let the door close behind you.

§

Henry Volkening's office was only a block or two distant, and you went there at once to report the break with Harcourt Brace.

He deplored it, saying, "There goes the best house in America."

"It can't be helped. Try the next best."

"I'll submit the book elsewhere, but for a writer like you—and writing like yours—not all doors are open. Very few houses will read it, let alone publish it."

"Are you saying what Woodburn said—that I ought to tone the book down?"

"Not at all. You aren't the only one who hates injustice, poverty, prejudice, but many of us don't pin the evils where you do. In that manuscript there, you make a big to-do, for instance, over the Sacco-Vanzetti case. Your main character, your Dan Johnson, is all wrapped up in it—*you're* all wrapped up in it—but the fact is, those two men were tried before a judge and convicted by a jury, and most of the world accepts the verdict.

"They were tried before a hangman and convicted by half-wits! Don't tell me *you* think they were guilty!"

"This isn't a quarrel between you and me. It's between you and the people who publish books. They're not bound to back what they don't believe in."

"That means I don't get published unless I accept what is! I piss on what is, because it isn't right!"

"Alexander Pope thought otherwise."

"I piss on Pope! What a creed the bastard had—God meant me to be rich and you poor!"

"You have dangerous thoughts," Volkening said. "In Japan once, they'd've arrested you for that."

"I've heard people say they had a good idea."

You left the manuscript with him. He'd try his best for you, he said, but he could promise nothing.

§

On your arrival in New York, you'd gone directly to your Aunt Sarah's apartment on Central Park West, and when you returned after the funeral, she refused to let you leave, insisting that you be her guest while you were in the city. During her husband's illness, she'd occupied the spare bedroom, and there she'd remained, assigning to you the one in which your uncle had died.

"That is, if it wouldn't upset you," she'd said. "You know, to be in such a place."

"It won't upset me."

"The bed, Julian. It's the one that—"

"I wish he was still alive. I'd be glad to sleep on the floor."

"And what would *I* not do?" she'd said.

While awaiting word from Volkening, you'd roamed streets you knew well among people who were strangers. Now and then you'd see a reminiscent face—had you seen it in some class, some courtroom, some concert hall?—but you were not impelled to stop and say *Aren't you Ormond Eberle?* or *Didn't you go to P.S. 10?* For a tick of time, you'd be living in the past (*Ormond is manly, and you're a kid*), and then the suggestive face would be gone with the crowd, and you'd be walking the other way.

It was with your aunt, though, that most of your stay was spent, and from a facing chair of green velour, you watched her sew, crochet, read, or simply sit and stare through a window. Others sometimes came, bringing tokens of sympathy, bread, ginger, home-made jelly, but you took little notice of them and less of their gifts: your eyes were almost always on your aunt. Regarding her, you recalled a saying, *Among the Jews, it is the old men who are beautiful.*

28

Rarely, you knew, was it a beauty of feature, the conformation of the head, say, or the tint and texture of the skin, or the space between the eyes: it was rather what the entire face expressed, the certainty of finding favor in the sight of Adonai.

But that and more emerged here, and you said, "Aunt Sarah, you're a beautiful old woman."

She looked up from her book, her needle, her crocheting hook, and she said, "And you, Julian, you're a *Schmeichler,*" and then she returned to whatever she held in her *goldene Hande,* saying, "Tell me about Philip my brother."

"He'll ask me about Sarah his sister."

"I love that man."

"This may surprise you, but I do too."

"What are you saying, surprise? A son loving a father, that's no surprise."

"I haven't been the best of sons."

"I know, but you changed."

"I did? How?"

"In regards to your father."

"You mean I provide for him. But you understand, of course, how I manage to do that?"

"Who does not understand? You tell *die ganze Welt.*"

"Why not? There's no shame in it."

"Not by me. By other people, a man could not take pride his wife supports him."

"In supporting me, my wife pays me the highest honor. It means she thinks I'm *worth* supporting. How could I fail to feel proud of that? Some men can make money; I can't. That doesn't make me hide my face. I can write, and Maggie thinks so too."

"And how is that writing going, Julian?"

"I saw my publisher the other day, and he isn't my publisher any more. I'm out in the street again."

"There was a quarrel?"

"A disagreement. He asked me to water the book down."

"And you refused, just like that?"

"I have to write what *I* want to write. If I write what *they* want, I'm nothing."

"And out in the street, you're something?" your aunt said. "My Harris, he used to say, 'Don't slam the door going out. Who knows? You might want to come back.' "

"Did I tell you this? You're a beautiful old woman."

§

29

Henry Volkening had chosen Reynal & Hitchcock as the publisher most likely to be receptive to *A Man Without Shoes*, and within a week, Frank Taylor, one of its editors, had read the extensive manuscript and proposed a meeting at the Algonquin. During a two-hour lunch, he made *most eloquent music,* but it was another man's book that gave rise to his song, and the man was Malcolm Lowry, of whom you'd never heard.

You can't recall having ordered food, nor can you say now whether you ate whatever it may have been. You do know, though, that you were being sung to of a prodigious drunkard who yet was composing a work as dark and dazzling as jet. In a stupor that rarely wore off, lurching about in a half-daze, puking himself, stumbling once into an open pit of shit, still, Taylor said, the swiller was making a book* that would long outlast his liver.

There was something in his own recital, you saw, that fascinated the editor, and in the all-around of dining-room sound, the chime of glassware, the sharps and flats of silver, you found that you were wondering what it was that cast the spell. Was there magic in the wild and wayward ones that the less conspicuous lacked? Were the decorous dull after all. . . ?

When your mind came back to the table, Taylor was still full of the Day of the Dead, of Yvonne the inconstant wife, of the horns on the head of the British consul, and you heard yourself say, "Why celebrate a bottle-sucker for falling into a sewer? Would he seem to be so laudable if you had to pull him out?"

"Sanford, I'm afraid you're a puritan."

"This squanderer of yours reminds me of a trick glass in a store-window. Water keeps pouring in, but the glass never fills."

"His drink, I believe, is whisky."

"I wonder if he'd be able to write if he swore off."

"You'll never know. He's going to drink and write till he kills himself."†

He gazed past you, so far past, it seemed, that he might've been seeing the people and places he'd been speaking of and hearing voices use their names.

"Taylor," you said, and you reached across the table to touch his sleeve. "You're in Mexico."

His vision took a moment to clear, and he said, "Cuernavaca, or, as Lowry calls it, Quauhnahuac," and then as if he'd never seen the crater of Popocatepetl two miles up from a mile-high valley, he said, "Why don't we talk about *A Man Without Shoes*?"

---

* *Under the Volcano,* 1947.

† In 1957, Lowry drowned in his own vomit.

"All I have is a question," you said. "Does Reynal & Hitchcock want the book?"

"I thought that was understood," he said. "Yes, we do."

"Then I have another question. Will it be published as it is?"

"As it is—after you've put your critical faculty to work on it. After you've become your own editor. After you've remedied what's out of place, wrong in itself, extraneous, distracting."

"I take it you think I'll find such things."

"Albert Erskine is reading the manuscript. We've both found such things."

"You have a right to know that Harcourt wouldn't stand for my slant on Sacco and Vanzetti."

And he said, "Reynal & Hitchcock will."

§

"What were you doing just now?" you said into the mouthpiece.

"Sitting in the sun with my feet on Juno."

"I have some good news."

"What? What?"

"Reynal took the book."

"Good? That's the *best* news!"

"I'll be leaving for home tomorrow."

"That's even better—but please don't fly."

"I'm taking the City of L.A."

"Want me to pick you up at San Berdoo?"

"Too far for you. Make it Union Station."

"I miss you, Jabe."

"Bring Juno. I miss Juno."

"I do not like you, Dr. Fell."

"Call the Governor. . . ."

THE COLOR OF THE AIR, I

Nathan Hale, 1755-1776

A MARTIAL AIR AT A HANGING

> *Your music is excellent.*
> —Major André, to his guards

John André, Esq.,
Major, Fifty-fourth Foot,
Royal Fusiliers
at Tappan, in New York state.

Sir:

To be addressed by a stranger at a time such as this will doubtless seem to you a most unwarrantable intrusion, bold, gross, cold even to the point of cruelty, wherefore I beg leave to say that erelong we shall meet face to face, on which occasion what satisfaction you may require I shall readily accord. For all that, sir, I venture to suggest that upon our thus coming together, you will demand no *amende honorable* for my conduct. Nay, rather will you have come to feel that in accosting you as you went toward extinction—in plucking your sleeve, if you will, on the road to the grave—I was chargeable only with a wish to pave your way. Would that as much had been done for me when, four years gone, I trod that road myself.

Ah, but yes, my dear Major, he who indites these lines to the rope's next victim was once its victim too. Small wonder, then, that at this juncture my mind should be drawn to you, but be assured, sir, that I hold you to be more than a mere gallows-bird, more than my fellow following four years behind. Since my hanging, many another has swung for a crime, but until now none I know of has paid for one so very like my own: you spied for your country, I spied for mine. I feel, therefore, that we stand, you and I, in a quite special relation, more apposite than opposed, more like than not, indeed, more the self-same thing.

Being there still, being still alive, you may doubt the comparison, deny the alliance, but I urge you to remember that I am *here,* where the sole denial is the denial of doubt: here there are only meanings; here, sir, we see what you fail to see, the conjunctions you are unaware of, the presences that have you by the hand. Thus, I say that if we differ at all, it is simply in the respect that we each served our own—you the King, and I—well, I another George. Beyond that, like our deaths, our lives lie very near.

We began neither in the glare of wealth nor the glow of purple: we sprang from less well-lit loins, a merchant's you, a yeoman's I. Our early learning came from pastors, our later from within the walls, mine Yale's, Geneva's yours, and even as my *amorosa* would have none of me (marvel not that I know these things), no more would your Honora, blue and blonde, honor you. To our like annals, add that final correspondence, our melancholy fate on the gibbet, and, A to izzard, what you have, dear sir, is the illusion realized: parallels that meet, or, rather, parallels due to meet within the hour.

I know that hour well: I have endured it. Mine ended at daybreak, when the Provost sent his men to fetch me from the gaol. Some say I was then borne away to a place in mid-Manhattan, near a tavern named The Dove, but no such journey can I recall, nor do I remember my hangman as a beast. He did not deny me a Bible, he did not destroy my last letters, curse me coarsely, taunt me as a traitor to the Crown. He merely hanged me, as General Howe had ordered, and then he lived on, as your topping-cove will do—and my General.

Soon you will join me here, and then that which is now dim will clear, the presences you now but feel will grow, and you will know them to be real: in an hour, sir, you will be admitted to the mysteries of the future and the past. I learned them four years ago, but you will not share their meaning for yet another hour. Alas, and I tell you this with rue, it was a sell, our dying as we did, you for England old and I for England new—a sell, sir, and we were sold.

I changed nothing when I danced the Tyburn jig for Captain Cunningham, nor will you for Colonel Scammel. Our real hangman is the world, and it will make its round of itself and the sun never knowing we are gone since it never knew we were there. The same sovereign, your George or mine, will rule it forever, and the same rag-tag will be forever ruled. We spied each of us for his own side, thinking there were two, but here we know the tristful truth: there really is but one. I entered the British lines to learn how their forces were disposed, and you conspired with Arnold for the betrayal of the Point, but had we both achieved our aims, neither the King nor the people would have feasted: the fruits are for the few.

Go, therefore, on your morning's walk from Tappan. Go arm in arm with your guards while fife and drum play you *Roslin Castle* and say, as I know you will, *Your music is excellent.* Go now a mile or so to the gallows—go, my friend, and we shall meet within the hour. . . .

SCENE 4

REAL PROPERTY (October 1945)

You'd ridden with Maggie as far as the gate, opened it for her car, and waved goodbye as she drove away. Turning back toward the house, you saw Juno sitting in the gravel at the head of the drive, but instead of joining her, as she seemed to expect, you wandered off into the walnut grove over a parquet made of sun and shade. Every aisle ended at a woven-wire fence, the border of your four-acre domain. Outside lay the rest of the world, all encroachment stayed by the reticulated links; within, a small estate running from hell below to the heavens above, yours from the core of the earth *usque ad caelum.*

You brushed against a branch, and leaves, ready to fall, fell. Stooping for a nut, you shucked its shriveled hull and fingered the shell—a skull, you thought, that held the halves of a walnut brain.

You'd retained little, you supposed, from your long-ago study of the law, and therefore it was as if from nowhere, like carbonation, that proprietary phrases rose through your mind—estates at sufferance, estates at will, estates *pour autre vie.* None of these, however, described the acres underfoot—a freehold in fee simple absolute.

Ahead of you, beneath the slats of a drying-tray, a Barred Rock and two Wyandottes were worrying the burnt discards of the walnut crop, and in a flurry over a found meat, they suddenly fled in three directions.

Often had you seen Maggie on her way, but that day, and for the first time, the gate proffered itself as more than a portal in a cyclone fence. It had become the symbol of Property, and in your right to open it for any and close it against all reposed the essence of dominium: there among those trees, your sway was unlimited in magnitude, eternal in duration.

Shed of their leaves, the two persimmon trees displayed ocher fruit that hung rather like frillery on the naked branches, and recalling the one time you'd tried them, you felt your mouth astringe.

But what did ownership mean to you, who lately had owned nothing? Only a few years since, you'd gone whole days on a dole from your father—a nickel for a towel at the Y.M.C.A., a dime for a dozen cigarettes. You'd stared at no menus in savory doorways then, nor at window-displays of foulards and hose; quite beyond your means the scarves, the shoes, the roasted chestnuts on an autumn afternoon. In all weathers, you walked to where you were going, and you did the same on coming back; you made do without the girl, the book, the tweed that caught your eye, and you dined on aroma while others ate the bird; and to mend tears and frays, you learned to sew, and you saved half-burnt snipes to smoke on flat-broke days.

In a small paddock near the four-stall barn stood the brood mare September Child, brought home in foal to the stallion Top Row. Her belly had begun to round out, and dozing in the sunlight, even so she chased flies with an occasional twitch of her hide.

Had you then, when all you owned was you, concerned yourself with other selves, with the insulted and injured, the poor, the put-upon, the more ill-used than you? Had you looked in on their crate-and-carton dwellings, had you seen the view through the cracks in the walls, had you tried their tin-can cuisine, their beds of rags and burlap bags stuffed with leaves? Or had they been beyond the range of your interest—outside your gate, would you say? Had only your own skinful distressed you, did you grieve for no other, was none your brother, O beggarly Jew?

The mare heard you wading through the brash beneath the trees, and when you reached her paddock, she came slowly toward you, as though with conscious care. Staying quite still, with an arm resting on the topmost rail, you let her inhale your identity, after which she butted your fist for the sugar it contained.

Now, you thought, instead of having nothing, you lacked nothing—and yet, though dead to the world then, now you'd come alive. Why?, you wondered. Why, no longer in need yourself, were you aware of need round-about? Had owning freed you, had you at last taken on the color of the air. . . ?

At your feet sat Juno. While the mare nosed into the sugar hand, all the dog sought was the touch of the other.

SCENE 5

. . . OR THE LEOPARD HIS SPOTS? (November 1945)

"Several times lately," Maggie said, "I've caught you with a most unusual look on your face: you seemed to be thinking."

"That's bad," you said. "You should've stopped me."

"You were in deep."

"The truth is, I was asking myself a question I couldn't answer."

"Ask *me*."

"There was a time when fifteen cents had to see me through the day. It didn't trouble me then that others had less than I did—had nothing, in fact. But I'm troubled now, when I can lay hands on fifteen cents a minute."

"And what was the question?"

"How do I account for the difference?"

"Maybe there isn't any."

"I guess you weren't listening."

"What I mean is, maybe you were always—I hate the word—compassionate. Tender, my folks would say. Human."

"Where was my humanity before? I had no regard for others; I thought only of myself."

Maggie laughed. "That's the humanest thing that humans do."

"I want to know why I care about the hungry when my own shirt is full. I didn't give a damn for them when it wasn't. Why now? What happened? What changed things?"

"Having no money turned you in on yourself. Having it lets you expand."

"Like a rosebud blooming in one of those trick films," you said, and it was you now who laughed. You soon stopped, though, saying, "What am I laughing about? What's so funny about the turn I've taken? Two years ago, I started to write a book about a typical American named Daniel Johnson. I wound up with a Daniel Johnson who was onto more at twenty than the average American at seventy-five. He knew about the poor and the rich, and he knew what happened to those who tried to close the gap . . . How did that come about? At Dan's age, I knew nothing. Debs was a jailbird that my uncle supplied with cigars. John Brown was an old fanatic, a crazy-ike. And as for Sacco and Vanzetti, I never heard their names till the night they died in the Chair."

You rose and crossed the room, but having no purpose there, or none that you recalled, you returned to where you'd been.

"Is it possible that there's no such thing as the past?" you said "That whatever took place is still part of now? That once it came, it stayed and forever colored the air?"

"It's possible."

"And that sooner or later, it colored everyone who breathed it?"

"Is that what you think may have happened to you?"

"In my case, later—but, yes, maybe it did."

"It isn't much of an answer," Maggie said, "but it doesn't have to be. The question was the important thing. It showed that whatever you were once, you're—compassionate—now."

"Tender," you said. "I like what your folks call it."

SCENE 6

A SMELL OF SMOKE (November 1945)

For several weeks, Maggie's brother Dan had been troubled by a cough, and when it failed to respond to the usual remedies, the linctus and the lozenge of the pharmacy, she'd asked you to consult with the family physician. As a preliminary, he'd arranged for the taking of x-rays at the Cedars of Lebanon Hospital, and on the day fixed, you accompanied your brother-in-law to the Radiology Department. After a technician had summoned him from the waitingroom, you went out into the corridor to smoke a cigarette.

From behind you, someone said, "Give us a light."

You turned to find Gustave Holmgren, a doctor you'd become friendly with during the previous year. He was shaking a Fatima up out of its yellow package, and as you let him use your coal, you said, "Do they still make those things? You must be their only customer."

"What's *your* brand, comrade?"

"Chesterfields, the workers' choice."

"What're you doing in this place, Vladimir Ilyich?" he said.

"Maggie's brother is being x-rayed."

"For what?"

"A cough that's been hanging on."

"Does he smoke?"

"All the time. Three-four packs a day."

Holmgren dropped some ash into a sand-tub, but he said nothing.

"What do you suppose is wrong, Gus?"

"I'd be guessing. A local irritation, maybe—from the smoke. Chronic bronchitis. And of course, tuberculosis."

"Could it be anything else?"

"Yes."

"What?"

"You know, or you wouldn't be asking."

"Is there really a chance of that?"

He nodded, saying, "For all of us, not just for him."

Using your cigarette to indicate his, you said, "Knowing that, why do you do this?"

"I don't much care whether I live or die," he said, and he indicated your cigarette. "But why do you?"

You glanced away down the long converge of the hall. "I went to a funeral a few weeks ago," you said, "but death still seems a long way off."

"It's all around you, kid. It's never a long way off."
"Kid—that's what my father always calls me."

§

The x-ray report was unfavorable—a reading of the films had shown a shadow on one of the lungs. A biopsy was thereupon performed, and under microscopic examination, a piece of tissue from the affected lung confirmed the presence of carcinoma at the metastatic stage.

Conferring with the surgeon out of earshot from Dan, you said, "What can be done?"
"He can be kept out of pain, and that's about all, I'm afraid."
"No operation? Nothing?"
"If the tumor hadn't spread, the lung might've been removed. It's a new procedure, though, and his chances would've been poor."
"But as things are . . . ?" you said.
He completed your question by shaking his head.

§

How would you tell Maggie?, you wondered. Dan had been her favorite from the earliest days *and extra-special ever since a colt he was breaking tangled him up with the gyp-rope and drug him around the yard. It was six months before he could walk again, but he was left with a gimpy leg, and he himself was never the same either. To his mind, being half-crippled made him half a man, and after a while he only felt at home with animals—horses, dogs—maybe because they didn't know he limped and wouldn't ask what happened. These days he's happiest under a shed-row.*
And smoking a cigarette, you thought.
From the porch, you saw Maggie's car coming up the driveway toward the house.

SCENE 7

BLUES FOR *A MAN WITHOUT SHOES,* 1 (NOVEMBER 1945)

> I have seen this people, and behold,
> it is a stiffnecked people.
> —Exodus 32.9.

The contract for *A Man Without Shoes* had been signed at the offices of Reynal & Hitchcock in a room looking down on Bryant Park and the rear entrance to the Public Library. More than likely, all three of your editors were present at the ceremony, and doubtless each had something to say, but you can recall none of the faces, none of the words, and you seem to have taken away little but the sense that the book was acceptable as written. You may have understood that there'd be editorial comment on matters of form — an overuse of italics, perhaps, or your spelling of grey as *gray,* or your free and easy way with the colon and the dash, as though either could serve as the other. How galling, then, to be followed to California by a twelve-page screed demanding changes of substance!

If a letter accompanied the imperative, it exists no longer, and you can't say, therefore, whose book-fed heart had faltered; but since in one place or another the trio are identified by initials (*AE would cut this; HF disagrees; marked passages FT's*),[*] it must be supposed that three hearts misgave as one. However composed, though, nowise has time remitted the pain of such censure as *stilted dialectical muddle; section clogs narrative; contributes nothing,* and as hard to bear as ever are *hackneyed; wooden; impossibly pedantic.* The phrase *In the Way* appears often, tolling the knell of entire sections of the manuscript, one of them ninety pages long; but beyond all in harshness is the mandamus in Paragraph 1: *Bulk of book must be reduced by at least ½.*

The allegations — *forced; badly stated; scene appears in every proletarian novel* — read like counts in an indictment, and if true, they spelled out a crime, but it was one of which your accusers were as guilty as you. Having endorsed the book in the first place, they'd become your accomplices, and it was no extenuation that they forswore now half of what they'd approved before and blistered the half that remained. You'd never thought the book perfect.

---

[*] Albert Erskine, Harry Ford, Frank Taylor.

You knew well that weeds would show up with the grass, but you also knew that you'd find them and that what you'd have left was a lawn.

Had you written *A Man Without Shoes* when you were older, possibly it would've been a better novel; surely, though, it would've been a different one. Age might've enlightened you, and in enabling you to see where you hadn't seen before, it might've brightened the black lines, the lackluster pages — but would there not have been a price to pay, the loss of force and fire? Worse, might you not have done what others did, grown weary with time and begun to go with the stream?

As published,* *A Man Without Shoes* varies almost everywhere from the original manuscript. Fully two hundred pages have been deleted altogether, and of those that survive, few have escaped the blue pencil. The changes, however, are largely your own: the editors' tone had made you balk, and you gave ground grudgingly where you gave at all. In the margins of their list, *No* is scored against forty-two directives, sometimes backed by a screamer. Always you resisted their orders to expunge your *evocations of history,* as they chose to call your commentaries on the American past. With the writing of *The People From Heaven,* these had become part of your signature, like a musical phrase, and it was a mark of your style to intersperse the narrative with blank verse, say, on the Pilgrims, the Indians, the black-robed Jesuits, the runaway slaves. In *A Man Without Shoes,* the usage became broader: there, instead of illuminating the narrative, history became a part of it; there it was the climate in which your principal character grew, the color, so to speak, of the air. The removal of pieces on John Brown and Gene Debs, on the surrender at Appomattox and Paul Bunyan, was not to be endured, and you did not endure it, nor did you yield on the sequences dealing with Sacco and Vanzetti: They're all there yet.

What did you accede to, then?

Behold, it is a stiffnecked people.

SCENE 8

MISTY MORNING AT SANTA ANITA (DECEMBER 1945)

Standing near the half-mile pole, you watched your breath unravel in the atomized rain, a fine fall that glassed your clothing, the rail, the infield grass. The

---

* In 1951, after being rejected by Reynal & Hitchcock and thirty-three other publishers.

low-slung sky, almost within reach, erased the grandstand, the tops of trees, and all but the base of the San Gabriel range. Horses were being worked on the vaporous track, and long before they faded into view, you could hear them coming, their hoof-pound and exhalation, the *Ha!* of their riders, their jingling bits—and then a pair or a set, almost of vapor themselves, would pass and vanish, sending back the sounds of going away.

For the race-meeting soon to open, Maggie had only one runner, the two-year-old America Smith,* by Top Row out of September Child. In the absence of her brother, now in a nursing home, the colt was being handled by Lee Montgomery, a former exercise-boy, and today, preparing for his first start, the horse would be worked six furlongs. Somewhere in the blur across the track, with Montgomery up, he was nearing the pole from which he'd break. You'd driven to Arcadia that day to see the move, but you saw little more than what lay before you, a few yards of fence standing free in space. You listened, hearing only a dog-bark in the distance and nearer voices (those of clockers, you supposed) that also spoke no words.

Top Row, you found yourself thinking, *by Peanuts out of Too High—and you frowned at the ease with which such trifles came to mind. What had you to do with bloodlines, what did the Stud Book mean to you? And then, as though to measure your store of picayunes, you asked yourself the breeding of the sire, and at once a streamer of memory seemed to ripple by—Peanuts, by Ambassador IV out of Agnes Sard, she by Sardanaple.*

You thought of the thousand-page novel on your desk at home, all of it against the grain of the age. The main character was you as you wished you'd been, aware instead of walking in your sleep, doing instead of letting the Georges do it. It was an act of contrition, and so known to you, a token atonement for your ignorance and your emptiness of spirit on a night, eighteen years past, when two Italians you'd never before heard of were put to death in Massachusetts. You must've been less benighted, though, when the novel was completed: Sacco and Vanzetti imbue every page; they gauge the road you've come since the day they died.

And yet here you were, weighing minims of lore, the ancestry of a half-ton horse about to come out of the mist. What of those Italians—had you forgotten them, put them aside, changed your views, or were they still there behind the pedigrees so insistent in your mind? *High Time,* you thought, *by Ultimus out of Noonday, she by Domino. . . .*

---

* Named not for the character in *The People From Heaven,* but for the prevalent Smiths.

A horse rushed by, a hazed-over bay—Maggie's colt, was it?—and soon he came walking back with Montgomery patting his withers.

"How did he go?" you said.
And Montgomery said, "Like he was on wheels."
"How fast?"
The rider showed you a stop-watch tied to his wrist with a thong. "One-seventeen breezing," he said.

Domino, you thought, *Nicola Sacco. . . .*

SCENE 9

CHIEF JUSTICE OF THE ONTRA* CAFETERIA (December 1945)

In *A Man Without Shoes*, the father of the principal character was a hackdriver working in and about the city of New York. His occupation was one that suited his migratory nature, for it took him time and again to places that he'd never have seen but for the bidding of his fares. But these excursions, by definition only a going forth, always implied a coming back, and back he came each night to his wife, his son, and his cold-water flat in Manhattan— and to a great colored map of the United States that hung on one of the walls. On this, rulings in red crayon marked his trips that had been out of the ordinary way
and you'd written

Long before, the five boroughs of New York had been overrun by a slick of red wax, and from this always-growing trespass, there were now paths to Port Jervis and Princeton, along the Sound to the Saugatuck, down the Jersey coast to Barnegat, and, longest of all, to Saratoga Springs. In time, the man thought, there would be lines to every name in the nation; in time, he thought, the record of his trips would be the nation itself; in time, he thought. . . . *Ah, God, to see it all! To see it all some day!*

Yes, you thought, that was what you'd written for the father of Johnson, Daniel, but despite the vast promised land he'd thumbtacked to the wall, he'd see little more of it than he'd seen before—there'd be a crayon line to the Finger Lakes and another, perhaps, to the Falls; for the rest, it'd be uptown to the ball park and downtown to City Hall; it was his son who'd see it

---

* On Wilshire at Burnside, pronounced *On-tray.*

all. In creating the character of the hackdriver, you'd drawn nothing from your own father, no trait, no feature, no fact from his history; still, in reading of the one, you felt the force of the other, and as though magnetized, you drove fifteen miles just to sit beside him and smooth his hair.

§

At a long table in the rear room of the cafeteria were gathered a dozen or more elderly men (olderly, your Grandma Nevins would've called them). All were well past the age of participation: they brought no wares to their time, and they served it not with their capacities. Whenever you saw them, you thought of the mothballed ships at Tappan Zee, rusting side-by-side till they rusted away.

Among these one-time traders of goods for money, these former factors, shippers, actuaries, these makers of something once, and these fixers of something else — among these acquaintances of the park bench and the barbershop sat your father. He occupied a place at neither end of the board, and therefore he did not seem to preside. To eyes at other tables, he might've been indistinguishable from the rest of his company, one of the relics, a power spent earlier in the century, and seen at a distance, he might've been thinking what his fellows did: *How endless it all seemed at the beginning!*

As to your father, they'd've been in error, those observers from afar: he was not one of the many, rueing the flight of time over a nickel cup of coffee and a dime piece of pie. There at that table, he was the Law-giver, and as you approached him, you felt that you were coming before the Bar, and in your fancy, you saw him in robes. Nothing in his voice or manner, though, indicated that he so pictured himself: he was mild, deferential, even, and never final; he wore no pontiff purple. All the same, he was The Authority, and his strength came from those with whom he sat. To them, he was *der Richter,* the judge, and to him they brought their claims of right and plaints of wrong.

Drawing a chair from an unoccupied table, you placed it near him in the aisle, where you were able to do what you'd come there for, to touch him, to touch his hand and hair. Absently you heard some plaintiff or defendant speak — Mr. Rapaport, was it, Mr. Walcoff, Mr. Weiss? — but clearly you heard your father's reply, reasonable and *richterlich,* and in amity was some nuisance abated, some injury appeased. And all the while, you smoothed and smoothed his hair.

At length, the group began to disperse for the day. You and your father were the last to leave, and as he rose, you took his hand and kissed it, and then you followed him toward the door. On the way, a woman reached from a booth and touched your sleeve, and you stopped.

"I've been watching you and your father," she said.
And you said, "How do you know he's my father?"
"A person can tell such things."
"I love him."
"A person can tell that too."

THE COLOR OF THE AIR, II

George Washington, 1732-1799
THE LAST GENTLEMAN

> His integrity was most pure,
> his justice the most inflexible.
> —Thomas Jefferson

He knew, when the ague shook him in the night, that the way would not be long: the winter without had come within, entered the room, entered him, and soon now he'd be one with the season, die of cold that had become his own. He knew, even as Mister Lear was sent for, Lear his aide and very near his son, that all the small and useful things would be done for him, that a fire would be lit and a linctus brewed, that someone would be summoned to open a vein—and indeed it was so. His blood did flow, and syrups were tried, and the hearth was made to glow, and still he knew that death alone would end what chill had begun. When physicians came, he suffered their auscultations, and he let them bind his throat and bathe his feet—as if remedy lay in some affinity of extremes—but never was he beguiled by their calomel, or their sal volatile, or their cataplasms of wheat: they were trying to treat what was almost a corpse.

He let his mind float from the faces roundabout, from hands doing futile this and needless that, from the aroma of sage tea, the mordancy of embrocations, let his attention wisp and wander, go as smoke and fray away. It was as though he were being borne on some current as gentle as time, but not for very far, for he had not far to go, a day's drift at most, and even now, not yet there at the end, he could see what lay beyond. He wondered as he neared it why it was known as the great unknown. Had not he soon in life seen

44

the coming of the only death he feared, the end of order?, and had not he so lived as to fend the change, the winter on the way?, and, sad to say, had not he no more done so than if he'd never lived at all?

They wrapped his neck in flannels, and there were vapors of vinegar that they caused him to breathe, and he heard them say *quinsy,* and they bled him thrice, turned him to ease his pain, and twice he was dressed and placed in a chair. But through all the send-and-fetch, all the vain ado, he was most aware of Toby, tender Toby Lear: he could sense his nearby presence, hear his voice through other voices, feel the warmth of his furthersome hands. How lonely going, had he not been there!

The end of order, he thought, and what came to mind was the nation as a river, and powerless to stop it or change its course, he watched it join the sea's commotion. Order lost in disorder, and he rued it that he'd failed—and yet how should he not have failed when from the far first days he'd known that forces were stronger than men? His *Rules of Civility* recalled themselves, and a smile briefly marred him like a grimace. What did civility mean to the uncivil many or even the civil few—and for the matter of that, what now marked the few from the many, who now knew a *Superiour* from *One of Low Degree?*

It was hard to breathe, and what breath he drew seemed drained, as if used before, and it left him with little more than the will to breathe again. He was well on the way by then, but someone was still trying to stay him, someone was still raising his head, salving his throat, sponging his mouth. Lear, it must've been, and he wanted to speak of many things: had more snow fallen, he wondered, and had the creeks begun to freeze, Little Hunting above the Mansion and Dogue Run beyond the trees? were the Quarters snug, were My People well, were the horses being walked each day and the dogs allowed to run? The dogs, he thought, Taster, Cloe, Captain, Mopsey—Mopsey the bitch, he thought, and it was as though her feel were in his hand. Mopsey, he said.

The end of order was what he saw, and he'd helped to bring it on—who, indeed, had done so more? He'd written his Rules and lived them all, set them down by number and let them guide his life, and then—for what reason?—he'd put them all aside. It was the day of Rules abandoned now, of craft and chicane, the day of the blow-horn, the plebe, the pig in clover. All men equal? In what these days but this—that none rose higher than low? But if all were low, some were lower (among the less, the least), and to such lords would go this land. Of what use then to say *Labour to keep alive in*

45

your Breast that Little Spark of Celestial fire called Conscience? The fire would be out.

It was going out now. *I am just going,* he said to Toby Lear, and then, though none could hear him, he called to Mopsey, but she could not come, being thirty years dead. And yet in another moment he saw her find at Muddy Hole Farm, and he followed her baying a long way through the woods. . . .

SCENE 10

DANIEL WEBSTER SMITH (January 1946)

At the time of his death, late in the month, you'd known him for almost ten years. You'd seen him so often and in so many places that none of them comes to mind without his image on the screen: there he is at his parents' home, a small figure in a large chair, and there at the Pomona fairgrounds, where he's mixing a bran mash or limbering a new set of reins; but it's silent film that your memory runs, as if you'd never heard him say a word. His had been a visual presence only, and mute in a nebula of smoke, he'd let smoke kill him at the age of sixty.

In the days after the funeral, Maggie was no little time with her family, and on many a visit, you went too. Dan, as you knew, had always been her favorite, and she his. Self-sustaining and solitary, they were much alike, and almost without speech they responded to each other, eloquently, it seemed, when some animal was in view, a running horse, a riding horse, any sort of dog—it was through such speechless things that they endlessly communed.

The father, the mother, the four daughters, they sat at table or did the chores just as they'd done before their loss. Dressed in their usual clothes, they made their usual rounds, and then they read the papers while they rocked their chairs, speaking a word or two to someone and nodding at someone's reply—but they wore no black nor did they cry. An only son was gone, an only brother, but their mourning was not for the world to see, and they tore no garments nor shed a tear. Never did you suppose, though, that they did not grieve.

In your own family, lamentation was what the word connoted, a bewailing. It was the performance of a tragedy, and while played for the player, it was open to all. Sorrow, and well you knew it, was not to be contained. You yourself, through the course of a year, had displayed its badges for your mother's repose, the slashed jacket, the band of black on the heart-side sleeve. You were ten when she died, and signs of the heavy spirit were heavy in themselves, the crape, the notched lapel, they weighed you down, they were measurable in pounds. It was not enough to have a mother dead at thirty-three; you had to show that you were nearly so at ten.

These Smiths that were now your family, they yielded their son no more easily than the Nevinses their daughter; the Christian, surely, was as bereft as the Jew. The difference lay only in what the eye was shown of the desolation and what the ear could hear of the heart.

SCENE 11

ON THE SPORT OF KINGS (February 1946)

He said, "Certain people have been discussing an activity of yours, and they've asked me to give you their views."
And you said, "The activity being. . . ?"
"Horse-racing."
"And the views. . . ?"
"They feel that the sport is inconsistent with the politics you profess."
"What *would* be consistent—weight-lifting?"
"They're not joking, John."
"I know they're not, and that's what grinds me: they never joke. Lenin himself could laugh, but not our peerless leaders. They're always in that sealed railway car, riding toward the Finland Station."
"You take the position, then, that what you're doing is acceptable conduct."

His name was William Latham, and he was an agent, or, as he preferred to be called, an artist's representative. His labors were confined to the motion picture industry, where, for a fee of ten per cent of their earnings, he sold the services of a string of writers. He did not represent either of the Sanfords.

"I take no position, Bill," you said. "Maggie and I happen to own a few horses, and we race them because they're race-horses. There's nothing else you can do with them."
"Yes, there is—you can dispose of them."
"We see no good reason for that. They give us pleasure."
"What about the economics of the thing? Can you afford to compete with Louis Mayer and Jack Warner?"
"The economics is our affair," you said. "As for competing with the Mayers

and the Warners, of course we do nothing of the kind. We have a dinky two-horse stable that's trained by Maggie's brother. She got into the game, in fact, to give him a job."

"Is that all he can do?"

"He died last month."

"There you are, then," Latham said. "You're free to get rid of the horses."

Why didn't you get up and walk out of his office?, you wondered. To hell with him, and to hell with all those clients of his who were grinning down from the walls. Instead, you sat there, reading an autograph: *To Bill, with sincere gratitude.* You glanced at others. Would you find one signed with *in*sincere gratitude. . . ?

You said, "These horses of ours—you won't understand—they've gotten to be part of the family. We shelter them, shoe them, and doctor them, and no one would dream of feeding himself before feeding them."

"That's touching," Latham said. "Some of us are foolish enough to do that for people."

You gazed at his display of tithed writers, and then you returned to him who was housed, shod, doctored, and fed on the exacted ten per cent.

"According to a man named Marx," you said, "capital is created by the appropriation of surplus value from the worker. Isn't that what you're doing with your stable of quill-drivers?"

"They'd have no work if I didn't find it for them. I'm entitled to get paid for that."

You laughed, saying, "You sound like the guys we're supposed to be fighting—the Henry Fords, the John D.s."

"Look, Jack," he said. "We're far afield. We started with horses."

"For no particular reason," you said, "I'm going to let you in on something; I *don't* feel easy about the horses."

"Good," he said. "What word do I take to the boys Downtown?"

"They're always holding forth on the contradictions of capitalism. Tell 'em there are also contradictions on the Left—and I'm one of them."

Again you surveyed the photographs arrayed on the walls—a display, you thought, of highly-paid wage-slaves, creators of surplus value, like their brothers at machines.

"Horse-racing *doesn't* square with socialism," you said. "I know that as well as Downtown does. What I don't know, though, is how I got to both from where I began. I never knew a working-stiff in my life. I've never been in a mill or a mine. I never punched a clock or walked a picket-line. But dressed in the best, I've eaten in dining-cars and passed the hungry on the roads. . . . The race-horses I dimly understand, but nothing explains how I arrived on the Left. What brought me here? And why do I mean to stay. . . ?"

48

SCENE 12

A DAY OF NO PARTICULAR SIGNIFICANCE (April 1946)

Or none at all, for that matter, since you can't recall what you were doing that made it stay in mind. You may have been revising the manuscript of *A Man Without Shoes*; or, having done with a morning's culling, you may have been roving the orchard along with your nose-down dogs; or, as you often did, you may have been listening to records on the

talking-machine, as they called it in 1914 when you were walking on the Atlantic City boardwalk, past shop after shop of seashore things — shell necklaces and shell rings, tin-types, parasols, toy-size buckets and toy shovels — and suddenly a dark door-way, an open mouth!, began to sing. You didn't know that you were hearing the Habanera, but the opening bars stopped you dead, and stock-still you stood in the wheelchair traffic and the quivering idiom

Atlantic City, where your mother had gone on her wedding-trip in 1903, and where eleven years later she'd gone again, that time for her failing health, as if the sea-air would restore it, the daily hour in the sun. You were ten at the time, and for a reason that only she was aware of, she'd taken you along. She alone knew what was on the way and not far off, and she wanted to enjoy her son, the Boy King, before it came. But his mind was on a roller-coaster ride and the Barrel of Fun, and while she tried to inhale life on some warm verandah, he was bound for the Steeplechase pier. First, though, he had to pass through those Moorish quavers that rippled from an open door-way as from a minaret. They were only the effect produced by a needle in the grooves of a rotating cylinder, but

you could think of nothing else, no other sound, not the voices around you, the laughter, the scuff of shoes on the weathered planking, certainly not your mother's constricted breathing as she strove to last for another season. Why, you wonder, why do they bespell you, those moresque tones and Iberian rhythms, what do they mean to a Russian Jew — and why do they always lead back to that angular hole in a building wall?

Your mother would be dead in three more months, but just out of sight and just out of hearing, she'd be there still for every jota to come, every malagueña.

On the calendar above your desk, red-letter days marked the Easter Week, and if you were there before it that day, you may have remembered another April, when your mother was trying to live a long-gone summer through.

You were ten years old, you may have thought, and now you were forty-two. Forty-two!, and in disbelief, you may have sought proof from the calendar. . . .

As you say, though, it was a day of no particular significance.

SCENE 13

HARRIET ESTHER NEVINS (1881-1914)

Sixty-five years after her death, you'd write of your mother for the first time. All who'd known her would be gone by then, your father and her friends and blood, and none would be left to add to what you yourself had seen and heard and saved against the day. Photographs and letters had come down to you, but only a few of each, and when you tried to assemble her from such remains, they became immaterial, and their shape was that of smoke. She was thirty-three when she died—or was it thirty-four?, you wonder, for you never learned her date of birth.

When your mother went, with her went the world you understood, and the new one so stunned you with its strangeness that you rejected both the death and the change it had brought about. For years, you refused to believe that there was anything in the box you'd seen lowered into the grave; and everywhere, as if your mother were merely absent, you sought her in crowds, in windows, in passing cars, in the woman across the street. But if her death was inadmissible, if she must be somewhere else and alive, why were you never able to use the word *mother,* why could your mouth not produce the sound? Even when referring to a mother other than your own, your voice would fail you, and on reaching the word in speech, you'd stop, as if there the sentence ended. But why, since she really wasn't dead?

Even when you came to know that her death was no mere going away, no game with a secret conclusion, even when it was plain that wherever she may have gone, she wasn't coming back, even then she was not to be spoken of, least of all to your father, the one who'd known her best; nor did he, long her survivor, ever open the doors to the private rooms. What you have of her, then, is those letters and photographs, still telling the discontinuous story that nothing now can fill. How often you thought of her when you were with your father, how often in what you were saying you neared the unspeakable word! What would he have told you?, you wonder, how would he have answered?—but no question was ever asked.

50

SCENE 14

ANOTHER OBITUARY* (June 1946)

Nathanael West

You take up a paper sometimes, intending to fritter away a few minutes chasing type across a page. You're expecting someone, maybe, or you're waiting to put in a call, or maybe you just want to look busy while you waste a small part of your life. And later, you rarely remember what you read, because you read it during a piece of time that you had no use for and that you're glad is gone. But one such time you've not forgotten, nor will you ever, and that was when the paper you happened to take up told you coldly of the death, in an auto-smash near El Centro, of a guy you'd gone to kindergarten with: Pep West.

He's been dead six years now, you tell yourself, and you write that down, as if it were an important thing to say about a dead friend—and so it is, but only if it makes more vivid the time when he was a living friend. And on that thought, you find yourself looking up, and you see alongside you the manuscript of a novel, and you look beyond that to a bookcase where, under glass, you've carefully preserved the first and only editions of your four other novels, and you think: Why, there's half your life! in those five books, there's half of all the days and nights you've spent on earth! And you shake your head, not to get rid of the thought, but to settle it, to sink it in, and the reason you do that while you have Pep West on another level of your mind is that you'd never have written a line if it hadn't been for him. And it really doesn't make much difference whether the lines you've written have been good or bad, and whether the lines to come will be better or worse. The point is, at his example and with his encouragement, you went and used half of yourself on words. That's why you shake your head when you think of him as six years dead. It isn't that you mean you'd change places with him if you could bring him back. Few men, and not you among them, could say that and not lie. But it's that you so very earnestly wish to God he hadn't been such a damn poor driver, which you and many others knew he was long before his poor driving killed him.

And yet it bears in on you that Pep's poor driving was Pep, that it was something he could no more have unlearned than he could have unlearned his way of walking, which was a sort of shamble, awkward and out of sync,

---

* Written at the request of *The Screen Writer* and published in Vol. II, No. 7, December 1946.

or his way of putting on a coat, which made you think he was trying to climb down the arm-hole and come out of the cuff, or his way of picking up change, which couldn't have been harder for him if the coins were made of water. He was always tripping, always fumbling, always ill-related to still objects, and he was like that in everything you'd seen him put his hand to—everything but writing, and there alone he seemed to be at home, moving language with such ease and grace as he could never master in so little a thing as lighting a cigarette.

So you come to understand that he died more because he was Pep West to the end than because it fell that two cars were nearing an intersection out of El Centro at the same moment. And this too you write down, as if this too were an important thought—and then all of a sudden you get sick to hell of important thoughts, thoughts that explain the smash-up, maybe, that take the dents out of the fenders of that station wagon, and that pump air back into the blown-out tires, but thoughts that heal no fractures in Pep's skull and breathe no breath into his lungs. . . .

And then you had *un*important thoughts, about your days with
him in Harlem, about the games you played, the books you read—
and then came a rush of thoughts, all of the very least importance

. . . his pet phrase, "to coin a phrase"; his habit of speaking clichés in italics; his fat-lady joke, which he must've told you a dozen times; his being fresh out of matches everywhere and always; his odd stunt of buying a pack of butts, offering you one, taking one himself, and then giving you the pack as if he'd gotten it from you; his other nickname, Tweedy Boy; his pointer Danny; his Brooks valise, five feet long and two feet wide; his collection of Beerbohm caricatures; his little brag that he could rewrite Dostoevsky with a pair of shears; his agony in the presence of sentiment, his physical agony; his good imitation of The Schnozzola; his trick of reading his own stuff back to himself aloud; his handing you a shotgun up at Viele Pond by poking you in the belly with the muzzle, all absently, understand, all awkwardly and out of sync, and with the hammer cocked; his honest and overwhelming desire to write a great book; and his very near miss with Miss Lonelyhearts.

And remembering how you wept after reading about him in the paper that day, you find yourself wanting to say, now after six years: "Pep, old kid, I hope you won't mind if . . . Well, I mean if you'll promise not to . . . That is, please don't be embarrassed if I tell you . . . But, damn it, Pep, you don't like it when people get sentimental, so you'll have to understand what I'm trying to say without my saying it. And you do understand, don't you, kid? You understand that I. . . ."

SCENE 15

SOMEBODY FROM DOWNTOWN (Summer of 1946)

When he entered the coffee-shop, he stopped to glance around, as if he'd been told what you looked like, and fixing on you, he came toward your booth.

"Sanford?" he said, and at a nod, he took the seat facing you across the table. "I understand you wanted to see me."

"Not you, exactly," you said. "Anyone who could overrule the Hollywood Comintern."

"I can do that, I suppose. Overrule it in what way?"

His age was hard to guess: he might've been fifty, you thought, or forty looking fifty years used. In trying to assign him a place in time, you found yourself thinking of his suit, one of no more than two, probably, and both of them worn to a shine. What rooming-houses had they hung in, you wondered, what picket-lines walked in the rain, this wrinkled worsted, that shrunken serge?

"I'm a writer," you said, "but I never meet with other writers. It was decreed by the commissars that I belong with a housewife group, and week after week, that's where I've been. I want to be switched to a writers' group."

"You don't know when you're well off," he said. "If I had to meet with writers week after week, I'd switch too—to the Ku Klux Klan."

You gazed at him for a moment, and he at you, and you said, "I hear they had some funny guys at Smolny Institute. That baldhead Ulianov, for one."

"You should've caught Lunatcharsky," he said. "Tell me, what've you got against housewives?"

"Nothing, except that I don't know beans about them."

"You mean, they don't know beans about writing. Be honest, now."

"Well, it's true."

"You're wrong: you can benefit them, and they can benefit you."

"Oh, come on! I don't need any of that patent-medicine! I get my fill of it from the *Peoples World*."

Now it was he who gazed at you and you who gazed back, and finally he said, 'You give us a lot of trouble, more than most."

"I'm not out to do that, but, Christ, when I listen to some of those big red mouths. . . !"

"You like what we stand for, but you don't like *us*."

"That's a good way to put it. You're sharp."

"Not so very," he said. "Downtown knew I was going to see you, so they

53

gave me one of your books, *The People From Heaven.* I read it last night, and I found out what you want—a new world today, at the latest tomorrow. What you overlook is that we have to make it with the same bunch that made the old one—writers, housewives, Baldy Lenin, and me."

"We won't be there by tomorrow."

"At Smolny, Lenin said, 'We shall now proceed to construct the Socialist order,' but he never thought it could be done in six days."

And now you gazed at him again, and again he gazed at you, and you said, "Say it."

And he said, "Stick with the housewives."

You looked through the window beside you, but you hardly saw those who were passing in the street, hardly noticed the cars, the colors, the sun and shade. You were thinking of the man from Downtown, but not, you supposed, of his clothes. How thin he was! how faded and shrunken!—and then you knew that after all, you *were* thinking of his clothes.

"I'll give it another try," you said.

SCENE 16

A SWIMMING POOL?, YOU SAID (April 1946)

And Maggie said, "Why not?"

"Oh, a lot of reasons."

"Any good ones?"

"Well, the best, I guess, is just the *idea* of having a pool. It doesn't seem to go with what we believe in."

She laughed. "You mean a pool is inconsistent with what happened at Smolny?"

"It's inconsistent with the kind of people we come from. My father was a butcher-boy, and yours carried a hod."

"What a foolish thing to say! It's a bad argument for socialism that, under capitalism, the lowly can rise. If it's rising to fill a hole with water and swim in it."

"But you don't know how to swim."

"You do," she said, "and you'll teach me."

SCENE 17

WON DRIVING, SECOND AND THIRD THE SAME (June 1946)

red, red horse head in white circle on back,
white sleeves, red and white cap
—racing colors of M. Roberts

As the post parade passed the grandstand, your eye briefly turned it into a series of stills, a stopped carousel; you saw the horses clearly, noted the numbers they wore, caught them in a prop or a prance, a statuary stride. And then they were in motion again, a flowing heraldry of silk, fessed, diamonded, saltired on the breast. Fifth behind the outrider was America Smith, and in a few more moments, he would be sent seven furlongs out of the chute in a field of twelve at Hollywood Park.

You turned from the track to Maggie, who was seated beside you and aware of nothing but what her glasses were trained on, Number 5, her three-year-old bay colt by Top Row out of her own mare, September Child.

Shorty, you thought, she always called him Shorty.

Speaking to no one, she said, "I hope he doesn't get hurt."

You glanced across her at Charlie Leavitt, her new trainer, but neither of you spoke.

Without lowering her glasses, she said, "I don't care where he finishes. Just so he doesn't get hurt."

"He'll be all right," Leavitt said. "He was born to run."

Putting the glasses aside, she said, "He could've done that in a paddock."

"Horses get hurt there too."

Your mouth opened, and lo, words came out, and you said, "Their speed saved the species. They outran the wolves."

Maggie looked at you, and then she looked away, saying "Charlie . . . ," as she stared across the track at the disquiet near the head of the chute, horses, handlers, weaving colors—and slowly the flurry dwindled as the stalls began to fill. "Charlie," she said, "I married a deep thinker."

And Charlie said, "There they go!"

Exploding from the gate, the horses crossed the bend of the main track and fled down the backstretch, where, almost hidden by the rail, they created the illusion that only their riders were running a race, *green, white sash, green cap* showing the way, followed by *sky blue, blue and cerise cap,* and then *canary, apple green sleeves.*

55

"Where is he, Charlie?" Maggie said.

"Laying fourth," the trainer said, "and now third. Love's Over by a length, Miss Perifox by a half — and Shorty, going good on the inside."

As the field rounded the far turn, you lost it in a memory of what you'd read and heard of a race in Siena, the Palio, run each year on the stones and slopes of the Piazza; you could see the banners, the caparisons of the fifteenth century. . . .

And then you heard Maggie cry, "Come on, Shorty!"

And you saw *white sleeves, red and white cap* cross the finish line two lengths in front. . . .

Won driving, second and third the same

SCENE 18

THE LAST OF A POOR MISFORTUNATE BOY (July 1946)

When he died in the hospital ward of a state institution at Napanoch, New York, he was a boy only in his mind, which had failed to advance with his body to the age of fifty-two. Long before that time, it had reached the limit of its power to learn, and from then to the end, all he knew of the world, poor misfortunate boy, was what he knew at ten. He was your Uncle Jerome — to you, Romie — a tall blue-eyed blond, the chosen of the family once, brighter than any other, they said, graceful, deft, well-made, and mild, the pride of one and all. A day had come, though, when his mind ran into a wall.

There were changes then, but they were ascribed to approaching maturity. His childish rages were thus explained away, his frustration with simple devices, his difficulties with words. Such things would pass, it was thought, and in time, he'd be manly, as before. The family became less certain when he built a fire in a clothes-closet, and even less so were they when he picked a canary's eyes out with a hatpin. For the dead bird, his father had flogged him with a belt — continued, you were told, till the son was black and blue. But alas the day, those were the wrong colors: his body grew older; his mind stayed behind at the foot of the wall.

Poor misfortunate boy, his mother called him. Man-sized at fifteen, he was five years beyond the size of his brain, and though blond still, he seemed to have faded, like the brilliant bird he'd been impelled to kill. By then, he'd worked many a mischief, some of them ruinous and some merely spoilage, waste, but in none was there malice: the harm he did seemed to come naturally, as to others came the good. Standing before one of his squanderings, his undoings, all he'd show was a smile of surprise, as though he could hardly credit his eyes.

Your first recall of him is from that time, and he struck you as being . . . but could he possibly have been at home in that stunted world where he lived? Could he have been at ease there, you wonder, as he picked out tinkle-tankle tunes with a single finger? Was it pleasant, at fifteen, to cut coupons from a magazine and send away for sample-size carminatives, for jars of ointment and bars of soap? Could he have been content there? Didn't he understand that his head was stranded and that his body was flowing on?

The household, whatever household meant, was not a place that could hold him, and he was sent out to military academies, to trade-schools, and finally to work-farms, but late or soon, he'd run off and bum his way home. Sometimes he'd be days on the road, and with the lice and grime of the road, he'd turn up stained and stinking but ever with a grin to win you, and as the door opened, he'd flourish his greasy hat and say *Ta-da-Tsing!*

And now you were told that he was dead. There'd be no more poked-out tunes on the piano, you thought, no more tiny tubes of toothpaste in the mail. His body, fifty-two years old, had been sent to join his father's in the family vault, and you couldn't help wondering what would happen when he got there with his ten-year-old mind. Would he bow, would he sweep his soiled plumes, would he say, as so often he'd said before, *Ta-da-Tsing! Romie's home!?*

SCENE 19

BLUES FOR *A MAN WITHOUT SHOES*, 2 (Early in 1946)

After the death of Curtice Hitchcock, killed in an automobile crash, your editor Frank Taylor wrote to say that

> Eugene* is returning to the firm after five-years' absence with the Army, the State Department, USIB,† etc., and we go on where Curtice left off. As Eugene says, we are now the older generation and

---

* Eugene Reynal.
† United States Intelligence Board.

must act accordingly. Please don't for a moment think that there will be any change in house policy. We plan to go on in Curtice's liberal tradition. . . .

Taylor had misunderstood what *Eugene* had said or written or otherwise given off: *we are now the older generation,* he read or heard or drew from the composition of the air. In counting on *Curtice's liberal tradition,* he assumed that the tradition had survived the collision. It had not: it lay with Curtice in the grave, and what survived was Eugene. Long before his five-year absence ended, any liberalism he may have worn to Washington had long since been shucked for the uniform of the masters, and by the time he returned, he was well on the way to actions that suited his age.

The Army, you thought, the State Department, Intelligence—how could you not have known what was in store for *A Man Without Shoes?* Why did you forget the days of the war and how you'd fared with the Signal Corps? *Too red,* they'd been told by G2 (Intelligence?), and *too red* said Col. Capra to you. . . .

Reynal's meaning is so clear to you now—we must act accordingly, we must put away childish things—that you wonder how it could have been less than clear then. Even Taylor's letter, expressing belief, reveals doubt. He knew, and no one knew better, that Reynal could not have improved in the kind of company he'd been keeping, and uneasy in that knowledge, he'd sought to assure you (and reassure himself) that nothing would change at 8 West 40th Street. Everything would change.

SCENE 20

BLUES FOR *A MAN WITHOUT SHOES,* 3 (July-August 1946)

> Bartleby in a singularly mild, firm voice,
> replied, "I would prefer not to."
> —Melville, *Bartleby the Scrivener*

Though much of your attention that summer was on other parts of the book, you gave thought from time to time to your publisher's imperative: remove, as far as possible, the commentaries on American history. Your purpose with those pieces had been to illustrate for your principal character the nature of his country, the political and social climate,* so to speak, in which he'd grown. You'd done that by taking him on a long tour of the land,

---

* Done differently in this autobiography.

58

apparently aimless but in fact laid out to send him through those places that had witnessed the trespasses, the perfidies and overreachings, the injustices of the nation's past.

He'd gone down roads that led to where Gold! was found and where Brown was hanged for Harpers Ferry (or was it for saying *Had I so interfered in behalf of the rich?*), to Abe gravely speaking from the tomb. A year earlier, your publisher had endorsed such things. Would you now change or remove them as bidden, or would you, with Bartleby, say *I would prefer not to?* Leafing through the manuscript, you read parts of what you'd written of Virginia Dare and the Lost Colony of Jamestown:

> Had he stayed there longer, would he have found the fact of the matter: would he have found, in some Indian town, one hundred and sixteen mummied heads on poles; would he have found their teeth slung on Indian necks and their skin on drums; would he have found their pots in use, the rusted wrecks of tools, the torn Bibles, and the clothes again but wrongly worn. . . ?

and you read of the find at Sutter's Mill:

> By New Year's Day of '48, the mill-frame was up, and a brush dam and a sluice-gate likewise. He knew how to get a job done, that Jim Marshall, and there was only one thing gave him even a little bit of trouble, and that was the tail-race. It hadn't been dug deep enough for the mill-wheel, so one afternoon late in January, Jim Marshall took a stroll along the forty-odd rods of the tail-race to see whether it was coming to hand, and down near where it spilled back into the river, his eye was caught by something laying on the bottom against a slab of granite. He bent over and pulled out a nubbin of yellowish stuff about half the size of a pea. . . .

and you read of what John Brown might've said to Dred just before the trap was sprung:

> I could've lived to be older than fifty-nine;
> I could've lasted out this merchant century:
> I had the frame for it—but not the frame of mind.
> If I'd been blind to you and deaf to God,
> If I'd loved myself more and money most,
> If I'd kept my nose clean and my soul snotty,
> If I'd valued my skin, if I'd thrown no stones
> At the sin of slavery, if I'd passed the buck
> And left such truck as bravery and broken bones
> To fools—in short, if I'd been a sleeping dog,
> They'd've let me lie till the nineteen-hundreds. . . .

59

and you read of dead Abe, talking to all from his Springfield vault:

Tell fewer of the funny stories I told,
And make no further mention of my plug hat,
My rolled umbrella, and my outsize shoes,
Bury the legend that I was a bastard deep,
Let my mother's sleep be that of the just,
And if you must be heard, speak briefly
Of my wife Mary and my wife's madness,
But speak not a word of my spoken-for Ann,
Nor say that I loved her all my life. . . .

and you read too of how Yellowhair had fared along the Little Big Horn:

We refrained from eating his heart; we refused to taint ourselves
with the rashness, the disdain, that had made him attack four thousand with six hundred. We knew that one sent against seven must
die, and we thought this Custer very bold in the mind, very proud,
to offend Death as he did that afternoon. Not only were the Sioux
before him in great force, but also they were laden with ammuni-
tion and repeating rifles of good pattern, and more than this, they
were weary of being run like game from whatever country the whites
thought good for Gold; they wished ardently for one place from which
they would be harried no more, for one place in all this land that
did not promise to hold the Yellow Powder the whites so deeply
cared for and killed so much to obtain. . . .

Remove such passages, you'd been told, but in the end you said *I would prefer
not to.*

THE COLOR OF THE AIR, III

The *Amistad* Case, 1839–41
THE *AMISTAD*, FORMERLY THE *FRIENDSHIP*

*a Baltimore-built schooner of about 150 tons,
painted black with a white streak*
— New York Globe, Aug. 1839

When first sighted off the Jersey woodlands, she was sixty-three
days out of Havana with a cargo of fancy merchandise — crockery,
silks and satins, and four dozen Mendi slaves. On being taken in

60

tow by a government brig, it was seen that much of the ware lay about broken, its shards in the scuppers or rocking on the decks, and the fine and sibilant stuffs were streamers in the rigging or wound around the blacks. The Captain, Ramon Ferrer, was eight weeks dead by then, slain with a swipe of a sugar-cane knife and tossed to the deep with his mulatto cook to keep him company. The schooner itself was sea-bitten and now in need of a full refit. Her sides and hull were breaded with barnacles, and weed that hung from her cables seemed to curtsy with the ship. Torn and tattered all her sail, the fore, the main, the jibs, and from rail and gunwale, the paint had peeled away. Also in poor condition were two white and frightened Latin swells: one had owned the crockery, silks, and satins, and both had owned the slaves.

Arrived at New London, the two spics lodged a complaint alleging mutiny and murder against the blacks, and those that were left of them, only nine-and-thirty now, found themselves in the clink along with their leader

Cinque,

or Cinquez,

or Cingue,

a Mendi from Mani in Dzhopoa,
which is to say *the open land,*
ten suns away from the waters of the sea,
seized, taken hold of in a road,
and sold, and sold again, and sent
many suns west on the waters of the sea
(The phrenologist Mr. Fletcher
has expressed the opinion that Cinque

or Sinko,

or Singbe,

is of a bilious and sanguine temperament,
the bilious predominating)

On being sworn, the Cuban dons produced licenses from their Gobernador permitting them to transport the slaves from Havana to Puerto Principe, and they deposed that said lawful purpose was precluded by an act of piracy, to their grievous loss. They demanded, therefore, the return of the *Amistad*, repossession of the slaves and the cargo, and compensation for the merchandise destroyed. In their list of these, they itemized 40,000 needles, 48 rolls of wire, 45 bottles of essence, 500 pounds of jerked beef, sundries such as glass knobs, raisins, and 50 pairs of pantaloons — and of course the cambric and Canton crepe, the shawls of gauze and bombazine.

and from Fulu
two moons away from the waters of the sea
                              Grabeau,
                              or Gilabaru,
meaning in Mendi *have mercy on me,*
caught at Taurang on the way to buy clothes,
sold to a Spaniard in Lomboko, and shipped in a hold on
the waters of the sea,
speaks Vai, Konno, and Gissi,
four feet eleven inches in height,
very active, especially in turning somersets

Aside from those relating to the rights of salvage, doubts arose
as to the propriety of a slave escaping slavery *vi et armis,* to wit, by
inflicting death on his owner. It was urged that the black pirates
of the *Amistad* were merely runaways, in no better case than their
like in the States. Argument was offered that were the law to
distinguish between domestic and foreign ownership, the entire institution of slavery would be open to question.

by Kimbo, meaning *cricket,*
born at Mawkoba in the Mendi country
far from the waters of the sea,
knows numbers

                              one *eta*
                              two *fili*
                              five *loelu*
                              six *weta*
his father was a gentleman

Per contra, it was maintained that the slaves so libeled were not fugitives
within the meaning of the Federal Constitution. They were not, it
was claimed, persons held to service in one state who had sought
to escape such service by fleeing to another. Cuba was no part of
the Union: the decks of a ship lay outside its jurisdiction, which did
not extend to the waters of the sea.

that was what Bartu would have said,
                              or Gbatu
meaning *a club or a sword,*
                              and Kwong,
who was sold for crim. con.,
                              and Fuliwa
                              and Pungwuni,

who was sold by his uncle for a coat,
>and Moru

would have said the same when sold
to Belawa, which meant *great whiskers,*
the Bandi name for Spaniard,
>and Fuliwulu,

who had a depression in his skull,
would have said it too,
>and Bau

from the Wowa River would have said it,
he who paid a goat for his wife
and plenty mats and a gun—
ah, they all would have said it,

>Faginna,
>and Bagna,
>and Shuma,

who also said *No one can die but once*

In the end, the case reached the Supreme Court, where John Q. Adams, in a two-day speech, spoke a hundred thousand words for the blacks. He talked one judge to death (he died at fifty thousand), and he made the others find that the slaves were slaves no longer: they were free.

They were sent back to Africa on the waters of the sea, and there they shed their clothes, the God of the whites, the manners learned in Connecticut, forgot the words of J. Q. Adams, the verdict of the Bench. It is said that in 1879, Cinque, or Cinquez, or Sinko, died at a mission, in Freetown, it may have been, or along Boom River a hundred miles away. Some say he had become a trader, a bandit, a dealer in slaves, but such things may not be true.

SCENE 21

FATHER TO THE MAN* (1946)

> *We had our arguments within the family and*
> *there were times when I suppose we were tempted*
> *to run away. None of us ever did.*
> —Richard M. Nixon

No, none of them ever did: they stayed for more, they never strayed. But what, he may have wondered, what if he'd done what he thought of, scribbled a screed, pinned it to the screen, and gone out into the suspiring night, drawn deep of jasmine, orange, oleander, and run . . . to where? how far toward where? But *none of us ever did,* he said, none, and least of all he, had ever forsaken himself and fled, none had ever taken the road that led . . . to what? to where?

It was just as well he never tried: he'd hardly have gotten to the door. For him, and he knew it, there was nothing outside but danger that began where the five stone steps descended from the lawn, went down into the swirl of an unknown world. It drew him, that roundabout suction, but never through his skin of windows, walls, and shiplap siding. He was safe there within . . . but all the same he was tempted, he said, he could feel the force of the outer persuasion, and when his feet failed to run, to walk, to stir, even, he may have tried to respond in his mind—to *imagine* going, just to *imagine!*—but when fancy faded, he was still inside.

He must've been aware early that he was sequestered by himself, container and contents in one, his one restrainer, and he studied not to care for the things he saw through his look-out eyes: he'd live on the safe side, he must've resolved, the inner side, the white-frame four-square skinful of *him.* Thrice on Sunday, therefore, he attended church (some say more), and he gravely fished, bent pin and pole, in the water-district reservoir, he stole fruit and swam in ditches, he split his scalp in a fall from a wagon (eleven stitches!), he chored, he odd-jobbed, he read useful books, wrote themes on topics of public interest, made his schools' debating teams (Resolved: that insects are more beneficial than harmful), won this game, lost that race, boned up, burned the midnight oil (or gas), earned the name of Iron-ass . . . but he never ran, he must've rued, never ran away.

---

* From *The Winters of That Country.*

There were Nixes in the thirteenth century and Nikesons in the next, but what they did before they died no Nixon ever knew; clay once, they were dust now, and so too such as may have fought on the Brandywine, fallen between the graves on Cemetery Ridge. There were no immortals among the family dead, no suns that would never set: there were only fading records in nutgall, only stories told at reunions spun thinner all the time — it was a low-lumen line.

The lessons taken on the violin, the work done in orchards, fields, packing-plants, the goods sold in stores, the windshields wiped, the *helping out* at home, the activities, the activities unending! He entered contests, edited papers, stood for student office, he danced, he tried out for no matter what, he cheered for 'varsity, he thrashed, throbbed, whirled around, some part of him always seemingly involved in sound or caught in motion, oscillating, reciprocating, grinding — he was one of his own beneficial insects, chafing, rasping, as if to set himself afire.

It did no good. He could see all his life from his near beginning, there from the foot of the Chino Hills, he could see year after year of the rest, a strung-out procession of identicals, and though he must've longed to make it change, he knew he never would. When the parade ended, he'd be just where he started, still in his house of skin and quite as ill at ease. He must've felt that he had no real right to be anywhere, out there in the cold or holed up in his pelt, and from afar, across that Yorba Linda lawn, he must've seen a day dawn when he was only a Nikeson of the past, an entry made in fading ink.

What was there about him, or what was there not, that cost him quality, lost him poise? what did he comprise that diminished him, what did he omit? why did he perform for mirrors and memorize? why was he always urgent, even while silent, even standing still? why did he seem to plead, and for what and from whom, what did he need? what did he have too much of, too little of, nothing of at all — taste? tact? the *bon ton*? dash? why were his clothes correct but wrong, why were his postures *im*posture, his gestures apt but for other meanings, his phrases coined from tin? why did he try so hard? why did he feel less than the least. . . ?

None of us ever did, he said, but oh God, if he could only have run away!

SCENE 22

POGROM

> *an organized massacre of helpless people,*
> *usually with the connivance of officials;*
> *specif., such a massacre of Jews*
> — Webster's International

In the late afternoons, a time would always come when you found yourself listening for her return. It would make no difference where you were or what engaged you: when you sensed her nearness, you'd suspend talk if you happened to be talking, you'd go more softly if you were walking the grounds, you'd quiet the dogs if they were vying for your hand, and you'd sit or stand where you were, and presently you'd hear the sound you'd been waiting for, tires grinding gravel in the driveway—and she'd be there.

On that day, though, the sound went unheard. She may have driven very slowly from the gate, or you, stalking some word or phrase, may have been trailing it through your mind, and not until her footsteps preceded her along the hall were you aware that she'd entered the house. From the pursuit of a thought, you turned to the doorway, expecting her to appear: she went instead to the bedroom, and there the footsteps stopped. Why had she come so quietly, you wondered, and why the quiet now, and why above all had dogs so clamorous been so subdued?

You called out her name, and at her failure to reply, you followed her to the bedroom, where, clutching a script and still wearing her coat, she was staring at a blank space of wall, as if there some enactment were taking place that held her in thrall.

"Maggie," you said.

The illusion seemed to have lost little when she spoke, saying, "I'd hardly gotten to my office this morning when Mayer's secretary called to invite me to a showing of film in the Executive projection-room. There must've been a hundred of us down there, producers, directors, actors, and half a dozen writers. None of us knew what we were going to see. We guessed it'd be some feature from another studio, but what Mayer sprang on us was three hours of U.S. Army footage shot in the Nazi concentration-camps. . . !"

She must've been seeing them again, those images that were funneled through the darkness and spread across the screen, they must've been as plain as before.

"I think of myself as a writer," she said, "but the writer never lived who could describe what we saw. A painter, maybe, one of those Dutchmen born and raised in hell, but no words could tell the story. Long before the film ended, half the audience was gone — they just got up and fled. The rest, those that weren't stupefied, they just couldn't stop crying, and there was one, a man, who threw up in the aisle, but he wouldn't or he couldn't run away. . . ."

She was hugging the script with both hands, clasping it as though it offered protection against the sights she'd seen. It did not; she saw them still.

"The camps," she said. "I don't remember them all, and I couldn't pronounce them if I did. One was Dachau, I know, and one was Belsen, but we were shown a dozen others. Three relentless hours of barbed wire, open ovens, holes filled with bones. . . ."

Treblinka, you thought, *Maidanek, Theresienstadt* — the pleasances, the amusement parks of Greater Germany. *Auschwitz,* you thought, *Sachsenhausen,* and you tried to visualize places to illustrate the names, to dream up staring faces that were little more than eyes, but your fancy broke down under the weight of what they'd beheld, and only when she spoke of spectacles — a great mound of spectacles — did you begin to see through the dark. There was a shot, you were told, that showed a prisoner kneeling beside the pile, seeking out a pair to fit his sight, to bring the far nearer, to merge his double vision. It was those lenses, some of them refracting light, it was those rims and frames of gold and silver and tortoiseshell that enabled you to see, and you saw backward into all kinds of people, all manner of minds, and for a moment you became all the wearers, now dead, who once had done all things, read a score, scanned Alexandrines, descried the colors of bacilli on a slide. . . .

"It lasted for three hours," Maggie was saying, "and when it was over no one said a word."

SCENE 23

PEOPLE'S EDUCATIONAL CENTER (Fall of 1946)

It was located on the second floor of a building on Vine Street that later became known as the Little Red Schoolhouse. In its several rooms, courses were given in a variety of subjects, all, however, having some basis in sociology; its faculty, drafted from the Left Wing, included you in a once-a-week series of lectures and discussion concerning the modern American novel. The most unusual feature of the work, perhaps, was that it demanded the didactic powers of *two* instructors, as though through one alone, a class of a dozen novices could never be shown the way to the mantle of Henry James.

Your fellow instructor was a fellow novelist named Jasper More, and in the field of fiction, he was quite as unsuccessful as you. A man with a family to support, he drew his earnings, scanty enough, from the occasional screen-writing assignment that came his way; thus torn, he was able to complete a book but rarely, and then, due to his bizarre turn of mind, only to see it fail. Seated side-by-side against a blackboard, you and he must've seemed a most peculiar pair to your weekly gathering of—what were they, you wondered, and where had they come from, and why were they there?

Two or three were housewives, you supposed, on the run for an evening from children and chores; and others doubtless were salesmen, clerks, secretaries, all of them yearning to express the unique stories of their stifled lives; and surely too there were strays, a few who seemed to have wandered in for no better reason than that the door was open and there was light in the room. It was these last, come only to be among others, that affected you the most.

Those two or three who traded the loneliness of the street for the loneliness of company, what could it profit them, here where such names as Kate Chopin and Stephen Crane and Harold Frederic were on the air? did they care, did they even listen, when *The Awakening* was spoken of or *The Damnation of Theron Ware*? How were they assuaged by such things, how were they changed, were they not the same when they went as when they came? And yet willingly they paid their fees, those strays, and raptly they sat through words that taught them nothing and to which they added no word of their own.

During those sessions, more than once were you put in mind of a story your father had told you:

"My mother, may she rest in peace, knew a lonely old woman who spoke nothing but Yiddish. This woman, she said, was walking home one evening on the lower East Side, and on the way she reached a banquet hall where a party was assembling for a Polish wedding. Once among the crowd, she was mistaken for a guest, this old one with a wig, and over her protests, which were not understood, she was escorted inside. Each family thought she was a member of the other, and both of them honored her. The people, the food, the music, all of it was strange, but she was lonely, as I said, and she stayed. . . ."

Those strays, you thought—all you ever said in that room was addressed to them.

SCENE 24

THE LITTLE RED SCHOOLHOUSE (January 1947)

Classes were over, and standing in the street-level doorway, you awaited Maggie, who earlier in the evening had left you off and gone up the Boulevard to the Chinese. It had rained during the afternoon, and the pavement was still dappled with dampness that caught the lamplight and faintly shone. You watched your breath, lavender in the blue night, and you read a sign on the bank at the corner, and you heard a streetcar's brakes as it stopped at Vine.

And alongside you, a voice said, "Just the guy I wanted to see."

It belonged to George Sowle, the director of the school. *I do not like you, Dr. Fell,* you thought, and you said, "Hello, George."

You wondered how long it would take him to reach his favorite phrase: *as it were.* Apt at times and at others not, it was all things to him, that elegant subjunctive, that boutonnière of speech.

"I left a note for you in your box."

"I never look in my box," you said, and you remembered someone in New York who'd say *title* when what he meant was book—*Julian,* he'd say, *let me show you my new titles.* Why had the word ground you so? And what was wrong with *as it were?*

He said, "I've been delegated to ask whether you'll lend a sum of money to the Center till the end of the summer."

"Delegated by whom?"

"The School Board, and Downtown too."

"What would the sum come to?"

"Five hundred dollars."

"I think I can swing it. I'll speak to Marguerite."

A question climbed his throat and died there. You brought it back to life.
Speak to Marguerite?
Of course. She's my wife.
What's your wife got to do with this?
It's her money you're asking for.
You used to be a lawyer. Don't you know about Community Property?
I'm still a lawyer. But Marguerite made the money, and it's hers.
That's foolish, comrade. It's half yours.
Who makes the money in your family?
I do, thank God.
God, comrade?
As it were. . . .

You laughed, saying, "I thank Marguerite."
And he said, "What're you talking about?"

At the curb, a car-horn sounded, and you waved as you crossed the sidewalk
to the curb.

§

As Maggie headed for Cahuenga Pass, she said, "Who was that back there?"
"One of your favorites—George Sowle."
"Oh, *that* one."
"He wanted me to lend the school Five Hundred."
"Whenever I think of him, I remember an evening at his house when his
wife tried to say something during a discussion—"
"—and he said, 'Why don't you shut up? What the hell do you know?' "
"What did you tell him?"
"That I'd speak to you about it."
"You never have to do that, Johnny."
"That's what he was thinking."
"Did he say so?"
"No, but I heard him all the same."
"You'll give him the Five Hundred, of course. . . ?"

SCENE 25

BLUES FOR *A MAN WITHOUT SHOES,* 4 (March 1947)

> . . . Please do not for a moment think
> that there will be any change in house policy. . . .
> —Frank Taylor

But now, less than a year later, he was writing to say:

> This is to announce formally that we are resigning from the Board
> and staff of Reynal & Hitchcock as of Friday, March the seventh.
> We have exciting plans, and we shall be writing you about them,
> with less formality, in the near future. . . .

The note was signed jointly with Albert Erskine, and suddenly, your editors
gone, you were in the hands of an unknown, a man five years exposed to
the weather and ways of Washington. What had been the effect of the exposure, you wondered: had it withered old beliefs or had it retarded new?

70

You were almost forty-three years of age then, and looking back at yourself from here, you marvel at your knack of living through a period as if it weren't there—a period in which, the wrong war over, the right one was being fought in peacetime, or what passed for peace with fools as sanguine as you. In those luminous days, had there not been a Second Coming, had not the world been cleansed of sin? How far the fall, then, when Taylor's letter came, telling little yet telling all!

"What do you think I ought to do?" you said.
And Maggie said, "Go to New York."

§

Henry Volkening's office was half a mile down the Avenue from your hotel, and you remember the walk that spring morning past mansions built in the previous century, past clubs, shops, cathedrals, all the way under an overhang of flags, a dancing pointillism of red, white, and blue.

"They wrote something about exciting plans," you said. "Exciting for whom?"
"Taylor and Erskine are both going to Random House," Volkening said. "And Harry Ford is going with them—he's Production."
"Which writers are they taking?"
"That's an odd question. None."
"I had a half-assed notion that a writer followed his editor."
"You'd better think with both halves. A writer's contract is with the publisher, not the editor."
"What kind of hairpin is this Reynal?" you said.

Volkening turned away to a window that overlooked a run of roofs to the west, and watching him across his stacked desk, you wondered whether he saw anything through the glass—sky, smoke, water-tanks, other windows.

When he spoke, he said, "Knowing you, I'm afraid to say."

§

Later in the morning, when you were shown into Reynal's room, you found yourself in the presence of a man who put you in mind of Albert Boni, so much so that never since have you been able to see separate images. When you think of either, you summon the same impression, that of a small animal in the mouth of a burrow, its nose twitching as it eyes you without a blink.

Before him lay the carbon copy of *A Man Without Shoes*. He flicked it, saying, "We're not publishing books like this any more."

And you said, "What do you mean by 'books like this'?"

"Communistic propaganda."

You stared at him for a moment, and then you said, "Are you pulling my leg, Mr. Reynal? Or just pulling your pud?"

"Language like that will land you in hot water."

"What'll you do—report me?"

He laid the flat of his hand on the manuscript, saying, "That won't be necessary. This tells where you stand."

"I'm glad that's clear," you said. "I was beginning to think you hadn't read the book."

"I've read it, and so have others, and we all agree that it doesn't conform to the new policy of the house."

"Which is—?"

"I'll put it this way—a policy quite different from Mr. Hitchcock's."

"Why? Was he a Communist?"

"When your book was accepted, I was in the Service. Had I been here, you'd never have gotten a contract."

"But I did get a contract, and there's the book it calls for."

"I hear otherwise. We never contracted for a subversive book, and it will not be published by this house."

"You just put in five years serving the country, which was admirable. What you're doing now is taking it all back. You'd be the first to say that they ban books in Russia, but what're you up to that's different?"

He pushed the manuscript toward you, saying, "This book is an attack on the American system from start to finish. Take it to Russia. Let them print it."

Rising, you picked up the manuscript. "Well, I can't make you, I guess," you said.

"No, you can't. But there's something else you can do—you can return the advance."

You stood there, looking down at eyes that seemed to be gleaming in a hole. "You've owned the book for two years. That contract has cost me two years' time."

"It's our right to withdraw. Which means that you owe us seven hundred and fifty dollars."

"You've got to believe in the whole constitution, Mr. Reynal, not just the part that suits you. So why don't you go fuck yourself?"

§

When you returned to Volkening's office to report the collapse on 40th Street, he said, "The same thing is going to happen again, and more than once, I'm afraid. All the same, I'll keep on trying. Meanwhile, go home."

§

At Frank Taylor's flat in Washington Square, you met with him and Albert Erskine the evening before your departure. They did not offer to show *A Man Without Shoes* at Random House, and you could not make yourself ask.

SCENE 26

A MOVABLE AND WANDERING THING (Spring of 1947)

You'd come upon the phrase in your study of the law, where, in the Commentaries of Blackstone, it was used to qualify water, a vagrant element that by its very nature was meant to flow free, to go as it willed unrestrained. Always you'd thought it might have described as well your Uncle Dave, a man as wayward as a running stream — the Wandering Jew, the family called him, and it was truly said, for no place on earth ever knew him long. And now, as you read the telegram, you thought of water again, but this time it was still, like water in a photograph, for the telegram told you he was dead.

When you'd seen him last, he was reading Braille. He wore patches where his eyes once had been, and when you entered the room, you stood watching him for a moment, saying nothing — watching his hands move over a domino arrangement of dots, drawing words through his arms to his brain, where in the night of space, there were memories of sight, a color, a page, a face. You recalled a letter he dictated a few months before: *I don't seem to have anything to cling to,* he'd said. *I can't conceive of a God who would subject the least and meanest of his creatures to live in perpetual darkness. Many times I feel that I was born in the wrong country. If I were a Jap, I would soon find a way to join my ancestors, and everyone would be happier — except, perhaps, the ancestors. . . .*

At last you spoke, saying, "You old Bolshevik! How the hell are you?"
And he said, "I'll be damned — Julian! When did you blow in?"
"Yesterday. My publisher gave me the gate, and I'm here to find a new one."
"Write about the rich. Publishers will be looking for *you.*"
"Maggie sends you her love."
"Write about the rich," he said. "That's where the dinero is."

"I don't write for money, Unc."

"Everybody writes for money. Everybody does everything for money."

"What about Gene Debs?" you said. "When I was a kid, all I ever heard from you was Debs, Debs. You sent him cigars when he was in jail—and once, I remember, a Panama hat. He never went after the money, did he?"

"Forget about Debs."

"To do that, I'd have to forget about you."

Facing the place your voice was coming from, he seemed to be staring at you with those eye-patches, and you wondered what he was seeing in his head. His nephew at nine, when he took you to Washington? At ten, when he told you your mother had died? At thirteen, fourteen, when he carried on about *wage-slaves* and *the running dogs of capitalism*, about *Eugene Debs* . . . ?

"Did I really teach you anything, Julian?" he said.

"As much as anyone," you said, "and more than most. Whenever I write a line for the people, I feel I owe it to you. And now you say write for money."

"Ah, that's my father talking, your Grandpa Nevins, may he rest in peace. He's the one who set so much store by money, and in the end it drove me away—to Peru, to Chile, to Bolivia, to Debs. That's the only home I've ever had—socialism."

His fingers passed across a page of dots, but not, you thought, for pictures or meanings: he was only (only!) feeling his way in the dark.

"That trip to Washington," you said. "I wonder how often I've thought of it. The box at Ford's, where Lincoln was shot. The house across the street, where he died. I never forgot those things."

"Well," he said, "don't forget Debs, either."

And now a telegram was telling you he was dead.

SCENE 27

MAGGIE'S STORY (April 1947)

On her return from the studio, she said, "When my phone rang this afternoon, I thought it might be Berman or the director calling from the *Sea of Grass* set for a line-change, a piece of business. Instead, it was the cop on the downstairs desk. He said there was a man in the lobby asking to see me, a Robert Ives. I told him to put Ives on the line, and when he did, Bob spoke in a low voice, or maybe he cupped the mouthpiece to stop the cop from hearing. He'd just gotten out of jail, he said—probably for passing a bum check or raising a good one—and he was dead broke and needed money."

She paused, as if giving you a chance to speak, but you did not speak.

"I called a messenger and sent down all I had—fifty bucks, maybe. I suppose he needed more, but I couldn't take a chance on giving him a check."

Again she paused, and again you did not speak.

"I had to give him the money, Jabe. After all, I'd lived with the guy for five years. How could I turn him down?"

You said, "Do you remember the day Joe March introduced us in the Paramount elevator?"

"Of course."

"That was the best day of my life."

SCENE 28

JOHN'S STORY (May 1947)

"I knocked off for a while this morning," you said, "and I was sitting on the front stoop fooling with the dogs when I saw a car coming up the driveway. It was one I didn't recognize, and when it stopped in the turnaround, out climbed a woman I didn't recognize either, a woman of sixty, maybe, sixty-five. 'Are you John Sanford?' she said, and when I said, 'Yes,' she told me she was Mrs. Doty, Ed Doty's mother."

"Did you tell her how he queered the atomic-bomb thing?" Maggie said.

"I said I knew her son well, and I was glad to meet her. What could I do for her?, I wanted to know. Guess what came next—try and guess. 'Mr. Sanford,' she said, 'I want a job.' "

"A job?"

"That's all *I* could say—*a job?*—and she said, 'Cooking, cleaning, washing, anything.' I just sat there dumbstruck. Ed Doty, that loudmouth Leftie, that man of the peepul who makes a grand a week—here's his mother asking a stranger for a job!"

"What did you say? You had to say something."

"I said, 'Mrs. Doty, we have a housekeeper, but even if we didn't, I'd have to refuse you. If I let you work for me, I'd have to refuse you. If I let you work for me, I'd be shaming your son.' She said, 'It would deserve him right to be shamed; *he* shames *me*. It's a *Schande* the way he scrimps on his own mother.' Now I began to catch on: she could use the job, all right, but her other reason was humiliating her son, and maybe that was the real reason. I said, 'Mrs. Doty, I'm going to be frank with you.

I don't like your son any better than you do, but we're on the same side politically, and it's the Left that would suffer if we showed him up. It's too bad that our beliefs have so little effect on our natures. What God gave us, the Manifesto hasn't changed. Not yet, anyway. . . ."

SCENE 29

BROTHER AND SISTER (Summer of 1947)

In a corridor of the Good Samaritan Hospital, you were waiting for your father to be brought from the operating-room, where his prostate had just been removed. At length, he was wheeled from an elevator, followed by his surgeon, a George Cecil, who bore on high a cloth-covered tray, rather as if he were a waiter with a culinary surprise. As he neared you, he whipped the cloth away, revealing a small and irregular mass of tissue unexpectedly pale.

"Isn't that a beauty?" he said, and on he strode along the hall.

As you watched your father, still under the anaesthetic, being transferred to the bed, you wondered at the surgeon's plane of admiration. *A beauty,* he'd said from where he dwelt, far above or far below what he might've felt for a rose. He'd excised from your father what had allowed you being, but to him it was merely evidence of his skill. And where was he going with it—to be photographed, like a chef with a display of his four-star cuisine? *Isn't that a beauty?*

In a room dimmed by a dark green blind, you stood at the bedside, looking down at your father and remembering another time in another hospital, when another doctor had given him only a short time to live—*two years, Julian, three with great good luck*—and here he was, ten beyond the prophesied span. Those diviners of the day, you thought, what did they know, what that in the past had not been gleaned from footprints in ash, from sounds heard in shells, from the behavior of birds? You touched your father's face, running your fingers the wrong way of the grain. He was in need of a shave, you thought, as he'd been before, when the prediction was made from the patterns of scattered stones. He needed a shave, you thought, and when he came out from under, you'd lather his face and do what you'd done in that other place and that other time.

§

76

Later in the day, when he was fairly awake, you took his hand and held it while you said, "I have some bad news for you, papa. A wire came from New York today. Aunt Sarah is very sick."

"Ah," he said, "that *is* bad news. My wonderful sister Sarah."

"They wanted to know if there was any chance of your coming east."

With his free hand, he made the mild gesture of helplessness. "I'd go in a minute," he said.

"Would you want me to go in your place?"

He gazed up at you for a moment before saying, "You'd do a thing like that for me?"

"I'd do more, and I'd go further."

"What do they say is the matter with Sarah?"

"It's her heart."

"Not good, not good," he said. "When would you go?"

"Tomorrow, on the Superchief."

§

Your sister offered to drive you downtown to the station, and on the way, you stopped at the hospital to say goodbye to your father. He'd passed a poor night, you and Ruth were told, and it was plain from his look that if his physical pain had been deadened, his other had not. Lying there between you and Ruth, he seemed to have shrunk during the night, as if for him the speed of time had been vastly increased. You could see that he was uneasy (about your going?, you wondered), and you thought of offering to stay. In the end, though, you left it to him.

And he said, "Julian, wait a few days."

§

You waited four, and then he let you go, but you reached New York too late.

SCENE 30

CONCERNING REMISSION OF SIN (Summer of 1947)

"I'll never forgive myself," your father said. "If I hadn't stopped you, you'd've gotten there in time."

"You couldn't've known she'd go so quickly," you said. "And I'd've gotten there in time if I'd taken a plane."

"I wouldn't've wanted you to fly. Planes fall."

"That's why I took the train. So if the criterion was getting there before Aunt Sarah died, we're both at fault."

"I blocked you. I was uneasy about your being away if something went sour at the hospital."

"Nobody can fault you for wanting me here."

"I have no excuse. I put myself ahead of my sister."

"When you were sick ten-twelve years ago, Aunt Sarah called me up to her house and gave me a lecture. At a time like that, she said, a good son would give up what she called *the writing business* and provide for his father. I stuck to the writing business. I put myself ahead of you, but you forgave me."

"True," he said. "But you've never forgiven yourself."

"True," you said.

A day before your arrival in New York, your Aunt Sarah had become comatose, and though you'd seen her alive, it was through the transparency of an oxygen tent. She'd be dead in two more days, but in the little pavilion that covered her bed, death was already with her, and you could only watch its slow and overbearing way. At the time, you hadn't thought of her reproof of you, hadn't brought to mind the words she'd used to dress you down. It was only now, a week later, that you heard them coming from another world.

You said, "This is what she told me: 'Julian, your father is a sick man. He can't provide for you like ever since you were born. He can't even provide for himself. So things are turned around now—the providing falls on you.'"

"Are you still rending your clothes over that?" your father said. "It's forgotten."

"Not by me. Guilt is a dirty shirt that you can't send to the laundry."

"Do you have many such shirts, kid?"

"Quite a few," you said, and you saw that he doubted you. "There was a girl I went with back in '25 or '26. It only lasted a summer, but we were pretty friendly, and I stood in well with her family. She called one day to tell me that her father had died, and she wanted to know if I could come over. I could, of course, and when I got there, I was asked to stay till after the funeral. In the morning, they offered me breakfast, but there there was no cream for the coffee. I said, 'No cream!' That's one of my dirty shirts."

Your father gazed at you for a moment, and then he said, "No wonder they refuse them at the laundry."

SCENE 31

ART IS A WEAPON (Fall of 1947)

You thought of him only as *somebody from Downtown*. In a cast of characters, he'd've been one of those without a name, merely the performer of a function, the bearer of a spear. Where had he come from, you wondered, how had he gotten from there to here?

He stood in the doorway, and with a lighted room behind him, he spoke from his own shadow, saying, "Who invited *you*?"

Beyond him, in a cube of blue and gray smoke, you saw faces you knew, a few of them turned toward the door. "Nobody invited me," you said. "But I should've been. These discussions mean as much to me as anyone in that room—more, maybe."

"Quite possibly, but you weren't wanted," he said, and he stepped outside to the verandah, closing the door to a chink of gold. "I told you once before that you give us a lot of trouble. We have enough as it is; we don't need more from a maverick like you."

"But what's going on in there *concerns* me! I'm one of the four-five novelists in the section, and still, when principle is being argued, I'm left out in the cold. Don't you think it matters to me whether art is a weapon or only decoration?"

"You were left out because we knew what you'd say."

You stared at him. "Knew what I'd say!" you said. "They knew what Lenin would say at Smolny, but he was there!"

"Lenin and you," he said. "Pretty soon, it'll be you and Lenin."

"I've had enough of your Downtown bullshit," you said. "Either I go in there—or I go *out*."

"Hold your horses, Sanford. When I said they knew what you'd say, all I meant was that your point of view was well represented."

"What *is* my point of view?"

"That art *isn't* a weapon. That it's a thing in itself, existing independent of the condition of society. That it's true if beautiful and beautiful if true, which is all you know on earth and all you need to know."

"Well met. I must be talking to John Keats. But whoever you are, you can't be the man who read *The People From Heaven*."

"Can't I? Why not?"

"It didn't register," you said. "If that book isn't a weapon, I never saw one."

"Because it ends with a black woman blowing a white man's brains out? You think that makes it a weapon?"

"What would you call it?"

"Anti-social," he said. "A book in the service of the people will not instruct people to kill."

"I don't agree one damn bit. A book should tell people what they're up against and persuade them to resist. If resistance leads to killing, that's not the fault of the weapon."

"We had one reason for not inviting you; now we have two. But if you think you've got something to say, go in and say it. Take my advice, though—don't mention Lenin in there."

As you passed him, you said, "What's *your* name, by the way?"

He didn't answer, and you thought *somebody from Downtown.*

SCENE 32

BENJAMIN THAU* (Late in 1947)

You'd spoken to him only once, some three years earlier, but you'd seen him so often—in studio hallways, in restaurants, and week after week at the racetrack—that you came to feel you knew him well. Whenever encountered, he was like a supporting player caught off-screen, familiar for his image rather than his person, but you confused the two and assumed you knew the man. He was in his late forties, you judged, a lean, a compressed figure in bespoke clothing, neat, quiet, inobvious, and secretive—a repository of secrets, you fancied, forever locked within him against the persuasions of the world.

You knew almost nothing about him, neither his origin nor his capabilities nor such of his career as would account for his name on the door of a suite on the executive floor. What marvels had he wrought, what miracles had he brought to pass at other times and other places, what had led him from there and then to here and now, to these antiques and orientals, this power you could feel in the air?

He'd changed little since your first meeting. He was the same indrawn man you'd seen before, held together still, it seemed, by some effort of the will; it was as if at the least easing, he might go off, explode through his custom tailoring, and wind up sparged on the ceiling and the walls. He was on guard even there in his room—against what?, you wondered, against whom?—and to foil the eavesdropper, he kept his mouth tight and his voice low, letting words fall like letters through a mail-slot, and at times he could not be heard at all.

---

* One of the vice-presidents of Metro-Goldwyn-Mayer.

In response to a call from his secretary, you'd driven with Maggie to Culver City, seen her to Room 243—where her Manet print again hung askew on the wall—and climbed a further flight to Thau's suite. There the secretary announced you and indicated a door.

After seating you, Thau said, "I asked you to come here today so as we can discuss about Maggie's contract."

"What is there to discuss, Mr. Thau? It still has several months to run."

"Till March, April, somewhere in there. But now, before it runs out, is when terms should be on the table."

"Terms?" you said. "The terms are stated in the contract."

"What I'm talking is a *new* contract," he said. "Other writers, a contract is running out, it runs out—goodbye and good luck. Not Maggie. We want her to stay where she is."

"I'm glad to hear that, Mr. Thau. She'll be glad too. She likes it here."

"She's been on the lot since—when is it, 1939?—and we look on her as a company asset. So what I'm exploring is, on what terms could we renew her contract for, say, three more years? That would be three years straight, you understand—no options."

"I understand that," you said, "but I don't understand what you mean by *terms.*"

"Terms, demands—what's the difference?"

"But, Mr. Thau, Maggie is making no demands."

"No? Then she don't know how good she is, and you don't either. The kind of work she does for the company, the company remembers it. Look how versatile she is—vehicles for Gable and Turner and Ava, for Tracy, Hepburn, Liz Taylor. And for Garson—now there's a tough one to write for, Garson."

"She was paid for all that, and well paid. Seventeen hundred and fifty dollars a week."

"And she don't want more now?"

"Everybody wants more, I suppose, but Maggie would never demand it. M-G-M has been good to her."

"Let's stop beating around the bushes. Would she accept a three-year contract at two thousand, twenty-two fifty, and twenty-five hundred, no options, and six weeks off each year with pay?"

"Certainly, Mr. Thau."

§

You went downstairs to Maggie and said, "Bennie Thau thinks I don't know how good you are."

"Well," Maggie said, "what happened up there?"

"He's a company man, but I like him, and I wish I knew why. He's the enemy."

"He isn't. I know him, and you don't."

"He doesn't speak; he conspires. He slips you the lowdown, like a spy in a crowd. All the same, there's something appealing about him."

"He's the nicest man on the Metro lot," Maggie said. "He's for the company, but he never lies, and he never says what he doesn't mean. That's rare in these parts . . . By the way, what do I have to do before you tell me what the meeting was about?"

"It was nothing important," you said. "Some nonsense about extending your contract for—what was it, now?—three years."

"And what did you say?"

"I said Yes."

"I'm surprised. You're supposed to be a deadly negotiator."

"I fought hard, but you're going to be forced to take a raise. To two grand, twenty-two fifty, and twenty-five hundred."

She crossed the room to kiss you, saying, "Go and tell the Governor—and take him a bottle of Johnnie Walker Black."*

§

You poured a jigger of Scotch for him, and raising it, he said, "To you and that marvelous *schicksa* of yours—and to Mr. Walker, who should never had died."

And you said, "*L'chayim!*"

On the wall beside him hung a photograph of your Grandma Shapiro, his mother. Ruch'l, her name had been, Ruch'l Lieberman, and there she was as you'd always known her, in a black *sheitl* and a black dress and wearing her golden earrings.

"Julian," your father said, "do you ever wonder about your luck?"

"Bad?" you said. "Or good?"

"What bad luck have you ever had? Apart from having me as a father, of course."

You looked past him at the old lady (to you, you thought, she'd always been old), but gazing straight at you with those dark brown, those iodine eyes, she seemed to be seeing something through you, as if you weren't there.

"Let me ask you another question," your father said. "I think I know the answer, but I'd like to hear it from you."

"Ask," you said.

"How do you feel about being supported by your wife?"

"There are guys, I suppose, who'd be ashamed to appear in public, but

---

* Note: It would last him a month.

I'm not one of those guys. I'd be ashamed only if I *refused* her support, because she believes in me. So—I feel fine. Is that the answer you were expecting?"

"That's the one, kid."

And now it was he who turned to the photograph, and he said, "My father never did a lick of work in the family butchershop. My mother did it all while he sat in the synagogue and *dovvened*. That is, while he was *supposed* to be *dovvening*. Actually, he was playing chess."

"How did he feel about being supported by his wife?"

Had he heard you when he said, "Playing chess. And he thought she didn't know. . . ."

§

And you returned to the studio for Maggie.

THE COLOR OF THE AIR, IV

JOHN CHAPMAN — 1847
BUCKEYE JOHNNY APPLESEED

They say he first turned up in Ohio around about 1801 — on Zane's Trace, it was, along Licking Creek — and they say he come leading a pack-horse loaded to the hocks with burlap bags, but they didn't say, because they didn't know, what-all was in the bags. Being he was a black-eyed man, a queer thing in those parts, and being he kind of kept to himself, which was all the queerer, he let himself in for a little side-watching, and no matter if he did overlook to bring a gun.

They say, the ones that made it their business, that he marched out onto a cleared piece of land and drawed something out of the topmost of his bags, which he buried it in a slew of shallow holes and went away, and when he was gone, it still being their business, they say they got down on their shins and poked about for whatever he'd cached (it figured, God knows how, to be gold). Only finding dirt as deep as they dug, they tried to pass him off as addled, but all the same they felt like chumps for being hankypankied by an out-of-stater.

They say this identical black-eyed man shown up next along the Muskingum, still with that pack-animal and still with those bags, and they say that there too he made some hocus-pocus over holes in

83

the ground, and there too nobody got richer for scratching where it itched. And now the story began to get around, to pass from hand to hand like the gold they hunted and never found, and you heard that the black-eyed man and his monkey-shines had been seen wherever there was bottom-land—on the Scioto and the Hocking, on White Woman Creek, on all the Miamis and the Maumee, on the Big Walnut and the Black Fork of the Mohican. And you heard other things as well, how he played with cubs while the b'ar looked on or snoozed, how he walked barefoot and damn near b.a. in the snow, how he found his way just by following his nose, like a bee or a bird, and you heard how he'd douse his fire if insects flew too close to the flames.

After a time, they say people took to expecting him in the spring, looking forward to his freak but quiet ways, and when he would finally arrive—with his horse and his bags, but never with a gun—they would feel good, like they did about a rain, and they would talk to him sometimes, and some would be sad as he went about his fruitless work of hiding nothing in plain view of all. They dug no more now in the loose soil after he'd moved on: they let it lay, out of respect, you might say.

Fruitless? Not by a damn sight and a long chalk! Nobody said fruitless when the apple trees came, because that's what he'd had in those burlap bags—orchards for Ohio!

It's a good thing you're dead, Johnny. It's a good thing you didn't live to see what they did to your trees. They're gone, Johnny, the trees and all that grew from the other seed you scattered—catnip, snakeweed, hoarhound, dog-fennel, and pennyroyal. It's a good thing you're all done coming down the pike in your coffee-sack clothes and that stew-kettle you wore for a hat— you'd've been hot, Johnny, because there's very little shade.

They say you could stick pins in your flesh and feel no pain, but you'd've flinched for your trees if you'd seen them brought to their knees. They took fifteen years to grow and fifteen minutes to whack down, and even the axe was held to be slow—only one would fall at a time—and so the speed-crazy fell to using fire, and whole districks went to hell in a handbasket. It's a good thing you're someplace else now, Johnny, a good thing you're never coming back to a world held together by concrete and lashed down with steel rail and copper wire, a spoiled world.

They say you died up around Fort Wayne, and while they don't say where you went from there, a lot of us have a fair idea. We don't know the name of the state, Johnny—let's just say it hasn't been admitted to the Union yet— but whatever it's called, it must be pleasant up there under trees that'll never be snags or sawyers in some spring flood. Trees must grow better when they know they'll not be harmed: their fruit must be prime.

*Are you running short of seed, Johnny? We could each bring a bag when
we come. . . .*

SCENE 33

DISHONOR AMONG THIEVES (Fall of 1947)

When you returned from the meeting, the house was dark save for slats of
light across the bedroom windows. Leaving their boxes, lined up on the porch,
the outdoor dogs came around to the garage to greet you, and after giving
each of them a rough-up, you went inside through the kitchen, where the
family-dog Juno vacuumed your sleeve before letting you pass.

Propped by her pillows, Maggie was reading. You kissed her, and sitting
on the edge of her bed, you tilted her book to learn the title. "*McTeague,*"
you said. "I saw the film twenty years ago, but I've never forgotten that gold
tooth on a black and white screen."

Maggie said, "Stroheim shot enough footage to run all day. The story goes
that he'd never look at the cut version."

"*McTeague* is Norris's best book. *The Octopus* and *The Pit* come nowhere
near it."

"Stroheim was so good that I confuse the book with the picture."

You listened to the dogs coming back to their boxes; as they arranged
themselves, wood shavings ground in their pads, and the ropes beneath them
creaked. Off at the middle of the orchard, water fell on water in the artificial
well.

"Was it a good meeting?" Maggie said.

For a further moment, you listened to outside sound, and then, looking
away from Maggie, you said, "I heard something tonight that beats the
Dutch — and the French too. Remember that Jim Chilton — the one who insulted Mrs. Inge? Well, he and another Left-Wing screenwriter named Henry
Samson got together to dream up an original screenplay. It was original, all
right — original with de Maupassant, who called it *Boule de Suif.* These lads
simply stole the plot, changed the names, the time, and the place, and offered
the work around as their own."

"I hate to say this," Maggie said, "but I'm not surprised."

"I am," you said, "and I haven't even finished the story. The screenplay
got nowhere at the studios — they should've tried to fence it — and finally Samson

said the hell with the thing and forgot it. Imagine his rage when he found out that Chilton had taken his name off the script and sold it as his own for eight thousand dollars."

"Poor Samson," Maggie said. "Hoist with his own petard. . . . I've always wanted a chance to say that."

The dogs sprang from their boxes and raced away through the orchard after some fancied intruder or real, and you heard their faroff barking and the sound of flurried leaves.

"Samson took his grievance to a committee," you said. "A hearing was held, and Chilton was forced to cough up four thousand dollars."

"To whom?" Maggie said.

"To Samson."

"Why not to the French Academy? Or de Maupassant's heirs? All the committee did was take half the loot from one thief and give it to the other."

"I know," you said.

"Yes, *you* know, but the committee doesn't."

§

Later, lying in the dark, you heard the dogs sigh and stir in their sleep, and you heard waterpour, and the wind, and the house itself as its timbers strove within the walls.

And then Maggie spoke from across the room, softly saying, "Are you awake, Jabe?"

And you said, "Yes."

"I've been thinking about that committee. It made an immoral decision."

"What would've been moral?"

"The story was stolen property. Nobody should've gained by it."

"Who'd get the eight thousand?"

"There's something here that's more important than money—and that's guys who steal from the dead and then from each other. The committee hasn't put a stop to that."

"What else could it do?"

"It could've kicked those crooks out. Because next time, they're apt to do worse."

"Like what, Mag?"

"John, are you easy in your mind about being in the hands of such shameless bastards?"

"No, but I don't know what to do about it."

"Did you ever think of this? If they're capable of stealing, what would stop them from giving you away, giving everybody away?"

"You're running off with yourself, Mag."

"Am I? You come home with an appalling story like that, and it doesn't remind you of Judas?"

The question seemed to stay on the air, to keep on asking itself with undiminished force—*Judas,* you heard, *Judas.*

And you said, "You can't stop believing just because of Judas."*

SCENE 34

SOMEBODY ELSE FROM DOWNTOWN

His car came slowly up the driveway and stopped beneath the stone pine in the parking, and as you watched him step out onto the gravel, you found yourself wondering what kind had fared forth on this occasion from dreary rooms near Tenth and Main. Was he merely one more party priest rounding up a stray, or was there something in his survey of the grounds, something in the way he stood, the stance itself, that set him apart from the servers of time? It was odd, you thought, that the Airedales were caught regardant, as if they too could not make up their minds.

It was a Saturday, you remember, and Ruth Borne, your housekeeper, was away for the weekend. Alone in the house with Maggie, you opened the door for the visitor as he mounted the steps to the porch.

"I'm Rich Gardner," he said. "From you know where."

"And we're the Sanfords, of course," you said. "Marguerite and John. Come in."

"It's a nice day," Gardner said. "If it's all the same, why don't we stay outside?"

"We have some chairs over there," Maggie said, indicating the grass around the pool, and then she moved past the man and led the way toward a great white oak that ruled the lawn. Across her shoulder as she went, she said, "Did you think we might record this meeting, Mr. Gardner?"

And he said, "Yes." And then he said, "You might."

The chairs were in the fretted shade of the oak, and now and then a leaf danced down to float on the water, a small brown boat with its sharp oars shipped.

---

* In the hearings of the House Committee on UnAmerican Activities during 1951, both Chilton and Samson were informers.

"Mrs. Sanford," Gardner said, "I was sent here to get you to change your mind."

"I'm afraid you're not going to have much luck."

"If this was a matter of luck, I'd've stayed downtown. I thought it had something to do with principle."

"It certainly has," she said, "and that's why you'll have no luck."

"As I hear it, you want to withdraw because of that de Maupassant thing."

"That settled it for me, but there are other things."

"Let's talk first about the quarrel over the story."

"The *theft* of the story," Maggie said.

"All right, theft. What did we do that was wrong? What *should* we have done?"

"You should've kicked those people out, that's what."

"How would we have gained by that?"

You were gazing at the oak, at its six-foot bole, at the deep grooves in its grayed bark, and you wondered how old it was, what its rings showed of dry years and wet, of frost and fire. From a muscle-bound branch, a jay berated the world below.

"You'd've been rid of a couple of thieves who stole from de Maupassant and then from each other. You don't keep that kind around unless what they did doesn't trouble you."

"We looked into the background of those two—thieves, you call them," Gardner said, "and what we found was this. Like it or not, they were shaped by the society they grew up in, a bourgeois society, and its morality was their morality. We felt that it was more to blame than they were, and, besides, they hurt no one but themselves."

Maggie stared at him for a moment, studied him before saying, "That will never do, never. They hurt us all—you, me, everyone. And in not getting rid of them, in keeping them around as if they were more sinned against than sinning, you've given a signal that anything people do, no matter how evil, can be explained, justified, by the system they live under. I think it's disgraceful to defend no-goods because they grew up in a no-good society. We all did, but we're not all knaves!"

The jay flew off through the foliage. Its flight shook the leaves, dislodging dust that descended slowly, like sediment, in a jar of sunlight.

Gardner said, "There are more knaves than you think, Mrs. Sanford, and it's my job to work with them."

"That's your lookout, but my advice is, don't ever let them get behind you—they'll do you in." And then she shook her head, saying, "All those high principles you talk about, and still they stole *Boule de Suif*!"

"There's nothing magical about a political principle," Gardner said. "It won't make saints out of sinners."

"If your principles are no better than anybody else's, what do we need socialism for?"

A light air struck the surface of the pool, and as if a solid had fallen into it, concentric ripples made heavy seas for a fleet of leaves.

"Under capitalism," Gardner said, "there's very little chance for people to change. *Their* character is formed by *its* character, its acquisitive character, and they—well, they steal *Boule de Suif.*"

"If people won't change till they get to Utopia, how do you know what they'll do when they get there? Maybe they'll corrupt Utopia."

"Maybe," Gardner said, "but we have to believe in a Utopia."

The jay had returned to the branch overhanging the lawn, and again it was complaining against what it saw below.

"I'll tell you what I believe," Maggie said. "I come from a working-class family, a low-income family—so low, in fact, that we sometimes lived in a tarpaper shack. So I don't have to be told about the poor, the sick, and the old. I've known about them all along, and I've always wanted to make things better for them. But at heart, I'm a reformer, not a rebel, and I went to meetings for one reason only, to be with my husband, who *is* a rebel. At those meetings, even the few I attended, I saw and heard more than enough to put me off. I'm naïve, I guess, but I expected that noble deeds would go with noble words. Your people, our people, had to be better than others, but in many respects, they weren't as good."

Gardner spoke to you now, saying, "Does your wife do all the talking for the Sanfords?"

It was Maggie, though, who continued. "Actually, I do very little talking, and I'd not be talking now if I thought John would tell you the things he's told me. Week after week, I've watched him go off to those meetings like an eager pup, only to come home like a whipped dog, and when he tells me why, I ask him when he's going to quit."

"And what does he say?"

"Never."

"And what about you, Mrs. Sanford?"

"I'm out of it, from this very moment."

"I'm sorry," Gardner said.

Now there were two jays on the branch, and they seemed to be decrying each other.

§

You walked Gardner to his car, leaving Maggie where she was, in the sun and shade under the oak. From the driver's seat, he reached through the open window to shake your hand.

"Tell me something, Sanford," he said. "You know your wife better than anyone. Why didn't you stop her from joining the Party?"

"A good question," you said. "I've asked it myself."

"And how did you answer?"

"All I've ever come up with is this: it was a test."

"Of what? Of whom?"

"Of me."

"I don't understand."

"Joining the Party isn't like joining the Scouts. There are dangers, political, social, economic, especially the last. If I had stopped Maggie, I'd never have known whether I was protecting her or protecting all this," and you made a gesture that took in your surroundings, your condition.

Gardner studied you, down to your feet slowly and slowly back to your eyes, and then he said, "So what you did was nothing: you stood aside while your wife walked in harm's way."

"I'm afraid that's true."

"All to prove that your socialism was pure."

"It was the worst mistake I ever made: I let her act against her inclination."

"You regret, then, that she joined."

"I could rend my garments," you said.

Gardner worked the steering wheel as if he were driving, and then he removed his hands as if the car had come to a halt. He said, "You're one odd cove, do you know that?"

"I know it now, too late."

"We've been talking about *your* motive. Let's talk about your wife's. Have you any idea why she joined?"

"To go along, I suppose."

"How about this — to make herself perfect in your eyes?"

You stared at him. "But she *was* perfect!" you said. "I'm the one who's not."

And now Gardner drove away.

SCENE 35

RUTH BORNE, HOUSEKEEPER (1946–1948)

Through the rear window of your room, you could see her on the lawn, seated in a welter of dogs, a black and tan and tumbling mass, and as you'd now and then do, you wondered why she'd chosen her line of work. She'd responded to an ad you'd placed in the *Valley Green Sheet,* and when she appeared for an interview, you supposed at first that she'd come by mistake, that she'd taken a wrong turning on her way to another place. It was you, though, who'd made the mistake: as she approached you from her car, parked in the turnaround, you saw that she was carrying a folded paper colored green.

You'd not have guessed her to be a housekeeper. Indeed, she seemed more like the lady of the house, a far cry from your beloved Ingeborg Emil, who was a housekeeper at her own insistence, who allowed herself no liberties, who if persuaded to sit in your presence would use only half of a chair — Ingeborg Emil, to whom you were Mr. and Mrs. Sonnfort and never John and Marguerite. But if Ruth Borne was a housekeeper, the house she kept was her own — and that was it!, you thought. She looked like the lady of the house because in her mind she *was.*

Why had it taken you so long to understand what was plain at the start, there when you watched her come from her car with the *Green Sheet* in hand? What you'd seen was a woman of forty-five, give or take a year, comely enough, and trigged up as if to receive for an afternoon tea — *receive!*, that was what you should've guessed from the way she bore herself, the way she was dressed. Out on the lawn, the Airedales were dozing now, lying anywhichway around her as if slain, and she was idly twirling a dandelion while gazing at some blur in the distance that had meaning only for her.

You thought back to the day of her arrival, when you'd mentioned your — how had you put it?, *requirements?* — and you recalled her smile as she spoke of a twenty-year marriage and a home of her own that had never known disorder or an ill-prepared meal, spoke past you at the same blur, perhaps, that she was fixed on now.

Only little by little had you learned of those twenty years. Her husband, a flyer during the Great War, had taken thereafter to barnstorming while she held down the fort, as she put it, somewhere in Illinois. Always, she said, the house was ready for his return, but a time came when he did not return, and your thought, of course, was that he'd crashed. You were told, though, that he hadn't been killed; he'd met a girl, and he'd stayed away. *Stayed away,* she said, and you remembered trying to fathom the words. How could he have gone off to do loop-the-loops over a cornfield, barrel-rolls, Immelmann turns, and then meet a girl and just *stay away?* What about his orderly wife, his paired shoes and brushed clothes, his preferences in food, his unused half of a bed?

Willingly had you let her keep on holding the fort, for you and Maggie now instead of Arthur Borne, that blur in the distance, he who'd stayed away with his Mexican girl in Amarillo, Wichita, Albuquerque — and your house (her house) was orderly as once in Illinois. You came to admire and pity her greatly, but you could never make her stop hating the Mexicans, all seventy million of them.

SCENE 36

ART ROWLEY, HANDYMAN (1946–1948)

You hired him to look after the horses, but that was only one of the things he knew how to do; in fact, there was nothing he couldn't do except do nothing. You saw him sitting down only when Ruth Borne fed him lunch; the rest of the day he spent on his feet with a rake in his hands, or a hay-fork, or a wrench, or a post-hole digger, or cutting an eye-fringe for the horse-fly season. *Jack-of-all-trades,* you'd think as you watched him devise whatevers and jigamarees, but they all worked, he was master of them all. What did you not learn from his innumerable skills? What were you not taught of pipe, stone, wood, and wire? What, as you fetched for him, helped him, or got in his way and heard him say *John, why don't you get your ass behind you where it belongs?*

He was a secretive man, in particular about where he lived. He'd come and go by bus, and only when it rained would he accept a lift, and even then never all the way to his door; he'd have you set him down at some corner, and there he'd stand till you drove away. It was many a day before you found out that he was hiding from a wife he hated and living with a woman named Mae, whom he loved. Truart, she called him.

And he was secretive about another thing, one you'd still be unaware of if he hadn't told you of it himself. Even so, he might not have spoken if he hadn't expected to die. He sent for you from the Veterans Hospital at Sawtelle, where he was to be operated on the next day, and when you saw him lying in a ward, cinder-colored for want of a shave and staring off at whatever he had on his mind, you too thought he was nearly done with the world. When you stopped at the bedside, he looked up at you as if taking your measure, as if he were at one of his chores and gauging the dimensions of a board.

And then, taking you tightly by the arm, he said, "I'm from a little town in Idaho. I had a nice place there, sixty acres, a tight house, some timber, and a few head of beef cattle. I was doing pretty good till I come down with the same sickness I got now, and I run up a slew of bills getting better. The man with the mortgage, I begged him to give me time, but he was hungry for his money, and he foreclosed me out of everything, house, timber, stock, and all. He was a Jew, and ever since I've hated Jews."

He paused, looking away at the rest of the ward, at other beds, other patients, looking away from himself, really, but not releasing you.

And finally he said, "When I started working for you, I knew you were a Jew, and I hated you along with the rest. I can tell you that now because I don't feel that way any more."
"Why not, Art?" you said.
"You taught me something."
"I did? I thought I was learning from you."
"Thanks for coming, John," he said. "I just wanted you to know."

He didn't die then, and he was your friend till he did.

SCENE 37

DR. GUSTAVE HOLMGREN, cont'd. (Fall of 1947)

He'd moved his offices from Sixth Street near Alvarado to a more modern building on Beverly Drive, and on your first visit thereafter, he received both you and Maggie at the same time. He seemed ill at ease, possibly, you thought, because of his new surroundings — the fashionable location, the new furnishings and equipment — and his tic, the spasm that wried his neck, was worse than before, and in its embrace, its thrall, he anguished all the more. Seated at his desk, he twitched a greeting to each of you, but his chorea made him appear to repeat it, to greet you again and again until at length you ignored it. But even as it faded in your mind you knew that it was still clawing at Holmgren's, riding him like a witch.

"What're you here for?" he said.
And Maggie said, "The yearly go-over."
"What about him?"
"The same," you said.
He opened a newspaper and folded it back to an inner page. "I thought maybe you came to say goodbye."

"Where would I be going?"

"To the slaughter," he said, "along with these lambs," and he tossed the newspaper across the desk.

It landed the wrong way to, and letting it lie, you scanned an upside-down headline: TEN IN HOLLYWOOD SUMMONED TO WASHINGTON.

"Read it," Holmgren said.

"I read it this morning."

"We both read it," Maggie said.

"And still, there you sit, ready for your yearly go-over. For Christ's sake, wake up!"

"From what, Gus?" you said.

"You're dreaming if you don't think this means you!" he said, and reaching out, he slapped the paper. "You know these guys?"

"All of 'em."

"You got any idea what's going to happen to them?"

"The way you go on, they're going to be shot."

"Just as good as: they're going to get fired. Director, writer, actor, or just plain *schmuck*, they're going to be out on their ass."

"For what?"

"Their nutty political beliefs."

"Wouldn't that violate their Constitutional rights?"

"Rights!" Holmgren said. "Where Communism is involved, they've got no more rights than a phone-book in an outhouse!"

He sat there trying to confront you steadily, but over and over as some nerve or muscle pulled it, his head made a quarter-turn aside and then a quarter-turn back.

"I like you kids," he said, "and I don't want to see you hurt. So when I say you're heading for a fall, I'm not giving you any secondhand stuff from the Jonathan Club. I get it straight from Louis Mayer. He's one of my patients, and when his pants are down, he talks."

"What does he hell you, Gus?" Maggie said.

"That there's no place for Reds in the picture industry."

"That's a dangerous stand to take. What if there was a movement to kick out the Jews?"

"He'd join it!" Holmgren said.

"I've heard him on the subject," Maggie said. "I'm sometimes invited to the executive diningroom, and I was at Mayer's table when he claimed that if there were Communists on the lot, they'd never managed to get a line of propaganda into his films. As far as I know, he lets it go at that."

"You're kidding yourself," Holmgren said. "If he tolerates Reds over at M-G-M, it's because he can't identify them. If he finds out who they are, they'll wish they were dead."

94

"I came here for a drink of barium," you said.

"You have no ulcer—not yet, anyway," Holmgren said. "but if you want to throw fifty dollars away, it's your lookout. I'll give you a tip for nothing, though—steer clear of your Commie friends, or you'll live to rue the day." He drew the newspaper back over the desk, and then he held his head with both hands in an effort to keep it still. "But it may be too late already."

SCENE 38

A FEW QUESTIONS AND ANSWERS (Fall of 1947)

It was late in the afternoon by the time you left Holmgren, and you did not return Maggie to Culver City. Instead, you drove toward home through Cold-water Canyon and the hills. For a way, the car was filled with soundless repetitions of the words and phrases just now spoken, a silent mile of speech within your head. You'd crossed Sunset, you remember, and you'd passed the palm driveway of the sprawled hotel when Maggie made herself heard for the first time.

"That Committee in Washington," she said. "Has it got the power to ask those people about their political beliefs?"

"Yes," you said, "but they don't have to answer."

"What good is power if you can't use it?"

"It's still power. The Committee is legal, and it can drag people clear across the country and ask them any damn thing it wants to. That's power, and that's using it. But people have power too, and if the Committee goes too far, they can balk."

"What would be too far?'"

"Making them testify against themselves. Under the Fifth Amendment, they can refuse."

"This'll surprise you, but I've read the Fifth Amendment. And this'll surprise you even more: it has to do with crime."

"What's your point?"

"Is it a crime to be a Communist?"

"No."

"My point is this, then: if it isn't a crime to be a Communist, why can't those people be asked if that's what they are?"

"Because the day may come when it *is* a crime."

The road was climbing now, winding upward between sagebrush slopes that ran like a firebreak along the spine of the rise.

You were at the crest before Maggie spoke again, saying, "So you think those ten people will go to Washington and refuse to answer, and the Committee will just say, 'Shucks'?"

"What else can it do?" you said. "It can't put them on the rack. The Star Chamber is gone."

"John, my beamish boy, *Alice* was written for children like you. You live in Wonderland."

"Where do *you* live?"

"Where I was brought up, the world lay in wait for you just outside your door. One mistake, and you wouldn't even make it to the mailbox. You say the Star Chamber is gone. I say the *Committee* is the Star Chamber, and it can torture you just by making you stand before it."

"You're seeing things," you said.

And she said, "Johnny, my dear Jew, don't the Jews ever learn?"

SCENE 40

SENDOFF AT THE BURBANK AIRPORT (October 1947)

You know those guys?
All of 'em.

The exit to the runway was almost blocked by the rally. Around the ten who had been commanded to Washington, a centripetal crowd of dozens was gathered, each of them trying to pat a back or shake a hand or, from the fringes, to raise a fist above the heads that intervened. You were one of several who merely looked on, standing over against a wall and apart from the commotion. For all you can recall of your thoughts, you might've been there not in support of a cause, but to hearten a team out to do battle for an ellipsoidal ball.

You know those guys?

What of the ten and the others?, you wonder. Did they see further than you, did they know or apprehend what lay ahead? Was any of them a Daniel, that read and knew the meaning of the words on the wall? Or were they all like you, believers in spite of misgivings, hopeful still that the grass would kill the weeds?

You know those guys?

At an announcement over the loudspeakers, the tumult grew. Farewells were cried out now, even by those who were near at hand, and then, as the doors opened, the crowd seemed to be drawn into the four-engine roar outside, and it streamed away toward a barrier of wire, a filter for all but the ten who were due to fly.

You know those guys?

Facing the backs of the party, you saw your team, your warriors, climb a gangway, punch once each at the sky, and disappear into the plane. And then, after slowly moving a long way off, it came back at speed, and soon the swan was in the air. But did you really think in metaphor? Was all you saw a bird?

You know those guys. . . ?

SCENE 40

ARE YOU NOW OR HAVE YOU EVER BEEN. . . ? (October 1947)

A real American would be proud to answer the question.
—J. Parnell Thomas, Chairman

Late in the afternoon, you'd sometimes wait at the gate for the paper to be flung at the driveway from a passing car. With your arms resting on the topmost bar, you'd gaze across the road at an alfalfa field where hay lay curing, and at the dairy beyond, its barns and sheds gilt-edged by the sun. In the windrows, there'd be flocks of starlings, and you'd watch them at their insecticide, their hue changing as they worked, from black to green to navy blue, and then at some alarm, there'd be a mass takeoff, a synchronized maneuver, and a mass landing far away. And when the paper came, you'd read of the proceedings in Washington,

> or was it in Valladolid or Languedoc, in Lombardy or Strasburg that the Grand Inquisitor sat? But wherever it may have been, there testimonies were given against the witches of these latter days—the Reds. Heresies most grievous were imputed to them by heroes of the screen, riders of range, sky, and submarine deep, by celluloid doers of derring. Sworn, they were proud to answer the question, they said: *We never were, and we scorn, we abhor these ten who are. . . .*

Missing you at the house, the dogs, all four of them, would come to join you at the gate, nosing you first, then trying your hand for a wooling, and finally, heads to the ground, following cold and crooked trails into the orchard. The sun would ride low now, and its rays would lie almost level through the trees, sprays of light that the milling dogs would fill with dust. And you'd read of

> ten unreal Americans who did not feel as the Chairman did, who assumed that, being free, they were free to speak and assemble as they chose, even if they spoke and assembled with witches, with those hell-born sons-of-bitches known as Reds. They invoked the guarantees of the First Amendment, and so far from being proud to answer, they said *We're more than proud to refuse. . . .**

Ahead of you in the orchard, the sun would light an orange as if from within, and it glowed, the last one left on the tree.

SCENE 41

A RAINY EVENING IN ENCINO (November 1947)

"Well," Maggie said, "what do you think?"

"Think about what?" you said.

"The stand those guys took before the Committee. What do you think of it?"

You stared past her at a framed poster, a Bonnard, and you read its legend: *Salon des Cents — Août–Septembre 1896.* What made you remember that it was raining? What had fixed the weather in your mind?

"Answer me, John."

"I think there's a good chance they'll all go to jail."

"How about what you said the other day — that people don't have to disclose their politics?"

"They don't, but they have to invoke the Fifth Amendment, or they're not protected. All of them used the First."

Your gaze moved from the woman suggested by Bonnard to a perfume poster by Lautrec — hands flinging confetti at a yellow-haired girl. How many times, you wondered, had your eyes toured the walls? So often, you thought, that the posters would still be there after they'd been removed.

---

* All ten would be cited for contempt of Congress.

98

"Something's wrong with the law," Maggie said. "Why should people lose their rights just because they used the wrong number? First, Fifth, what difference does it make?"

"All I know is, if they'd used the Fifth, they'd've walked away. But, no, they had to take 'a principled stand'!"

Near a doorway hung Manet's *Fifer*, a sad-faced Zouave, ageless when painted, ageless at L'Orangerie, and ageless now.

"Principled stand!" you said. "As if principle meant something to the Committee! If principle counted, there'd *be* no Committee. But that wasn't the only mistake those ten guys made. A worse one was thinking they were tougher than Congress—shouting, interrupting, showing disrespect. *Contumacy*, the papers called it. Christ, there's a word I haven't seen since law school."

"At Greeley Business College, I *never* saw it."

"Whoever advised them should've looked up the meaning of *contempt*—because that's what it was. You can't behave like that and get away with it."

And there was a poster for *La Revue Blanche*. It showed a woman in a skating costume who reminded you of your mother—was it the feathered hat or the sway of the long blue skirt? How lovely! you thought, and you read the word *bi-mensuelle*.

"What would you have done?" Maggie said.

"Kept my trap shut," you said. "Nobody was listening."

Why are you so sure it was raining?

SCENE 42

THE LA BREA TAR PITS (November 1947)

They were in Hancock Park, only a short walk from where your father lived. On a mild day, you might find him there with his friends, and at times he'd be alone, reading or merely looking off through the trees and the buildings at seventy years of bygone days. Not wanting to startle him, you'd speak as you came near—*Counselor,* you'd say, or *Mr. Sappara*—and he'd return from wherever he'd been, saying *Well, if it isn't the kid!*

The park was of no small size, thirty or forty acres, you supposed it to be, and it contained pathways that were only faintly reached by sound from outside, by auto-horns and rolling rubber and the underlying residue of speech. It was pleasant to be there, to warm in your father's presence as much as in the sun, and you'd put an arm across his shoulders and smooth and smooth his hair, and he'd keep on talking of things old and new and pretend to be unaware.

On the particular afternoon, the path he'd picked for himself ran along the rim of the tar pits, and from his bench he could see their uneasy surface, a skin of opalescent water marred here and there by eruptions of oil from the fathomless asphalt below. He was seated, you thought, at the edge of an earlier geological time, one that was no longer lineal: beginning at his feet, it plunged, down, down, through a thin layer of water and then a black-brown smother that held all that was left of the age—bones. . . .

"Kid," he said, "I've been wanting to ask—are you mixed up in this thing?"
"What thing?" you said.
"The thing in Washington. Those ten Communists who were cited for contempt."
"We don't know that they're Communists, do we?"
And he said, "Don't we?"

Why, you wondered, had he chosen for the day the part of the park within sight of the pits, a great common grave for creatures of the past, it now as dead as they? To this place had come the peccary to drink, the camel, the sloth, the primitive horse, and venturing into its mask of water, they'd been sucked into the pitch, eaten alive and entire, the imperial elephant as well as the beetle, the bird, and the snake.

"I've read about this place," you said, "but I never was this close to it."
"My friends from the cafeteria," your father said, "they don't like it either."
"I can understand that. They avoid cemeteries."
His gesture was small, hardly more than a flirt of the hand. "Julian," he said, "it's all a cemetery."
"Every kind of animal came here to drink," you said. "They took it for a water-hole, and it was—if they stayed on the bank. If they waded in, and millions did, down they went."

You thought yourself back to the scene you'd described, and you saw mammoths floundering in the ooze, bison in a standpat stampede, and a frenzy of giant wolves, and you heard roars and screams and final sighs—while safe on the bank, the luckier ones, the warier, all but oblivious drank.

"You haven't answered the question, Julian. Are you mixed up in that Washington thing?"
"The ones that stayed on solid ground," you said. "They just watched the others sink."

100

THE COLOR OF THE AIR, V

THE WAR WITH MEXICO, 1846–48
POOR MEXICO, SO FAR FROM GOD

and so near the United States.
—old saying

They were nearer than near: they touched. They lay side by side along the *filum aquae* of the Rio Grande, the middle line, the thread of a stream that in certain seasons sank from sight, became a bed of silt, a dry and winding band of gravel, sand, and stranded reeds. They verged there, the two, in a concurrence of curves that was very like an embrace, but alas the day for poor Mexico!—the *abrazo* cost her Texas, and still more would be lost, twice Texas, before the gringos were through.

Her army was a press-gang army, indios and peons dragged or driven to some regiment, scrags even in uniform, for their officers sutled the mess. Thin men made thin soldiers, and when they were killed for running away, the ranks were filled with picaroons, assassins, and (far, far from God!) ravishers of boys. Their muskets were the discards of the British, and the French had cast their cannon for some long-forgotten war, but their lancers—ah, their lancers would ride through hell, and their bands would play them back! An army of put-upons, those mix-bloods and Yaquis, sad, hopeless, strange to Christ, but they tired never, like burros, and always they were brave.

On their north, the South—and having taken Texas, she looked beyond to what Texas led to, a bigger Dixie for her nigger slaves. And there it was, from the rise of the Colorado to Califa's paradise—a million square miles! If all went well, they'd make five more states for cotton, and well it went indeed. At Resaca de la Palma, with their secondhand guns and their know-nothing generals, the Mexicans fought for two days before being driven back against the river, leaving twelve hundred dead on the field, little piles of regimentals, rather like fallen flags, and then, *mala suerte,* three hundred more in water that was deep for the time of year

aye
                        it went well there for the gringos
and well at Monterrey,

101

where you would think the Citadel
might have stopped them,
the Black Fort, we called it,
with guns commanding two approaches,
the Monclova road and the road from Marin,
and we had much faith also
in the redoubts
that were placed about the city
and in the high hills that walled it
and the walls within,
and there was a river to be crossed,
a gorge to take in single file,
after which the massed houses
in the narrow streets—
you would think these things enough
to turn them away
and send them back the long march
to Port Isabel,
but they were not enough,
no, nor would more have been enough
and all the things that had to fall
before they gained the day
fell, and sad to say,
not even the lancers
with their red and green pennons,
their gold frogging,
and their bridles that seemed all silver
could keep the white flag
from being raised
above the Black Fort

        it went well there for them,
and at Agua Nueva,
where they were outnumbered
four or five to one,
and we were so positioned
as to be able to take them in rear
unless they fell back on the sheep ranch
at Buena Vista,
and burning their stores,
they ran for it,
and we pressed after with twenty thousand,

a third of whom were cavalry,
our best arm,
and our General,
the Lame Man we called him,
sent a flag to inform them
that he would grant a surrender
on liberal terms,
and their General
(may he be forgiven)
told him to go pull his popish pud,
and the attack began —
but it was the same as before,
it was all the same,
and a sad sight it was to see
our cavalry beaten again,
six thousand plumed horsemen
stopped by buckshot,
torn from their saddles,
fallen upon with knives,
and slashed to rags,
sad to see them so closely lying
as to interlace,
supplying missing parts for each other,
a head where a head was gone,
a leg for a blown-off leg,
and to see our eighteen hundred dead

                       it went well there for the gringos,
and well at Cerro Gordo too,
and at Churubusco,
and at Chapultepec,
and in the end over all Mexico
the white flag flew

it went well, that war, but not for us,
poor Mexico
we lost Califa and her paradise
and San Francisco Bay,
poor Mexico,
so far from God
and so near the United States

SCENE 43

A MAN, DESIRING. . . . (Fall of 1947)

Earlier in the year, while your agent Henry Volkening was offering *A Man Without Shoes* to publishers in New York, you'd begun to write your sixth novel.* Its central character was the wounded soldier you and Maggie had picked up in Hollywood one night near the close of the war. During the quarter of an hour that he'd been in the car, he'd revealed nothing of himself, not even so little as his name, and though you'd seen his face and heard his voice, neither the sight nor the sound had been remarkable, and soon they'd faded away. What did remain of him, almost as if he'd left it with you to make of what you could, was the bandage that swathed one of his hands to the wrist. A great white cocoon, it had seemed to be, and so it seemed still, and often you'd wondered how much of the hand it contained — four fingers? three? two? or (it shamed you to recall) had the hand been whole, had it never been injured at all?

The bandage, you'd thought one day. . . .

You'd heard the story once, at a bar, it may have been, at a party, a meeting, a streetcorner, and you'd forgotten who told it even as you'd forgotten where, but the story itself had been imperishable, however long it lived on the shady side of memory. The story was this: *There were two orphan brothers at a County Home, boys of twelve and thirteen. A man, desiring to adopt one but unable to choose between them, forced them to decide for themselves — by running a race against each other.* There was no more to the story.

And one day you remembered the bandage, and suddenly it began to unwind, a few yards at first and then miles of it, a stream of gauze that rippled away in your mind until, stunning you, it entwined with the boys of the story.

Steve Pierce, you'd call the brother who won. The other would be Carlo, and though beaten, he'd keep on running even after he was out of sight. . . .†

---

* Called *The Bandage* at the time.
† You'd find him for your seventh novel, *Every Island Fled Away.*

SCENE 44

WRITERS MEETING IN THE ROOSEVELT BALLROOM (End of 1947)

> *It is singular that such closely allied species as the dog*
> *and the fox are among the favorite prey of wolves.*
> —Encyc. Brit.

Your car was parked north of the Boulevard on Sycamore, where lamp-lit trees shed the shadows of their leaves on the pavement. As you drove toward Franklin,

Maggie said, "I wonder what the papers will say about the meeting."
And you said, "If they're fair, they'll say, *"Writers Guild rejects blacklist."*
"Is that what we just did?"
"So the vote went."
"Well, there'll be other nights and other votes. There'll be a blacklist yet."
"Not if the Guild stays solid."
"Nothing is solid," she said. "There's always a crack somewhere—and somebody's always out to make it wider. You heard Dore.* What do you think he was up to when he said everybody else would be safe if we threw the Hollywood ten to the wolves."
"He didn't get anywhere with that."
"He didn't expect to. All the same, the crack's wider than it was before he made his pitch."

Throw ten to the wolves, you thought, and the trope seemed to grow in your mind, to take on color and give off sound, and what you were driving was a horse-drawn sleigh, and you saw and heard a happening in the wintry woods. *It is singular,* you thought, *that the favorite prey....*

"Would people really do that to people?" you said. "Throw them to the wolves?"
And Maggie said, "Oh, John, my dear Mr. Dumjohn!"

---

* Dore Schary, a writer who had become a studio executive.

SCENE 45

THE LOUIS MAYER STOCK FARM (March 1948)

It was in Perris Valley, south of Riverside, and at her employer's invitation, Maggie and you had taken breakfast with him and a party of horsemen at the guest quarters; afterward, Alec Gordon, his foreman, had led the group on a tour of the paddocks, the stud-barn, and the foaling-sheds; and now, at mid-afternoon, you were heading home through the foothills of the San Bernardino range.

"His place has everything but beauty," you said. "I wonder why he didn't set himself up in Kentucky."

"Where the hardboots are!" Maggie said. "Back there, they eat Jews and wash them down with sour mash!"

You were passing Camp Haan, a treeless reservation with rows of featureless barracks and grounds without grass. Beyond the flying-fields, the brown earth rippled away like a wrinkled rug.

"A Jew never gets away from the Jew-haters," you said. "They're everywhere, on the Russell Cave Pike in Lexington and here in Perris. There were some at that breakfast-table. A couple of those Turf Club boys were drinking gall, not coffee. My father had a nose for those sons-of-bitches, and so have I."

"I couldn't hear you from where I was sitting," Maggie said. "You and Alec Gordon were going on like your tongues were slung in the middle."

"He was asking after the Alibhai* foal, but he really wanted to hear about the mare. He swears by her blood-lines — The Porter-Sweep-Ben Brush. He thinks it's the best in America. Then we discovered that we both like fillies more than colts, and we were off. He carried on about one called Rose of Sharon."

"It was fillies at both ends of the table, then," Maggie said. "L.B. was holding forth on girls. There were two kinds, he said — the kind you made stars of, and the kind you marry. Odd talk at a horse-farm breakfast."

"Not so very," you said. "He's a stone-horse, and that was a pass."

"A pass! Why, I'm just an old bag. He can find better stuff in the Metro commissary."

---

* Mayer's leading stallion, to whom Maggie's mare September Child (The Porter-Miss Fortune) had been bred the previous spring.

The sun was down low ahead of you, and glancing past the swales and canyons in the snow-topped range, it cast them into purple shade.

"There *is* no better than you," you said. "It was a pass."

SCENE 46

4912 WHITE OAK AVENUE (March 1948)

Alone in the house that morning, you listened to small sound on the Sunday quiet, leaves being blown along the driveway, water as it fell on water in the well. On the desk before you lay the manuscript of *A Man Without Shoes.* Shortened by deletions—phrases, paragraphs, entire pages, even, were gone—it was slimmer now and nearing lean. *Lean,* you thought: it was Pep West's word; *lean,* he'd say of someone's prose, meaning it as praise.

The blue and brown type began to blur, and to unfix your stare, you turned to things that were further off—a dictionary on its sloping rack (a musical score, you thought, three thousand pages long), walls papered with Geodetic Survey sections, bookcases, photographs. In the end, it came to you that in leaving behind what you'd been doing, you hoped to find something else. To find what?, you wondered, and, rising, you wandered through the hallway to the bedroom, where you stopped near Juno, coiled in sleep on the whorls of a braided rug. Venetian blinds laid ladders of light against the pine paneling, and bright was Lautrec's red gown on May Belfort, and glowing the yellow of Steinlen's cats.

Without opening her eyes or even coming to the surface of sleep, the little Airedale knew you were there—but you, awake, were still unaware of another presence, and yet it was the one that had brought you to the room. When you gathered at last that it was Maggie you'd been looking for, the knowledge seemed to have come by assimilation, as if chemically converted within you by the sun.

Your glance took in a cherrywood chest inlaid with rhombs of holly. It was a piece you'd always admired, and it held, as you knew, fractions of Maggie's attire. In its spaces, it held her too; she was in its silk and suede, in its textile air. Moving toward it, you reached for the knobs of the topmost drawer, thinking as you did so *When I open it, the gloves, the ribbons, the rolled stockings will stay where they are, but she will go.* You paused, fancying nothing you could see, only a flavor passing, as of someone unknown in a crowd. You did not open the drawer.

Juno made some comment from another world, but it was garbled and lost in her throat.

SCENE 47

BLOODLINES (Spring of 1948)

At the Circle S. Ranch in Canoga Park, Maggie's broodmare September Child dropped a foal to the cover of Alibhai, the Mayer Stock Farm stallion. The colt, a blaze-faced bay, was likely-looking from the start, and many a time you drove across the Valley as if to watch him grow by the day. He was about two weeks old when you took your father along, and you found the mare turned out in a paddock, where she was foraging for heads of clover buried deep in the grass. Never, though, did she fare far from her foal, and when you called her, she came, closely attended by the colt, who trotted at her flank as if tied.

At your feet in the access-road, you saw a spray of filaree,* and tearing it up, you offered it to the mare; she inhaled long before accepting it. "Suspicious critter," you said.

Your father reached between the rails to touch the foal, but he shied away from the hand and stood switching his miniature tail. "What do you think of him?" he said.

"I don't know much about conformation," you said, "but the foreman here is a friend of mine, Willis Reavis, and he says he's well set up — good feet, long shoulders, things like that. He ought to be good, though, on his breeding alone."

"You've made a study of that?"

"I wouldn't say a study, but I've learned something about pedigrees."

"That's interesting," your father said. "You must find it useful."

"It is. Some lines are better than others."

"What do you mean by better, Julian?"

"Higher class."

Hungry, the colt thrust his head under the mare's belly and began to suck. Impatient with a slow flow, he tried to milk her by shoving against her bag.

---

* So-called but actually afileria, or pin grass.

108

"In his bottom line, his dam's, that little gentleman has a double cross of Ben Brush, the best in American racing. And through his sire, he comes down from winners of the English classics—the Derby, the Oaks, the Thousand Guineas. The combination could give us a stakes horse."

"Or a plater," your father said.

"Or a plater," you said. "But I'd bet against it."

The colt seemed to suspect the mare of holding back deliberately. He withdrew his milk-smeared head, stared at her in anger, and then plunged back to work.

"You were a fast feeder," your father said. "You used to get mad too." And then he laughed, saying, "Of course, I didn't realize at the time that I was watching a colt by Phil Shapiro out of Hatty Nevins, two very distinguished lines."

"I know you're guying me, counselor," you said. "But the truth is, I never think about lineage when I think about people. It means nothing. Anyone's blood, even a writer's, is as good as a Howard's. Or as bad."

"That should make you wonder about horses."

"It doesn't, though. Once in a blue moon, a nothing horse comes along, but day in and day out, class tells."

"Blood is blood, kid, and if it tells in horses, it tells in people."

You shook your head, saying, "People acquire, and horses don't, and therefore people spoil, and horses don't. Very few of us are born with some natural preservative, very few. You're one of them, and Maggie's another—and come to think of it, her family's the same."

"Did you ever tell her that?"

"Often, because I think they're remarkable. I say, 'You know something about that bunch of simples you come from? They're not shrewd. They're not sharp. They have no guile.' "

"And what does she say about you?"

"She says you're just like her folks."

"About you, I said."

"About me? Well, her family always went by a certain rule: Never trust a brown-eyed man. And she says, 'John, you have the brownest eyes.' "

SCENE 48

IF I FORGET THEE, O JERUSALEM (May 14, 1948)

> *We, by virtue of the national and historic right of the Jewish people, hereby proclaim the establishment of the Jewish state in Palestine—to be called Israel.*
> —David Ben Gurion

Forty years gone now, that 14th of May, and with it all memory of where you were and what you were doing at the particular hour of the particular day. Written and read in Hebrew, there were nine hundred and seventy-nine words in that proclamation, and in the great hall of the Tel Aviv Museum, they were heard by a congregation of enraptured Jews; and elsewhere too they were heard, in public squares and private places, in shops and fields and vessels at sea; and there were those who, without seeming to have listened, suddenly began to weep, as if they knew in their bones that two millennia of wandering had come to an end at a luminous open door. They knew, those transfigured Jews, and their dead knew in the ash of bones, in pissed-on phylacteries, in mounds of mismatched shoes. They all knew, but what of you. . . ?

If I forget thee, O Jerusalem!

It was at four o'clock on a Friday afternoon—in all accounts, it was at four precisely—that he rose from his chair and began to read from the pages he held in his hand. In the half-sung speech of Canaan, it took him only fifteen minutes to reach the final clauses, wherein, as the Sabbath drew near, Jews were told that at last, at last!, the Dispersion was over, and the date was given as the Fifth of Iyar in the biblical year Five Thousand Seven Hundred and Eight. For all those there, and for all Jews everywhere, it would be the first Shabbas since Pharaoh that the Lights were blessed in a land of their own— for all, it seems, but you.

Where could you have been at that radiant hour, and what engaged your mind? Were you asleep, or, being blind to what was happening, were you unaware awake? Were you seated at table over unclean and abominable things, were you alone or in company, were you reading, and if so, what—the words of some master or your paltry own? Were you riding in a car, encysted in steel, glass, rubber, or were you supine in the grass unknowing of the zion-blue sky.

In that old building, decorated for the occasion at a cost of Two Hundred

Dollars, an old man was reading an old promise into history, and in the gathering before him and in the streets of the city and in the orchards beyond the city and in the cities and groves across all the waters of the world, there was gladness—and yet there was sorrow too for those who'd died before that 14th day of May in ovens and showers and at the edge of open graves—but, God Almighty, what of you? Were you raking leaves, walking the dogs, writing the dead language of an American Jew?

If I forget thee, O Jerusalem. . . .

SCENE 49

MESSALINA (June 1948)

Hip No. 99
by Roman out of Playfull
by Chance Play

On the table between you and Maggie lay an inch-thick catalogue of the forthcoming Yearling Sales, to be held at the Keeneland Race Course, near Lexington, Kentucky. Listed were more than four hundred offerings, each of them accorded a page citing the racing and stud record of its sire and the produce record of the last three dams in its bottom line.

Flicking the orange cover, you said, "Without this dope, a buyer would have to bid on color, looks, and conformation. Without this, he'd never know there hadn't been a winner in the family since the day of Darley's Arabian."

"And *with* this. . . ?" Maggie said.

"He can bid on the history of the line."

"The history of the line!" she said, and she laughed. "He'd be just as well off bidding on something with four white feet."

"A good sire gets good foals."

"Lincoln got crowbait," she said. "Good horses are where you find them. I didn't marry you for the history of your line, my dear Johnny, and you didn't marry me for mine."

"Why *did* you marry me?"

"Well, you came without a catalogue, so I had to go by—what did you say?—conformation."

"I'm not joking," you said. "Why?"

"I'm not, either. I married you because you looked like a stayer. I thought you'd be around at the finish."

"Remember what I told you once?: I hate to see you leave a room."

"I remember."

"Because when you do, the life goes out of the air."

She looked at her hands for a moment, and then she said, "I like that very much."

Opening the catalogue at random, you read aloud from it: "*Hip No. 332, chestnut filly by Count Fleet out of Banish Fear by Blue Larkspur, third dam Herodias by The Tetrarch.* They don't breed 'em any better than that."

"I'd take anything in that catalogue. It could be *by Very Little out of Even Less.*"

And you said, "Well. . . ."

And she said, "Well, what?"

"Why don't we go back there and buy us a horse?"

"Are you serious—go to Keeneland?"

"Why the hell not? Seppy's getting old, Mag, and we won't be breeding her much longer."

"We'd be looking for a filly, then?"

"Only a filly. I love fillies."

"Don't ever think *I* don't!" she said. "I'll go you, Jabe!"

And you went, and you bid on Hip No. 99, a bay filly, and when she was knocked down to you, you called her Messalina—and after one of her several victories in your olive green colors, the Racing Form would say of her: *Named for a bad one, she runs like a good one.*

SCENE 50

A WALK BETWEEN TWO SENTENCES (July 1948)

One had just ended, and the other had not yet begun, and in the void you wandered from the room and then from the house, wondering as you went whether it was the warmth of the day that made sound seem more distinct, that intensified color even in the shade. In the orange trees, the humming of bees might've been coming from the blossoms, their perfumed speech. In one of the paddocks the Porter mare stood sleeping in the sun, her dark brown tail slowly sweeping her chestnut hide, and beyond her, below the bottom rail, you saw a dog on its Airedale round. In the hen-yard, a few Barred Rocks sat dusting themselves while eyeing a meringue of chicks as they moved from place to place as one. They were there, those chicks, because of you. . . .

In the cellar of the house, where the former owner had left it, you found an old incubator. Long unused, it stood against a wall rather like a pin-ball machine, and there it remained until it took your fancy and impelled you to try your hand. Following the directions in the manual, you marked a clutch of eggs and set them in the tray of the heating chamber, and then once a day for twenty days, you gave each a partial turn to balance the growth of the embryo. On the twenty-first day, you were about to raise the lid when you saw a shell crack and a beak, pink and transparent, break through.

. . . That chick and fourteen others moved like foam across the yard, little yellow lives, you thought, that owed themselves to you. You remembered city streets, you remembered Central Park and law school, transatlantic crossings and summers at the shore — and then you looked about at a mare in foal, at a black and tan bitch called Juno, and back again at a hatch of chicks that, but for you, would've been viscous clots in a garbage pail. But for you, you thought — how far you'd come from where you'd been to where you were!

You returned to your room. The next sentence had taken shape in your mind.

SCENE 51

DR. GUSTAVE HOLMGREN, cont'd. (Summer of 1948)

Lying in deck-chairs near the pool, you and he were passing the time of a Saturday afternoon, a time that seemed made of undertone, of wingbeat at a distance and stirring leaves — or was time passing you?, you wondered, or were you and time on the move as one, so that you couldn't know whether you were moving at all. . . ?

"Why don't you go for a swim?" Holmgren said.

"It's the Sabbath," you said. "Us orthodox Jews don't bathe on the Sabbath."

"Or any other day, from what I hear around my clubs. But what's this about being a good Jew? Are you saying you're a good Jew?"

"One of the Hasidim," you said. "I'm letting my hair grow. I'll soon be wearing curls."

"You won't be loved where the Hammer and Sickle flies."

"I'm not loved here, either."

"Go to Israel. That's where good Jews belong."

"Why can't I be a good Jew here?"

"Here?" he said, and his gesture embraced your four acres and the contiguous millions as far as the shore of the seas. "Here you're an American."

"How about an American Jew, then?"

"There's no such animal. You want to be a good Jew? Go to the Promised Land."

"I never felt it was promised to me."

"You're no Jew," he said. "It's safe to go for a swim."

You laughed, and then, not knowing what you were laughing at, you stopped. "On and off lately," you said, "I've thought about the day that Israel became a state—the 14th of May. I hate to admit it, but it meant nothing. It was just another day. Why didn't it signify? I know I'm not a good Jew, but what kind am I, if I'm still a Jew at all?"

He turned to gaze at you, his twitch for the moment subdued, and he said, "I didn't realize I was so near the nerve."

SCENE 52

FIGURES OF SPEECH (Summer of 1948)

"While you were at your mother's," you said, "I had a visitor. Doc Holmgren."

And Maggie said, "He hates everything you stand for, but you love him. How do you account for that?"

"He doesn't hate *me*."

"I'm sorry I missed him. What did you talk about?"

"The usual, mostly. According to him, I'm in a canoe, and I'm drifting toward the falls—a red canoe, you understand."

"Very imaginative."

"I'm in trouble, he says, and I'm too dumb to do anything about it. Do what—jump?"

"Unless you think the falls aren't there."

"Then your advice is the same as his: get out of the canoe."

"I didn't say that. I'd never tell you to cut and run. If you think there's no danger, though, you're living in a dream. Of course, you *do* live in a dream."

"Maybe so. Sometimes the only reality is my sense of *un*reality. I don't seem to have experienced a thing—the Great War, the Jazz Age, the Depression, the war just ended. They were parts of my time, and I sleepwalked them all."

"One realist is all a family needs. In doubting that you're in danger, you show that you don't know the American people. I do. I was brought up smack in the middle of them—in Nebraska—and they won't lift a finger to stop you from going over the falls. Not in a red canoe."

"We talked about this too, the Doc and I—about whether I'm an American or a Jew. I claimed I was both, but he wouldn't allow it. I had to be one or the other, he said."

"And to his mind, you were which?"

"An American."

"He's wrong there, I think."

"There might be something in what he says. All my reading is about America, and all my writing. My only interest is America. Where's my connection with the Jews? I dropped my Jewish name. I married a Christian. . . ."

"I know you better than you know yourself: you were born a Jew, and you'll die a Jew. Of course you care about this country, and of course you read and write about it and want it to improve—but if you married a Christian, Johnny darling, I married a Jew."

SCENE 53

REQUEST FROM A STRANGER* (August 1948)

. . . I am currently engaged in research on Nathanael West and have discovered you were a close friend of his. I have read the article in the Screen Writer and it is evident that you could give me a lot of valuable information concerning West's life, his personality, his ideas about fiction, etc. . . .

Several weeks later, he wrote to you again, saying

. . . I would like to express my appreciation for your informative letter. . . .

§

Having kept no copy, you wonder what you said in your informative letter. Did you begin with this, that you'd known Nat West when he was still Nate Weinstein, a clunchfisted boy of nine or ten who'd stand and watch you and your bonehead kind at games of skill, such as shooting marbles and playing pitch-and-toss with bottle-caps?

And did you say then that when he played games, they were games of the mind, where he was the sure-shot and you were as good as blind?

And if you said those things, you said these too, that after his family had removed from Harlem, a dozen years passed before you saw him again, still the muff of old, with out-of-sync feet and hands he tried to hide. And you spoke with pride, did you not?, of attending law school, and he was offhand, was he not?, when he said *I'm writing a book!*

---

* Cyril M. Schneider.

Was it in your informative letter that the book was *Balso Snell*, and did you tell of your stare, your stupefaction, of how the air went out of the Law?

And was this there too, that you lived near each other now, and that for a reason you never learned, or for no reason at all, he was willing to walk the city with you, he talking and you listening to new ideas, new names, new ways of seeing all you'd seen before?

And in your letter, if it informed, you must've said still more, that you were no reader then, no concert-goer, no art-lover, no anything, that all you brought along was your ears, and that what they heard for the first time in those miles of street was couplets from *Mr. Prufrock* and bombast from Ezra, stories of Beerbohm wit, and the ineluctable *day of dappled seaborne clouds,* and they heard of a bright young guy named Hemenway or Hemingway and of a novel about a Theodore Gumbril and a pair of pneumatic pants—but, strangely, they heard about music never, never a single word.

And what of the smaller things, did you mention the smaller things, that he hated loud talk (only Jews spoke to the next table), sharpie clothes, banality, emotion shown in public, sentimentality, and most of all himself?

Did you deal with such matters, did you reveal his life, his personality, his ideas about fiction, etc. or didn't you know enough at the time. . . ?

THE COLOR OF THE AIR, VI

ABRAHAM LINCOLN—1865
SECOND INAUGURAL

> *Fondly do we hope—fervently do we pray.*
> —A. Lincoln

There was a spell of rain that day, a light fall and rather fine, they say, but enough to weigh on flags and strain festoons, and in the mousse it made of the going, skirts grew stiff, and boots and shoes seemed uppers only. It kept none off the avenue, though, and long before the swearing in, the lawns were paved with faces to a distant line of trees. A slow descent of rain, it was, measured, sheer, like crêpe de chine, and it settled on plume and braid, on sequin, fur, and pelerine. It stopped—all took note of the odd conjunction—just as he began to speak. The rain stopped, and the sun shone on the fallen drops, and each became a sun itself and burned. An omen, the people called it, and they gave heed to the words that were streaming toward the trees.

Seven hundred words, there were, and with them the South lost the war, and they knew as much when the speech was read in Richmond. There was no comfort for the Rebs in that seraphic final paragraph—their cause was gone before he ever got there. *With malice toward none,* he said, and in truth he felt no enmity of heart, no spite for those who'd laid five hundred thousand dead for the right to eat their bread in other men's sweat, other men's sorrow. He hated no one, even as Matthew and Matthew's master, but woe had been promised those by whom offenses came, and woe would come. They knew that in Richmond. They knew it was more than a promise in seven hundred words. It was a prophecy, grave but somehow glowing, and a multitude fled in dread of doom.

SCENE 54

PSHAW: an obituary (November 1948)

> *And don't ever think it ain't.*
> —Henry A. Smith (1861–1948)

On the night of November 6th, the Old Settlers, as he and his wife were called by their family, had gone to bed, just as they'd done for sixty-seven years, the length of their married life. From that particular repose, though, only one of them would awaken, and it would not be he, Henry Albert. At some hour while he slept, the periodic contractions of his heart would cease, and his blood, no longer forced through his body and brain, would begin to drain into his lowest level. By morning, he'd be cold to the touch, and his wife, somehow knowing even as she opened her eyes, would gaze on a dead face that still seemed to speak of those sixty-seven years, and when at last she was able to voice her regret, it would be contained in a single word—a sound, really. *Pshaw,* she'd say.

In the dozen years that you'd known him, he'd never called you John or Julian: to him, you were always Yonny, and it wasn't due to any trouble with his J's. You were just another equal in a world of equals, and you didn't bowl him over with your flow of words or your knowing ways: nothing made him smaller, nothing overawed him. He was a natural man, and being neither better or worse, you were only Yonny, never John or Julian, as if writing books were on a par with mixing mortar—which, come to think of it, maybe it was.

A natural man was Henry Albert, but he differed from many such in this: he had no cunning in mind for you, no lies behind his pale blue eyes. True, he never got to own much of the world; and true too, he never craved it. About all he ever had was what he wore and what a rope would lead away, a swapping-horse, say, or a cross-breed dog. But he was made without greed, and whatever *you* had was yours—and if you had need, whatever *he* had was yours as well. In that way too he differed from many—hell, from most.

His wife may have been thinking of such things as she stood beside the bed that morning. It was the last time she'd ever see him lying there, she may have thought. After all those nights together, in all those to come she'd be alone, and to fill the void, she may have tried to make him live again by remembering the days of his living.

In and around Clarks, Nebraska, Henry Albert was known as a man of many skills. To find his equal as a plasterer or a tile-setter, you'd've had to go as far as Grand Island one way or Columbus the other. If you were looking for a hand with horses, though, you could stay where you were, because he had no equal: his voice gentled, his touch cured. He was the strongest swimmer along the North Platte, the deepest diver, the hardest runner, and a bare-knuck fighter from who laid the chuck. Also, he was the catcher-captain of the Clarks ball-team, and he caught Grover Cleveland Alexander without a glove—and one thing more, he served as Town Marshal, and he never wore a gun. He didn't need one; he weighed a hundred and fifty pounds, and no man living scared him. For a man so handy, it was odd that he couldn't fix a thing, no machine, no device, no dingfod. Any gingalory with two or more parts was his mortal enemy.

For all that power of his, his wife may have thought, he was woman-soft with women, with foals, calves, chicks, and especially with his kids, who'd mess with him something unsightly, such as whilst he was reading the papers, they'd gussy him up in baby bonnets and powder his face like a clown, and he'd never even twitch or say a word. She had to admit, though, that he could heist a few, the old rip, and when he did, he was a regular staver, no mistake. Whatever was in dispute, he'd state the fact of the matter to one and all, and then he'd say *Don't ever think it ain't*—and, mister, you had better do as you were told. . . .

But all that was over now, she may have thought, and once more she may have said the word—*Pshaw,* she may have said for those sixty-seven years.

SCENE 55

A NOVEL CALLED *THE BANDAGE** (Summer of 1948)

Unless the reference is to penmanship, a writer is, by definition, one who engages in the creation of literature. After half a century at the art, for all you're able to say of the creative process, you might've been practicing the Palmer Method instead of writing eighteen books. As you read it now, this one in its binding of yellow linen gives you a sense of irrelation. The descriptive passages are unfamiliar, and the phrasing, the metaphor, the characters and the winding ways of their minds, all these too are strange, as though they'd been conceived by someone else. What the covers contain, of course—sight, sound, color, and history—came from you, but of the working by which experience had been transmuted into language, you can reveal nothing, for you know that you do not know. Here before you are fifty thousand words, all so unaccountable that they might well have originated themselves.

Your writing has always been entered upon without plan, and however schematic and sequential it may seem, it is never the result of ordered thought. Still, on the opening page of *The Bandage,* a mood is made that will pervade the book, a key for the writing of every other page. You speak there of an abandoned farm lying between the foot of the Santa Lucia Range and the Pacific. All that remains of it, you say, is *a wracked and rotten hay-barn long peeled bare by chloride fog and the wind,* and you go on to tell of fields gone back to sage, of the iodine savor of kelp and the thin dim cry of gulls. Those sights, sounds, colors, had you actually been there to record them, you wonder, or had you imagined the deserted air of the place—and the soldier in the barn as he lay watching the Piedras Blancas Light *brighten and blacken a crack in the wall?*

It's all a fancy—all but that soldier and the bandage on his hand. Risen from some fosse, some convolution, some depository of your brain, he's the one you once gave a lift in the rain. Nameless and unknown to you then, he's known now and named Steve Pierce, and with him has risen the story you'd heard of a race run between brothers—and here, years afterward, is the lonely winner, and in his mind there may be Carlo, the brother he left behind, and he may be thinking these things too:

---

* Published in 1953 as *The Land That Touches Mine.*

How would you describe yourself? At what point would you begin? Would you set out from your hair and descend, through neckband and chest-expansion, to the size of your shoes? Or would you bound yourself by inch, ounce, and year, or would it be better to open with your place of birth (the town, the house, the floor, the room, the bed, the one particular womb?)? Or would you simply list three persons acquainted with you since the Crucifixion and fill in the blanks necessary to establish you finally as an irredeemable son-of-a-bitch. . . ?

His bandaged hand has always been whole, and he, the winner of the race, is still on the run, a deserter.

SCENE 56

WHITE OAK EVENING, 1 (Fall of 1948)

"What're you thinking about?" Maggie said.
"I'm not thinking about anything," you said.
"But you are."

On the far side of the room, with a Steinlen poster in between, stood a pair of pine breakfronts. Of recent origin, they were the handiwork of a retired cabinetmaker indulging a love of wood and an aversion to metal: the boards were a close match as to color and grain, and, God forfend the screw and nail!, they were joined with glue and dowel. There were sets of drawers below, and there were glassed-in shelves above, where the lamplight shone on rounds of china and silver and the gilt of leather-bound books.

"You are," she said, "and it isn't those cats in that poster."

There were two of them, a black one seated and a crouching calico, short-haired street-cats, and they were gazing off at something outside the frame—at Aristide Bruant in his silk-lined cloak, possibly, or a scene in Butte-Montmartre. *A la Bodinière,* you read, *18 Rue S Lazare.*

"He was a good illustrator," you said. "And he could paint too."

And you read *Exposition de l'oeuvre dessiné et peint de T. A. Steinlen du 10 Avril au 15 Mai 1894.*

"I wonder who came," you said. "Lautrec, surely, and Forain, Bonnard, Cheret—or was Cheret dead by then?"

"John," Maggie said. "What were you thinking about just now?"
And you said, "My books! My God damn books!"

From the bottommost shelf of the right-hand chest, your four published novels showed you their spines, *The Water Wheel* in green morocco, *The Old Man's Place* in maroon, and *Seventy Times Seven* and *The People From Heaven* in black.

"Why do you God-damn them?" Maggie said.

"At the Educational Center the other night, I saw John Craxton in the hallway. Between his plays back East, he usually comes out here to give a course in the Drama—Ibsen, Strindberg, Shaw, that kind. I was about to pass him when he took me by the arm and said, 'You're Sanford. I just read *The People From Heaven*.' I said, 'Did you? It came out in 1943.' He said, 'Nobody ever told me you could write like that.'"

"And what did you say?"

"I said, 'What you mean is, the fuckers never told you I could *write*!'"

"And then what happened?"

"Nothing," you said. "I just walked away."

"That was foolish. You should've picked up on *Nobody ever told me. Why* didn't anybody ever tell him? The Left out here acts as if you don't exist, and you, proud guy!, you just walk away."

"I don't beg for approval."

"*You* beg? It's your party-line pals that ought to be begging. You're as good a writer for the Cause as they could ever hope to get, and all they say about your work is, 'It doesn't come off.'"

"Don't get me started on that shitty committee," you said. "I just might join the Gypsies."

"The committee," Maggie said. "Every time I think of it, I get sore. It was smarter than Harcourt Brace, it was smarter than Dr. Williams, it even knew more than Masses & Mainstream. I memorized what the editor said."

"Charles Humboldt," you said. "It's about the only good notice I ever got from the Left."

"Original is an overworked word, he said, but it would be hard to find a better one to describe John Sanford's extraordinary novel. A major event, he called it, not only for literature but also in the struggle for the liberation of all people. . . . And now along comes Craxton, saying *Nobody ever told me*! Doesn't the Left read its own press?"

"Sometimes I think it doesn't *read*."

"If you wrote for money or acclaim, I could understand. But you write to change things for the better, and still they pass you by. If Art is a weapon, why throw a weapon away?"

From four books under glass, light on gilded titles gleamed. In days to come, you thought, the number would grow to six, to eight, to other books bound in other colors, blue, perhaps, or brown, and you'd be gazing at them as now, wondering at someone's remark in passing: *Nobody ever told me.*

"John," Maggie said, "you've got to do something about it."

But the Steinlen cats, the crouching calico and the squatting black—they knew, back there in 1894, that people often stumbled. After all, feet were what they saw coming and going on the street.

SCENE 57

WHITE OAK EVENING, 2 (Fall of 1948)

It was still light outside, and standing at the door-screen, you were staring into the blue-green evening. From the artificial well came the sedative sound of water-pour, and you heard bated tones from the barn, September Child sighing and the whisper of stirred straw. Near you on the porch, lined up against the front wall of the house, were the Conestoga wagons of the outdoor dogs. Dozing within them now, they'd come awake at the utterance of a hinge, at a footfall on fallen leaves. Maggie was reading, you remember, and you were at the door.

But she'd stopped reading, and she was saying, "I've been thinking about something you said the other day. It must be important to me, or it wouldn't keep coming to mind."

"I talk a lot of nonsense," you said.

"You spoke of your feeling of having lived in your time without being part of it. That's important, or nothing is."

"What does it tell you about me?"

"That maybe you're a better thinker than you think you are."

"I don't think; I feel."

"Wherever it comes from, it was a good observation about yourself. It made me wonder how many of us are only spending time."

"All of us, I guess, but only a few have something to show for it."

"What's it like, turning back the clock—or worse, throwing it away?"

"My mother died on the first day of the Great War, and it's her death that makes the day significant, not the war. In some ways, I never got beyond it. The age fascinates me—the styles, the music, the trains, the slang, even the race horses, Commando, Peter Pan, Roseben. And the photographs—I *enter* the photographs! When my mother died, it was as if I'd run aground, gotten stuck in the stream. To me, an airplane will always be a flying-machine."

"How far does it control you, living in 1914?"

"I don't know that it controls me at all. No matter how I feel, I'm really right here, and the time is right now."

"Do you really believe that, Jabe?"

"Of course I believe it. Otherwise I'd be certifiable. I dwell on my mother's time because somehow it keeps her alive. That's all it means."

But she shook her head, saying, "It goes further than you realize. That was perceptive, about keeping your mother alive. But you're doing something else by living in 1914: you're *thinking* in 1914."

It had grown darker, and bare trees drew black river-systems on the sky. You heard a bird call and a bird reply.

"Those lambs sent off to be slaughtered in Washington," she said. "Doesn't it ever occur to you that the same could happen to us?"

In one of the little wagons, a dog rose, circled twice on its mattress of wood shavings, and then again lay down.

"I don't suppose it does," you said.

SCENE 58

THREE SHEETS OF PAPER (January 1949)

They came to light while you were searching for something else in your files — a letter, it might've been, a misplaced clipping, a passage culled from a book. Single-spaced on a well-used ribbon, they were notes you'd typed long before and long forgotten, but you had only to scan the heading to know that they'd not been forgotten at all: *All Jews according to one gentile,* you read; *A.S., at the Sutton, August 1932.* At once, like a fresh slide on a screen, A.S. appeared in your mind as you'd seen her then, unfavored rather than ill-favored, a pleasant enough girl from the right side of the tracks, but not as far right as the rich. Both of you, through the indulgence of Pep West, the manager, were living rent-free at the hotel, and having met each other in his office, thereafter you'd spent an occasional evening together. Once, you remembered, you'd taken her a little gift, a jar of brandied peaches, and it may have been then that you had your talk about the Jews. And now the still on the screen was still no more: figures stirred, cigarette-smoke flowed upward, and on your face emotion showed. . . .

§

"I don't like the idea, Julian," A.S. said. "I don't like it at all."

And you said, "I know so few Christians. I really have no one to ask."

"But it's such an unusual question: What do we think of the Jews? Among ourselves, we don't discuss such things."

Jews are always after money and will do anything to get it. It fascinates them. It makes them inhuman and unkind.

"I've been trying to write a story about a Jew among Christians," you said. "I know the Jewish side of it, but I'm vague about the other."

"You wouldn't like the Christian side. Take my word for it."

They're dirty. Entire families live in one house, one apartment, even, and when they travel, they travel in herds.

"I'm not asking for your own view," you said. "What I want is the general view."

"So you say, but you'd still think it was mine."

Christians never accept gifts from Jews. They always believe the Jews have a motive and expect a rich return.

"And who can say?" she said. "Maybe it *would* be mine. We don't analyze these things. They're there in us, and we feel them."

"You mean you just accept those feelings? You don't try to understand them?"

Whenever a Jew entertains a Christian, some social error is bound to be made. A Jew just can't "do it right."

"I wish you wouldn't press me about this, Julian. We've gotten to be friends. Why spoil it?"

And you said, "What you're holding back must be very hurtful."

Jews are too slick for Christians. They'll do them every time.

"I've been hinting at that all along," she said. "Why should I offend you? Why do you *want* to be offended?"

"I don't. I just want to be informed."

No matter how rich a Jew is, he's still cheap enough to argue over pennies.

"But, Julian, you can't guess what you're getting into. Why don't you leave it alone?"

"It's too late for that. You've made it ominous."

Jews are show-offs. Jews are loud. Jews are argumentative. Jews are poor sports.

"I meant to make it ominous," she said. "I thought it would make you sheer off."

"I can't. Not now."

Jews are ashamed of being Jews. They envy Christians. . . .

§

The typed-on sheets were testimony bond from your father's office. Their blue ruling was still distinct, but the paper had yellowed to the color of vellum. You carried them out to Maggie, who was reading in another room.

"Here," you said. "From one of your fellow gentiles."

"*A.S.,*" she read. "You never told me about an *A.S.*"

"I had so many girls. Too many, my dear, to weary you with."

"*A.S.* — what do the initials stand for?"

"I honestly can't recall her name."

"You type *All Jews according to one gentile,* you follow that with thirty-one numbered entries, and you keep the notes for seventeen years — and you can't remember her name."

"You remember, I guess, what you want to remember."

"*When a gentile imitates a Jew,*" she read, "*he always uses his hands.* How did you get this stuff from her?"

"I asked her for it."

"You should've waited. You could've asked me."

"And what would you have told me? There were damn few Jews where you hail from."

"True," she said. "But we had slews of gentiles, all as stupid as A.S."

And you said, "All but you."

SCENE 59

IN A BOX AT SANTA ANITA (February 1949)

The day was cold and so clear that the San Gabriel range, sheer and impending, looked much nearer than five miles off. On its steep slope, green-brown with masses of chaparral, slanting arcs of road could be seen, and along the summit, pines notched the edge of the sky. On a foothill beyond the infield, a mob of oaks seemed to be held in check by the backstretch rails — as if they were about to rush the track, you fancied, and then the view was filmed by drifting smoke from your father's cigarette. He too was gazing at the mile-high rise before him, but all he saw, you thought, was some vista in his head of another time and another place. You were wrong, though, for he wasn't as far away as you supposed.

"We've talked about this," he said, "but it isn't your favorite topic."

And you said, "What isn't?"

"The Committee. The House Un-American Committee."

"Oh, that bunch of bastards."

"You don't tell me much about your politics, Julian—not straight out, that is. But sometimes you sound like your Uncle Dave, and that's when you give yourself away."

"It's no disgrace to sound like him. He was for the underdog, and so am I."

"I admire that, but you didn't learn it from Dave. You were for the underdog when you were a kid of five."

"Was I, really?"

"Your Cousin Jassie was older than you, and bigger, but he couldn't fight worth a lick. You did his fighting."

"Did I win?"

"Oh, now and then you'd beat some bum."

Whenever he was near, you had to touch him, and touching him, you said, "Shappie, how come they never disbarred you? You're a tricky lawyer."

"To get back to the Committee. Maybe they *are* a bunch of bastards, but they're bastards with power, as your friends found out in the District Court."

"My friends?"

"The Ten are your friends, kid. Did you think I was born yesterday?"

Led by an outrider in a scarlet coat, a file of horses came from a tunnel under the grandstand. Bays and grays and chestnuts passed, some on their own and some being ponied, but all were on the muscle with their sunstruck silks, striped and slashed and polkadotted.

"Because of you," your father said, "I've followed their case from the beginning. I'll be damned, though, if I understand what their lawyers are up to—and I've been practicing for fifty years."

"What don't you understand, counselor?"

"Why they've based their defense on the First Amendment instead of the Fifth. The First won't protect them."

"It's a matter of principle—and I don't mean with the lawyers. I mean with The Ten. The Fifth Amendment, they feel, is for criminals, and they're not criminals. Even if they were Communists, they wouldn't be criminals: the Communist Party is a legal party; it's on the Ballot. So why should The Ten use the Fifth? They're not safe-crackers."

Your father said, "When the Committee asked them whether they were Communists, they had the right to keep their mouths shut. They got that right from the Fifth Amendment, not the First. You're a lawyer yourself; you ought to know that much."

"It seems to me," you said, "that the First ought to do the same. In guaranteeing freedom of speech, it guarantees the opposite—freedom *not* to speak."

He considered you for a moment, and then his gaze became long-distance, as if what he'd sought in you might be found far away. "Julian," he said, "The Ten are going to jail."

"The Supreme Court hasn't said so yet."

"It *will* say so. How will The Ten feel then?"

"To tell the truth, I don't think they'll be surprised. When you act out of principle, you take what comes."

"Let me ask you something. This is hypothetical, of course, but if you're ever in the same fix, which amendment will *you* use?"

"I don't know," you said.

Behind the starting-gate and half-hidden by a hedge, horses milled for position, their colors on the move like spilled spools of thread.

Your father said, "Can't principle be served *out* of prison as well as *in?*"

"Not always," you said. "In 1918, Debs spoke out against the war, and like fools, they put him away for it. They made a hero out of him."

"He was always a hero to your Uncle Dave."

"Convict 9653—and when they turned him loose, two thousand other convicts cheered him down the road."

The gate was sprung, and a dozen horses were running for a roaring crowd—and you thought of two thousand faces at barred windows, two thousand voices shouting after a car carrying a gaunt old man away.

"You *are* in deep, aren't you?" your father said.

SCENE 60

CONCERNING THE COLOR OF EYES (March 1949)

Lying on the desk before you was the manuscript of *A Man Without Shoes,* but at the moment, you weren't at work. You were listening to a long-play record so muted that the music seemed to be coming from far outside the room—as far as Spain, you may have thought, for it was Spanish or in the Spanish idiom, something by Lalo, was it, De Falla, Ravel? And were you thinking the word *Iberia,* and did that lead you to river Ebro and the Loyalist defeat, and was it there that the music ended. . . ?

From the doorway, Maggie spoke, saying, "These days, you keep kind of quiet about the book."

"There hasn't been much to report," you said. "Another rejection, and then another rejection."

"Even so, I'd like to know."

"Same story all the time. Scribners, Harpers, Little Brown, Knopf, and a dozen more of the best. It's a long book, but it comes back fast. I could swear they don't read it; they weigh it."

"Has it ever occurred to you that it might never be accepted?"

"Certainly not."

"Well, let it occur now."

"That's asking me to stop believing in the book."

"Just the opposite: it's asking you to believe in it even more than you do. And don't stare at me with those big Jew-brown eyes. What I'm suggesting is that you publish *Shoes* yourself."

Jew-brown eyes, she'd said, but what color were hers—green, green shot with amber, christian-green.

"Did you hear me? I said why don't you publish the book yourself?"

"Up to now," you said, "I've been rash, and you've been rational. All of a sudden, it's ass-end-to."

"Things don't change that fast. You're not as bright as you think, or you'd see the sense in what I propose. You're running out of publishers. Why not *be* a publisher?"

"I'm a writer, not a bloodsucker."

"If you published your own book, you'd be sucking your own blood."

"You know what somebody told me once? Every publishing house in America keeps going on unpaid royalties. Guess who I got that from. A publisher! And that's all I know about the beggarly game."

"Learn, then."

"But, Mag, it costs money to put out a book."

"We've got money."

"*You've* got money."

"All right, you fool, *I've* got it. And I want to spend it so that *Shoes* can see the light."

Were they green, you wondered, were they green and yellow?

And you said, "You'd do that for a brown-eyed man?"

"For this one," she said, "I'd do even more."

SCENE 61

THE PLANTIN PRESS (April 1949)

The proprietor was a typographer named Saul Marks. You'd met him first some ten years earlier when, as one of the editors of a Left Wing magazine,* you'd carried a batch of copy to his shop, a two-car garage built into a Silver Lake hillside. On entering it, you entered also a new stage of communication: there, you thought, there the word was readied for the eye; there was order further ordered, dressed for parade.

The Plantin Press, he called himself, after Christophe Plantin, the French printer and bookbinder of the 16th century. You learned that much from your Encyclopedia, but Marks never explained his attraction to the name. It may have been the Frenchman's weakness for books of a heretical nature, which, between missals and breviaries for the Church, he issued in secret — but you did not ask, for his manner of speech warned you off. His voice was low-toned and intense, damped, deadened to a mere disturbance of the air, as if once he lost control of it, he'd lose control of himself. And do what?, you wondered — but, as you say, you did not ask.

You knew nothing of Christophe Plantin at the time, but you know now that he'd not have felt disgraced by the use of his name. Saul Marks was even then a superlative letterpress printer, and evidence of it was everywhere to be found in his shop, on tables, shelves, and walls, and underfoot as well, since even his discards seemed to be paper somehow improved. In galleys, sample pages, finished sheets, everywhere his constructions of type, clean, proportionate, exact as notation; on benches it lay, on chairs and cartons, in fallen leaves on the floor.

When you called on him now, so long after the magazine had been discontinued, nothing but the shop had changed. It was larger, and it was on a different hillside — what virtue was there in hillsides? — but the man himself was still in a rage, still repressed and almost breathless, still *il miglior fabbro* of the printed page. As before, where your glance fell, there you saw his compositions (black lace, you thought), some of them passing through his old Heidelberg flat-bed rotary, some stacked in signatures, and some as always scattered on the floor. You stooped for one of these and scanned it for its

---

* *Black & White*, later *The Clipper*.

imperfection, but it was so minute, so inobvious, that only Saul Marks could've pointed it out.

"John!" he said as you stopped beside him, but you had to read the word, for all you could hear was the insistent machine, metal in tedious collision with metal. And then he switched off the power, saying, "what brings you to 1052 Manzanita?"

"This," you said, and you held up the manuscript of *A Man Without Shoes*.

"That's one big book."

"Too big, maybe. Nobody'll take it. Of course, it's also too red."

"Any paticalar reason you brought it here?"

"Maggie is after me to publish it myself."

"Oh, my God!" he said. "She got any idea what she's getting you into?"

"No, and neither do I."

"John, you go in the publishing business, you could come out with a pain in the ass."

"The book's been knocking around for three years. I've *got* a pain in the ass."

"It could get worse."

"How?"

"If you lay out good money and get nothing back."

"That's what I came for—to find out the price."

Marks shook his head, saying as he touched the manuscript, "How many words you got in there. . . ?"

§

Before you, on a half-sheet of newsprint, is Marks' preliminary estimate of what it would cost to produce two thousand copies of *A Man Without Shoes*. Over the years, the coarse paper has deepened in color from white to buff, and the pencillings of the typographer, spidery to begin with, have grown more than ever indistinct, but they still illuminate the browned half-page. It's ancient writing, you think: the numerals, the lettering, all come down from a bygone age.

§

"How was it left?" Maggie said.

"I told him I'd talk it over with you."

"We talked before you went. You didn't need my permission."

"To spend six thousand bucks for a book, maybe even seven?"

"Why not? We've got the money."

"But, Mag, it isn't mine."

130

"Tell me, how long are you going to keep that up?"

"Till I put some in the pot—and don't worry about how I'll feel in the meantime. I'm not ashamed of being supported. It doesn't diminish me. I'm not the man's-man type."

"You're the child's-child type. Half of the money is yours—so, please, Jabe, give Saul a call and tell him to go ahead."

"Some day, maybe. Not right now."

"When, then? I want to see that book in print."

"I do too, but I want to see it *published.* If I put it out myself, it'll just *look* like a book."

"Why? Is it only a book if Madison Avenue says so?"

"The way things are, yes. Nobody'll know about it. Nobody'll read it. It won't be there, like sound in an empty room."

"Suppose no one ever accepts it. What then?"

"Then I'll come to you."

"You promise?"

"I promise."

THE COLOR OF THE AIR, VII

THE BISON

A FLOOD UPON THE EARTH

> *a vast sea of animals*
> —a hunter, 1875

So spoke all, in infinitudes. To the eye, the creatures were more numerous than numbers, wherefore the mind abandoned figures and turned to figures of speech: where the herds grazed, it was claimed, there all the world was engulfed, as by the Waters once in the days of wrath. *A vast sea* said they that saw it, *a motionless ocean.* To the Indian, they were all his needs on the hoof—their flesh fed him, their hides robed him, their powdered horn would work his spells. They were living treasuries, and, best of many things good, though ever drawn on, they were ever full: they were killed, but still they lived; they died and were not dead. Indeed, it seemed, they multiplied.

And then, with the People from Heaven, the horse came, and the sticks-that-speak, and the Deluge began to recede. They were not the hungered that hunted now, not the naked, not the magician seeking medicine: they were the butchers, or, worse, the skinners, out for pelts alone, and a curse on what was left. And there were epicures

131

that, from a thousand pounds of meat, would only eat the tongue.
And there were toffs with their heavy Henrys, .50 calibre and deadly at a mile: they hardly had to stir from camp; they killed from
a chair in the prairie shade. And there were the marksmen, the firing-
squads, concerned not with food, fur, or trophies, but with scores.
And back and forth across the plains, the railroads ran excursion trains

> *will leave Leavenworth for Sheridan*
> *on Tuesday.*
> *refreshment on the cars*
> *at reasonable prices,*
> *and return on Friday*

and there was shooting from the windows all the way

> *a large herd seemed to go wild*
> *at the shrieking of the whistle*
> *and the ringing of the bell,*
> *and suddenly the animals charged,*
> *and down on us they came,*
> *trembling the earth*
> *as they plunged headlong into us,*
> *some becoming wedged between the cars*
> *and some beneath them,*
> *and so great was the crush*
> *that they turned three cars over,*
> *killing the ones*
> *our guns had missed*

And then a day came when the vast sea dried, when there were
Henrys by the hundred and nary a sight of game—the herds were
gone, the bands of strays, even the lone head on the ghostly ocean.
And there was silence now, there were no more downwind surrounds,
no more droves driven over cliffs, no more corrals of burning grass,
and the Grand Duke Alexis was back at Court, all such sport forgot.
There was silence and, when the bone-pickers arrived, one last to-do

> along the Santa Fe right-of-way,
> near Granada, Colorado
> there was a rick of buffalo bones
> twelve feet high,
> twelve at the base,
> and half a mile long,
> it would fetch ten dollars a ton.

It is related that one spring early in the new century, a party of
Indians was preparing for a ride into the hills when a white man
asked them where they were going. *To hunt the buffalo,* they told
him, and he said, *But there are no more buffalo,* and they nodded, saying, *We know that, but we always look at this time of year, and maybe
we will find some. . . .*

SCENE 62

JOSEPH McCARTHY, RISE AND FALL (1949)

And suddenly he was there and in being, he was in the air (Tailgunner Joe!),
and though you were unaware of him then, one day he'd bear down on you,
and you'd say of him, so:*

> *Oh God, when I go down, let me go down*
> *like an oak felled by a woodsman's axe.*
> —motto on his office wall

He went otherwise: his liver failed him, and he died of the poisons his body
produced. Toward the end, there was leucin in his urine, and tyrocin too,
and it turned yolk-yellow, almost orange. His head shook at times, and his
hands were never still, and, weak and somewhat vacant, he took to falling
down. The four-pound mass in his abdominal cavity was smaller than before,
harder in texture, and bile, instead of flowing into his duodenum, was absorbed by his blood, and he was soon dead of his own humors, a saffron suicide.
The jaundiced stiff was borne in a flag-draped casket to the Capitol, where
seventy senators came to view it and some of them to mourn.
A big, slovenly, jam-packed man, a whole kit and caboodle of pipes and
organs, he all the same made no few wonder whether he was quite as fraught
as he seemed. For all his fullness, were there not voids within him, were there
not dark intervals that he'd striven and failed to fill? There was about him
a suggestion of unstable rest, of a child rapt for the moment, but apt at the
next to self-excite, explode. A child—was that it? is that why little could
hold him long and less could take him away? is that what those who wondered
saw, the child expanded, larger, louder, more unstaid, but still as he'd been
before, timid, clumsy, friendless, shy? Was he a child, short-armed and thick-

---

* In *The Winters of That Country.*

fingered, without the skills of other children (a bear cub, his brothers called him, though unlike such he never played: he was a solitaire)?

Why was he so? What was in the blood he was given, the Wisconsin air, the one-room school he went to, the catechism? Why did he squirm among strangers, sweat, shake, look at the floor? What happened to him back there at the beginning, what made him run when callers came, what was said to him, was he doubted, slighted, denied, or was nothing said at all, had silence fallen, and did he fear it, flee it, hide? And where did he go in his flight, to which stall, which hayloft, and what did he hate when he got there, what did he try to kill? A drear time, he must've had of it, with himself his only company, with only himself to outdo. How young was he when he knew he was unequal to others, lacked their grace, their looks, their ease, at what age did his betters enrage him — they were all his betters — and make him take revenge?

If that was what he sought, a quittance of his condition, he never got it. He rose in station — for a time, he did outdo himself — but his arms were still too short to suit him, his head still trembled, and he drew no friends to the last. With those forepaws of his, he mauled his enemies — they were the people's enemies! he said — but the people were afraid of him too, and they shunned him, ran as he'd run once, and he was lonely of *their* choosing now, he was still in that stall on his father's farm, still trying to kill something and not knowing what till his liver gave out. He knew then. In the yellow haze of those final days, he knew.

SCENE 63

A LITTLE LOCAL COLOR (Summer of 1949)

Isaac, or Uncle Ike, as you called him, was your father's elder brother, now a man of seventy-five. Long since retired, he had once drummed the North Atlantic states for a manufacturer of shoes, working out of a city office in the Marbridge Building, across the way from Macy's in Herald Square. When in the neighborhood, you'd sometimes stop there to see him — and to see his showroom too, where samples, displayed on sloping shelves, seemed to be walking down the walls, shoes for the right foot only, as for a one-legged world.

He was a genial sort, your uncle, and those who knew him least might've supposed that his path wound through cordial places, especially the one at home; always he appeared to have just now come from some gaiety or to be just now on the way. In truth, though, he was vastly cast down by a wife who could've been the pose for *Sorrow,* brought to life from the Book of Attitudes. She mourned nothing lost, however, no parent, child, love, or cause. She was merely mournful, extinguishing day and so darkening night that she made you wonder what her bed was like, what pose she took in the gloom — was she *the Ill-used* there, was she *Hope Forlorn,* or there too did she simply mourn? You understood then why your uncle's territory beckoned, why he turned sadness to good cheer on the road.

Still, for all he may have done in one or more of those North Atlantic states, he remained surprisingly simple, as if untouched by wrong. He never became the jaded traveller in shoes, casual, wise, and unamused. Where he went, he brightened rooms, even those with drawn curtains, but he never came back the knowing rip; if he'd touched pitch, he was somehow undefiled. When his wife died, she took her pose with her, to the regret of the angels, perhaps, but not to Uncle Ike's; he removed to California to be near your father, who loved him for an innocence seventy-five years impervious to the world.

Often in the evening, you and Maggie would find him at your father's flat, a guest at dinner or *schmoosing* about the dwindling family, the new times, and what the old call better days. On one such evening, your sister and her husband were there too, and with your father and stepmother, you made a party of seven ranged around the parlor.

On your entrance, your father said, "What brings you to town, Julian?"
And you said, "We've been here all afternoon. We were at the doctor's."
"The doctor's! What for?"
"Our yearly physicals."
"Oh," he said. "You had me worried."
And then Uncle Ike said, "How much does your doctor charge for a physical?"
"A hundred bucks," you said.
"A hundred. You consider that's a bargain?"
"He's a fine doctor," you said. "Very thorough."
"I got a fine doctor too, and you know what I pay for a physical? Fifteen dollars!"
"For a *complete* physical?"
"Complete," he said. "From soup to nuts."

Silence was sudden and seconds long, void of all but a memory of your uncle's words — and then quite as suddenly sound resumed. Your father, trying to restrain it, only shook laughter loose, and you, thinking *Soup to nuts,* followed his lead. And four others must've thought the same, for all at once the room was aroar. And what of the seventh in the company, your artless Uncle Ike? It moves you yet to remember how he sat through the tumult looking pleased. He knew—how could he not know?—that he'd said something rich, but being too artless to know what it was, he sat there enjoying the enjoyment of others. . . .

And you think now of all those days and nights he spent on the road, and still he'd never grown wise on barbershop wisdom, still he'd only been hurt at home.

SCENE 64

LET BYGONES BE (Summer of 1949)

". . . I'm not objecting," you said. "I'm just asking you to explain."

And your father said, "You've been carrying a grudge against your Aunt Rae for thirty years—your own mother's sister. You're the one who needs explaining."

"You're inviting her to come out from New York and be your guest for the summer. It's as if you were the best of friends."

"You forget what I owe her, Julian. . . ."

(It was through your Aunt Rae and her husband Harry Perlman—indeed, it was in the Perlman home—that your mother and father had met, and from that moment until your mother's death eleven years later, the two couples had been inseparable.)

". . . She always sounded sorry," you said. "She'd say, 'I pity anyone who gets in your father's bad books.' "

"Ah, then you must've inherited your ill will."

"She called you a hard-hearted man. 'He never forgives,' she said, 'and he never forgets. . . .' "

(*Endocarditis*—the word comes up through memory from nowhere, like carbonic gas. It was only long after you'd heard it that you knew it described your mother's illness—an affection of the valves of the heart. It took years to kill her, years of dropsy, shortness of breath, fatigue, years of the blowing sound of her blood flowing in a narrowed stream.)

" '. . . That father of yours,' she'd say. 'Don't ever take after him, Julian. He's a hater.' "

136

"I'll bet she followed that with this: 'All the Shapiros are haters.' "

"As a matter of fact, she did. She said they could kill you with a look. Especially Aunt Sarah and Aunt Paulie."

Your father laughed, saying, "We'd scare people with that look. Did it scare you. . . ?"

(All your father owned and all he was able to borrow was spent in a vain effort to save your mother's life, leaving him a bankrupt with a neglected and ruined law practice. Unable to support himself and his two children, he was reduced to accepting the providence of his in-laws, your Grandpa and Grandma Nevins.)

". . . Did you ever know this?" you said. "When we were living with grandma and grandpa, you'd take Ruthie and me out to dinner every Sunday. Well, every Sunday Aunt Rae would be there when we got back, and she'd say, 'Did you see Josie today? Was your father with the painted woman?"

"And what would Julian tell her?"

"Not enough, I guess, because week after week she'd ask me the same old thing. 'So, Julian, what was Josie wearing? What did Josie have to say?' "

"Your Aunt Rae really had no idea of what Josie was like," your father said. "She was vain, I'll admit. She enjoyed attention, and she had the looks and flash to get it. But she was a far cry from being a woman of the world. In fact, she was kind of simple. . . ."

(The years of the Great War were lean ones for your father, but with the peace, as his clientele became active and his practice grew, he felt that the time had come to establish a home for his family. He told your grandma and grandpa of his intention, and he told them too that he meant to remarry. They were saddened by the decision, but when your father named the woman, your grandpa's sorrow gave way to rage: *A divorced woman! A woman with a child already! That's the kind you pick to take my daughter's place! A fine mother for your Ruthie and Julian! A stepmother she'll be, and her own will come first!*)

". . . Why didn't you set Aunt Rae straight about her?"

"Julian," your father said. "I was forty years old. I didn't have to account to anyone."

"Maybe she would've stopped steaming up grandpa."

"Maybe, but it would've demeaned me to defend the person I was going to marry. It would've demeaned Josie. . . ."

(Prevailed upon by your Aunt Rae, you refused to accompany your father when he removed to a home of his own. No sooner had he done so than your grandpa began a campaign to reduce him to beggary for yet another time. Withdrawing from your father's clientele, he then besought the rest of it to do the same, telling all who would listen the tale of your father's crime—a crime of the black heart, he called it, *der schwarze Herz*. Many heard it, but none came over to his side—none, though he told it until, after six half-touched years, he died. At his funeral, your father sat with your grandma and never let go of her hand.)

". . . And now," you said, "someone who injured you so badly is coming here as your guest. How does that come about? You're supposed to be a hardhearted guy. No forgiving. No forgetting."

"How do *you* think it comes about, kid?"

"You aren't hard at all. You're made of mush."

"Well," he said, and he looked off at whatever it is one sees when not really seeing with the eye. "Well," he said, "it isn't a bad way to be. . . ."

SCENE 65

A PILE OF TRASH (Summer of 1949)

The walnut grove on White Oak confronted a forty-acre truck-farm that began at the intervening roadway and ran off in rows that were bound, it seemed, for a single point in the distance. Whatever the crop, which changed each year, it was given care that even you knew to be rare. At almost any daylight hour, you could find a tractor plying the spread, with a ghost of dust in slow pursuit, and what it left behind was aisle on aisle steelyard straight and free of weed. You admired the green and brown perfection, but you never spoke to the man on the plodding yellow machine. Why, you wonder, why did you say nothing as he made his turns and passed, why were you more concerned with a gust of bluebirds, rust on blue, that landed in his wake one day? Thereafter, you sought them whenever you were near the gate, but, off-course only once, they never reappeared. You saw the man often, though, and the dust he raised with his yellow machine.

Each morning, when Maggie set out for the studio, you'd go with her as far as the gate, open it for her car, and then wave as she drove away. The dogs, all four, would be somewhere about, nosing at signatures in the gravel or the offcast of the trees. About to return to the house on one such morning, your sight was caught by a riddance of paper, tin, and glass lying along the opposite side of the road. The man on the machine, you thought—had he seen the eyesore yet, and if not, what would he say or do when he did?

Or, doing and saying nothing, would he simply sit there and stare, aquiver on his idling machine?

Heading up the driveway, you glanced backward once, and through the woven wire of the cyclone fence, you could see the disorder of paper, tin, and glass that someone *the son-of-a-bitch!* had wrought at the edge of the ordered field — and then, entering the house, you thought of it no more. Or, while trying to write a passage, were you thinking of paper, tin, and glass all along, of a ridge of rubbish that, strewn at the roadside, had begun to encroach on you?

You can still see yourself at the desk, still see your shored-up dictionary, your portable Royal of long ago, you still face, through three panes of glass, a grove of orange trees, and through the three above, the sky. All about you is the rigging of the writer, the gear for the conversion of idea to word — but the roller of the Royal holds nothing, and the paper before you is blank. The leavings that lie beside the road glint and glare in your mind now, and there too flimsy scraps tear loose and roll.

And then once more you went down the driveway and through the gate to stand and stare at labeled jars and labeled cans, at apple-cores and coffee-grounds, and as you watched, a timetable seemed to turn its own leaves, and now from afar off you heard the tractor, and you saw it a hundred rows away, slow as always but ever outrunning a cloud of dust. Melon-rinds, a wornout moccasin, stained rags, and, amid the scuff and scour, an envelope — and suddenly the son-of-a-bitch had a name!

His address was half a mile away, but he wasn't at home when you delivered three feed-sacks filled with his dross. You were about to leave them at his door when it occurred to you that there was no good reason for not emptying them on his lawn.

SCENE 66

THE PLUM TREE (1949)

From the steps of the porch, you could see it beside the path leading to the well. Its leaves were dark, almost black, like the plumage of starlings, and when a wind came to preen them, they'd change to purple-green. In the spring, the little tree was pinked with blossom, and as these fell, fruit would begin to form, and by summer's end, they'd reach the size of cherries. They never saw the summer's end. Each year, as ripeness drew near, a plague of birds

139

(the very starlings!) would come as if summoned and pick the branches clean.

The lawn, all day in the sun, made the air above it weave, and through it, as through water, images seemed on the move, like stones in a stream. Tobacco-smoke rose in a trembling column, and flies flew meanders and slow figure-eights. It was one of those time-passing times, you thought, with you standing still and something flowing by. You could almost see the ever-going, you thought, you could touch the endless funeral if you would. The endless funeral of time, you thought, and you a bystander till your own time came.

In the heated air, the plum tree seemed to shake, as if to free itself of birds.

SCENE 67

BLUES FOR *A MAN WITHOUT SHOES,* 5 (July 1949)

By midyear, the novel had been rejected twenty-four times, and before the year was out, it would be rejected nine times more. These last were yet to come when you applied to a literary agent named Desmond Hall,* asking him to represent you in what appeared to be a lost cause. A carbon-copy of the letter remains, four pages of typing still bold for all the wear and tear of forty years. *Dear Mr. Hall,* you wrote, and you told him the story, played him the blues, of the twenty-four failures of *A Man Without Shoes.*

Dear Mr. Hall, you wrote at your rear-room desk, facing a dado of books and a papered wall. *Dear Mr. Hall,* you said in a four-square of pale brown tracings, dust-jacket displays, pencil-jars, trays of bagatelles, and you knew without turning that behind your chair, a dog lay asleep on a Navajo rug. It's all still clear, *Mr. Hall,* still sharp in the mind, and you can even hear the sound of typing and the ringing bell at the end of a line. Everlasting, that little room, the dog on the floor, the Royal on the cherry table, and seated before it you!

Dear Mr. Hall, you wrote, and you took four single-spaced pages to say that your book needed help. But for *A Man Without Shoes,* no help would come. None ever does in the blues.

---

* Of the Jacques Chambrun Agency in New York.

SCENE 68

AN EVENT OF GREAT IMPORTANCE (October 1949)

Peking, October 1: From the balcony of the capital city's Gate of Heavenly Peace, Chairman Mao Tse-Tung today proclaimed the official founding of a new Communist state, the People's Republic of China.

On the evening of the 24th of October, you and Maggie boarded the Southern Pacific's *Owl* for San Francisco. On the evening of the 25th, you bought a newspaper in the lobby of the Fairmont, and on the sporting-page you read:

At Bay Meadows this afternoon, M. & J. Sanford's speedy filly Messalina won the six-furlong Kaiser-Frazier Purse in the good time of 1.11 2/5. Trained by R. Priddy and ridden by Johnny Longden, the daughter of Roman-Playful was only cantering through the stretch to beat the favorite Dateline by six lengths.

And aboard the *Daylight* on the 26th, what were you thinking of on your way back to Glendale? Was it the Gate of Heavenly Peace, where thousands looked up at a man in cotton rags — or was it the grandstand at Bay Meadows, where thousands looked down at a man in your silks. . . ?

SCENE 69

A SHORT WALK IN GRAUSTARK (1949)

and a long march in China

In photographs of that winter, bare trees are scribbled on the sky, and the water in the pool and pond is still, as if the wind too lay dormant for the while. Horses, dogs, and humans where humans appear,* all seem to have been suspended not only by a shutter but by the season of the year. Thin shadows, like erasures, smear the ground and its flaking of castoff leaves, and no birds can be seen in the prints, no hints of coming green.

---

* Of 111 snapshots, there are dogs in 13, horses in 84.

What went through your head as you strolled your domain well-fed and warm, what thoughts did you have as you ranged your reign?

> *Thousands froze to death. For months we had only corn to eat, and many could not digest it. It passed through them. Others gathered it up, washed it, and ate it again — only to expel it once more. . . .* *

Were you thinking of the Red Army on its blood-soaked plod through China, of the rivers, the gorges, the passes it crossed, the seventy thousand men it lost in floods, in falls from heights, in swamps and snow and daily fights with the enemy at their heels and hunger, the enemy in the ranks?

Many were so exhausted, you'd read, that when they squatted for a shit, they needed help to rise, and there were dry leagues where men, and women too, had to drink their own piss to kill their thirst — but were they on your mind when you sought signs of spring in the trees, for catkins to fringe the branches and leaves to duel in the breeze? But what of you, standing beside your pale blue pool?

SCENE 70

FROM EACH ACCORDING TO HIS ABILITY (December 1949)

> *to each according to his needs.*
> —Socialist motto

It was late, nearly midnight, when you came home from the weekly meeting, but stars brightened the grounds, and you made your way to the barn over stepping-stones of light and shade. At your approach, the horses stirred in the stalls, and you heard their soft utterances and the whispers of their bedding-straw. After refilling their water-buckets, you headed for the house, where you paused in the doorway for a last deep breath of the dew-damp air. It was as if you hoped to clear yourself of an evening of smoke and doctrine, hours of blue-gray smoke and the leaden spoken word. But nothing expunged the boredom, nothing the smell of smoke, and you stood where you were, listening to the pour in the well.

From the dark bedroom behind you, Maggie spoke, saying, "The dogs never bark when you come home."

And you said, "I thought you'd be asleep."

---

* A member of the Long March, in *Battle Hymn of China*, Agnes Smedley, Knopf 1943.

"How do they know it's you?"

"How do *you* know?"

"I can always tell," she said.

And you said, "So can they," and you went inside.

There was no need for light: after five years, it was a room you'd be able to see though you never saw it again. All it held had color and dimension and occupied space in your mind, and you knew that wherever else you might be, you'd find its images—the cherry chest inlaid with holly, the rag rug, May Belfort red-gowned on one of the walls, and Maggie in the bed below, she more distinct than the rest. You sat beside her and kissed her hand.

"How did it go this time?" she said.

"It didn't go," you said. "It never goes. The talk, the talk! They speak in editorials from *The People's World,* the dull stuff of Alex Bittelman, and somehow they make it duller."

"I'm sorry for you."

"I try not to hear them, but it's like trying not to breathe."

"Don't you ever say anything? Do you always just sit there and listen?"

"What would I say—'Pay attention to me, Comrades'? That's what *they're* saying. That's what they come there for—to get the hearing they don't get at home."

"You're blaming the wrong people, then. If women have to leave home to be heard, it's the fault of the men. Most women are married to bastards."

"But only one of them is married to me. The others make me twitch."

"How would it be in a men's group? Would you sit among the spellbinders then?"

From their beds on the porch, the dogs made a sudden rush into the darkness and thrashed away through last year's slough of leaves, and then, pursuit broken off, they came trotting back to recoil in sleep.

"They're no better," you said. "They just spiel in a deeper voice. The truth is, I'm not cut out for meetings."

"What *are* you cut out for?" she said.

But you were thinking of all those socialist oracles, those from whom fell the sibylline word, and you said, "I can't think of one who ever said, 'I don't know.' "

And Maggie said, "You're cut out for writing."

"For ten years now, I've been listening to two-bit Lenins, and I can't quote you a new idea."

"Did you hear what I said? Your lick is writing."

"They have two licks. They write movies all day, and they construct the coming order at night."

"I know what they do all day. I've read it, and I've seen it on the screen. It's writing of a kind, but it's nothing like yours."

"Did I ever tell you what one of them said about *The People From Heaven*? 'I never knew you could write like that.' "

"You told me. But you didn't tell me what *you* said."

"What *could* I say?"

"That he *should've* known. Somebody should've told him. What do those guys do—keep you a secret?"

"They have me down as hard to handle, and they don't like that one damn bit. Revolutionaries don't like rebels, so they keep me in the tules, where I can't do any harm."

"And where *they* can't harm *you*," Maggie said. "Do you ever think of that? If you were exposed to those coffee-housers week after week, they'd soon make one out of you."

"So suffer the housewives—is that what you're saying?"

"It's only for three hours," she said. "And then you can come home and listen to me."

SCENE 71

RICHARD NIXON (1950)

> *Who can bring a clean thing out of an unclean. . . ?*
> —Job 14.4

The young Congressman had a trick worth two of that one: he could do the opposite, for his clean clothes held an *un*clean thing. He wore, the story goes, a fresh white shirt to school each day, and if the weather allowed, he'd walk all the way rather than ride with a crowd. And it's told too that he was mindful of his breath, wherefore he must've been no less aware of his nails, his hair, the shine on his shoes: he was the kind, it seems, who bathed often—and twice as often he'd wash his hands. Poor early, threadbare, neat, and with breath sweetened, he'd fare forth pure to the eye, a grave boy with his feet on the ground and his head in the sky, a boy truly out of Alger, people said—but all the same, he comprised the knave, and so it was that from a clean thing an unclean came.

And now he was on the Hill, a far cry from where he'd started in Yorba Linda, a long road from the grind at the beginning, the galling chores, the odd jobs for small change, his mother's daily praying, the bad breath of his father's failures. It was half a life back to strivings on campus and nights of

144

dogged boning by the lamp. Wearing white shirts still and his owner's collar, Alger-boy was on Capitol Hill, bearing news of his dime-novel virtue and his dime-novel deeds — the runaway steed he'd caught (Bucephalus!), the flagging of the fated train.

With him, though, he'd brought his creed, which was this — *If you can't lie, you'll never go anywhere* — and because he meant to go, he lied and went. He lied out of fear, and he lied for favor; he lied to appear to be more than he was, to gain, to win, to explain another lie; but when all's said, he lied because he was a liar born, and falsehood was in his grain. Beautiful outward (cf. Christ in Matthew 23.27), he was full within of dead men's bones, because, alas, he also lied to kill.

Who can bring a clean thing. . . ? cries Job. Not Dick, not even on the day he dies.

THE COLOR OF THE AIR, VIII

HERMAN MELVILLE, 1819–1891
THE CUSTOMHOUSE YEARS

> *All Fame is patronage. Let me be infamous.*
> —Melville to Hawthorne

Each morning at eight, he'd set out from Madison Square, walking on a fair day and riding the stage in the rain, and two miles down Broadway he'd go — to Duane, say, or Jay — and there he'd cross to the Hudson, stopping on occasion to stare above the slips, where a palisade of rigging seemed to fence the Palisades. None can say what he dwelt on in such intermissions, nor may even he have been aware of what concerned his mind. There were matters of the moment, the names and berths of ships, the cargoes he was due to inspect; and there were matters of the past, sights once seen, words spoken (to whom?) and heard, the tones of certain winds. Nowhere could he have been free of remembrance, but here, so near to many reminders, the masts, the festooned canvas, the mewing gulls and chloride air, here he must've found himself living in more than one place and more than one time. He was an old man now on one of the days of his six-day round, he was weighing sulphur, counting pelts, stamping chests of tea; and he was also young, unknown as yet and not as yet forgotten, he was watching the *vahine* girls

swimming naked out to the *Acushnet,* he was seeing their wet brown
bodies, their wet and jet-black hair. So, though no one knows what
he thought of on those days beside the dull green river, he may have
seen its gulls mingle with other gulls, the ones that cried round the
Rock Rodondo, may have seen the hulls across the street meet and
gam with hulls across the world, may have seen drays transform to
pods of whales, and so faintly as to seem imagined, from no place
or from Paradise, he may have caught his hero's name and designation: *Jack Chase, captain of the maintop.* In that same moment or the
next, a sobriquet may have surfaced in his mind—*the Handsome
Sailor*—and, clearly but a fancy, it may have stirred and then
submerged.

Let me be infamous, he'd said, and Fame let him be, left him at
his sere and feckless four-dollar days on the wharves, sought him
not among his invoices and manifests, his table of tariffs, his stamping-
pad and its purple ink: there were twenty years of such days, and
Fame let him be. It was the only work he ever did for pay, and he
did it well and with honor, as if it were a charge that lay upon him,
for nearly a third of his life. And yet what could he have deeply cared
for in those daily dealings with the tricksters of trade, how could
his thoughts have stayed with ad valorems and specifics, with false
weights and misappraisals, with documents drawn by the light-of-
hand—how could he have lived on land those twenty years of days?
He was out of his element there, a drydocked ship or one on the
ways, a stranded creation, ungainly, exposed, of no avail. If he had
a place among the living, or even among the dead, it was where Jack
Chase surely was, on the seas or under: the things he did at desks
(did he really do them?) were contrary to his nature, were all against
his will.

Let me be infamous, he'd said, and so he was for twenty years.
Always, though, he was only there in part and only partly of that
time, and more and more did he dwell on Jack his hero and the Handsome Sailor, and in the end he may well have joined them, the three
becoming one. If so, he may one day have heard himself say *Sentry,
are you there?,* and for Ishmael, Jack, and Billy, the long last voyage
would have begun.

SCENE 72

PRISCILLA AND ALGER HISS (January 1950)

> Mr. Chambers: *They used to get up early in the morning
> to observe birds. Once, to their great excitement,
> they saw a prothonotary warbler. . . .*
> —House Committee testimony

Chambers, was it, Whittaker Chambers? They claimed they couldn't
remember a Chambers, but he knew a slew about them for a man they failed
to place—and it wasn't the sort of stuff that would bubble up in a dream.
He had to be there or nigh to say that the husband was hard of hearing, though
he might've been in doubt as to the ear, and he had to be somewhere about
to swear that Alger wore glasses while reading but otherwise not, and that
neither he nor Pross cared a toss about food—and that Pross, not Priss, was
what Hiss called her. All the same, more was needed, and more there was,
for Chambers reeled off in proper order their several homes, spoke of their
silverware and china, described the Bokhara rug (red) that warmed the floor.
He knew those things, those were the things he knew, and he swore to them all.

> Mr. Stripling: *You have never seen Mr. Chambers?*
> Mr. Hiss: *The name means absolutely nothing to me.*

Well, as far as it went, the answer was true: he *didn't* know a Chambers,
Whittaker or whatever. But ten years back, he'd met a George Crosley, one
of the pseudonyms that Chambers used, one of many—among them Phillips,
Cantwell, Dwyer, Breen, to name but a few—and therefore in knowing any,
Hiss could be said to have known the lot.

> Mr. Hiss: *To the best of my knowledge, I never heard of Whittaker
> Chambers. I have never laid eyes on him.*

His eyes, when at last permitted to lie on Chambers, lay on the guise he'd
known as Crosley, altered, he thought, coarser than before and heavier-set,
and even more regardless of his clothes, but he had the same fearful air, like
some lesser animal, the same whey face, the same clay look. Yes, he might
be Crosley, Hiss said, but to be quite certain, he'd have to see what he
remembered best, the man's badly neglected teeth—and, sure enough, there
they were, brown-stained still and some beyond saving.

Mr. Chambers: *The day after Hitler and Stalin signed their pact, I went to Washington and reported to the authorities what I knew about the infiltration of the United States Government by the Communists.*

In other words, he spilled, he puked up his life, and what a sight he must've made, what an eyesore, as he poured himself past those blighted teeth! And when done, what then—did he sit there and stare at the spew, did he see in the cheese on his chest, his knees, his shoes and socks, a few chewed lumps of what had once been trustful men?

Mr. Chambers: *I went to Hiss at considerable risk to myself and tried to break him away from the Party, but he absolutely refused.*

And thereafter, he said, he was on the *qui vive,* dreading the day and furtive by night, always fearful, always with a pistol near at hand.

In a later time, the face of neither man is clear in mind, but of the two, strange to say, it's Chambers who catches what light there is. It may be that, unlike the other, he requires illumination, for he brings little of his own to brighten the room, no ease of manner or natural graces, no flights of fancy, no lightsome ways or inner shine, and where he comes, the air goes stale, like the air in a mine.

Mr. Chambers: *The story has spread that in testifying against Mr. Hiss, I am working out some old grudge. I do not hate Mr. Hiss. We were close friends. But we are caught in a tragedy of history.*

He came from a rum line, that Chambers—or Crosley, or Dwyer, or "Bob," or "Carl," or whatever else he chose to call himself. He weighed twelve pounds at birth, he said, and he was so broad at the shoulders (fourteen inches) that he had to be taken out by instrument. This tore an artery in his mother's uterus, and thus he was born in blood, though none of it rose in the Howards. Memory of that flood stayed in her mind for life, and it stayed as well in his, for she kept it vivid by repetition. It made unhappy hearing (*I bled,* did she say again and again, *I nearly bled to death?*), and as he grew, guilt grew with him. The father passed as a painter—a kindly term, his own, perhaps, for all his work was illustration—and the mother, something of an actress, had briefly been on the stage. Neither profession had yielded wealth, and what Chambers knew was a straitened childhood, of which he recalled a shack house near Rockaway Bay, coal-lamp lighting, and brought-in water. In the village of Lynbrook, they were known as *the French family* and were thought peculiar.

And they *were* peculiar, one and all. His father, Chambers said, was quiet to the point of seeming mute, and the boy was rising seven when the man ran off with his lover, another peculiar man. And the mother too had her share of rareness, pacing the house and railing at a husband no longer there. As for the sons of the pair, one downed a bottle of whiskey and turned on the gas, while the other, born fourteen inches across the shoulders—guilty then and more so now—sought solace in Marx and Engels and in the embrace of peculiar men. Oh, they were queer coves, never fear.

> Mr. Chambers: *I served, chiefly in Washington, D.C., in the underground organization of the Communist Party. The purpose of the group at that time was not primarily espionage, but espionage was certainly one of its eventual objectives.*

Down there in the dark, he said, strike him dead if he hadn't seen the light. It came to him through all his many disguises, all his changes of place and name, his maneuvers in the night, and in dishing up his comrades (*I was very fond of Mr. Hiss*), he was only saving the world. How wrong to suppose that he hated Hiss for having been well-born and *bien élevé*! How could he but admire those eager ways beneath genteel repose, how could he begrudge the schools and honors (the Cane Club at Hopkins, the *Law Review* at Harvard), how could he feel diminished by the clerkship year with Wendell Holmes? Hate Hiss? Nay, he loved the man—and gave him away.

He didn't enjoy being Judas, he said. He felt sadness and loss and nowhere near the excitement of Hiss and Pross on spotting that warbler.

SCENE 73

A REPORT ON THE WEATHER (February 1950)

From the porch, you could see two wheel-wide rills running down the driveway toward the gate, and there were tufted pools in the paddocks and fringes of rain on the trees.

Maggie came from the house and joined you, saying, "One of those radio pundits was giving Hiss a going-over." She extended a hand to catch some drip-drop from the eaves. "When will *Chambers* get a going-over?"
"Chambers wasn't on trial," you said.
"He should've been, after that stuff about the pumpkin."
"You think he made it all up?"
"Of course he made it up."
"Too bad for Hiss you weren't on the jury."

"Hiding secret papers in a pumpkin!" she said. "I'd've laughed in Chambers' face."

"The jury didn't laugh. They thought *Hiss* was the liar."

"The way you talk, you seem to agree."

"It doesn't matter whether I agree or not. I wasn't on the jury, either."

"Are you making a point?"

"Yes," you said. "Scare a jury, and you can prove anything against anybody."

"How do you scare a jury?"

"Say *Communist,* and they'll go pissy-assed before you can get out of the way."

"Hiss denied being a Communist. Chambers is the one who admitted it."

"They knew each other, though, and it came off on Hiss. That's the beauty of using the word."

Again she reached out for the eavesdrop, saying, "Maybe it's time to wonder about a Chambers of our own."

In the wind, the grained air seemed to pass in review, a parade of rain.

"We don't have to wonder," you said. "Whoever he is, he's someone we know."

SCENE 74

JOSEPH McCARTHY AGAIN (February 10, 1950)

> *Get ahead! Be somebody!*
> —Bridget McCarthy, to her son

He was on the way the day he was born, and he'd still be going on the day he died. Always he'd be on the run from where he was to where he wasn't, and when he got there, he'd only keep on running: motion alone seemed the end in view. Nothing drew him, nothing detained—from the outset, he was bent on a career to no place at all, a solid that wouldn't fall for the pull of *g* and freer by far than a star. *I never saw anybody so steamed up,* a friend said. *He just couldn't relax. He was pushing all the time.* He didn't know that Joe was doing his mother's bidding, and Joe didn't know that getting ahead and being somebody were different things, one an endless road and the other a destination: he spent a lifetime on the road; he *had* no destination.

There's a photo of him as a shirt-tail kid, taken along with two of his brothers on the Grand Chute farm, they in the sunlight, he in the shade, and he's grinning at something beyond the lens, beyond you, something that not even his brothers can see, and they're at his side. That same grin would appear again and often, though never, it would seem, at another's face; instead, it would go off into space on the interminable road ahead. *He worked at everything he did,* said his friend. *He was pushing all the time.*

As a boy, he was called "the bear cub" for his paw-like hands, his thickness through the middle, and his weighty way of going, and when his mother prayed him *Be somebody!,* the plea stayed in his bearish mind, where all his life he'd claw it like a tin of food, never to reach its contents, never to understand. And the cub grew and strayed, taking with him little but Bridget's invocation and that photo of himself in the shade.

En route (to what? to where?), there were many stations—schools, the law, the Bench, the second War—but *pushing! working!,* he sped through them all on an express of lies and defamation, blind to the wrack and ruin he left behind, deaf to the cries of fear and rage. Had he seen and heard, though, he'd not have cared a pinch: he was bending to Bridget, he was getting ahead to her what and where. Indeed, only yesterday he'd traveled faster, he'd flown through the air for a spiel in Wheeling.

At the old McClure (12th and Market), he'd spoken to three hundred women after a Lincoln Day dinner, but for once the slap on the back had been barred, the glad hand, the poke in the ribs for an equivocal joke, and there'd been no well-met fellows to hail for once, only three hundred Republican girls. For once, therefore, he'd lacked force and faltered, and his smears and slurs had fallen on unreceptive ears; worse, tables near the doors had emptied to fill tiled rooms on other floors. He was failing, he must've thought, he was losing speed, descending—when suddenly, down deep in a pocket his fat fingers found a slip of paper. A slip of paper, that was all, but he'd drawn it forth and flashed it, crying *I have here in my hand. . . !,* and then he'd smiled, waiting for those tiled rooms to empty and those tables to refill.

What he'd had there in his hand was a laundry-list, a check-list of his hose, his shirts and collars and drawers, his week of soiled smalls, but flourishing it before the company, somehow he'd turned it into a roster of traitors, a roll of dishonor: *I have here in my hand,* he'd said, *a list of 205 known Communists still shaping the policy of the State Department.* In time, the number would rise to 207, fall to 81, and fall further to 57, but always there'd be those for whom it was still a tally of Joe's dirty linen.

He'd gotten ahead, though, and no mistake: the bear cub was now the full-grown bear. But a question remained, and the question was *Where to?* He didn't know the answer himself, nor could he know. He was still on the endless road, and having no aim, Bridget, he'd reach nothing, he'd never *be.*

151

SCENE 75

THE COLD WIND AS BEFORE (March 1950)

Maggie said, "You said something foolish the other day."

And you laughed, saying, "I do that often. Be more specific."

"We were talking about the Hiss case and informers like Whittaker Chambers, and I wondered whether we had a Chambers of our own out here. You said there was no need to wonder; whoever he was, he'd be someone we knew."

"And that was the foolish thing?"

"Why would *we* have to know *him*? Wouldn't it be enough if *he* knew *us*? Suppose he was one of the regulars at Musso's, like we were. Suppose he used to see us at the Pickwick, Stanley Roses's, meetings of the Guild, somebody we never even spoke to. What would stop him from naming our names?"

"He'd have to have something to go on," you said. "People don't just cough up names."

"Nobody knows what Chambers really knew, but he coughed up Hiss. Why not some local son-of-a-bitch?"

You said nothing.

"You don't think there are people out there who'd swear us away—the flag-wavers, the spit-lickers, the hacks who work only four weeks a year. . . ?"

But you said nothing.

"Well, I do, Jabe," she said. "And if they didn't squeal for Old Glory, they'd sure as hell squeal for a job."

When you spoke, it was to say, "Is this what you mean—that no matter how dirty the work, somewhere there's a man who'll do it?"

"It must be true," she said, "because so many dirty things are done."

And you said, "In one of my books, a character said, 'People ain't such a much,' and in another, somebody said they were. I still haven't made up my mind."

"You had it right the first time. I know, because I've been out there among them, and you've only watched from a window."

"It's such a bad thought to have—people climbing over people."

"They're good at it."

And you said, "So we're back to that foolish thing."

And she nodded, saying, "I wonder who'll give us away."

SCENE 76

KING OF THE KINDERGARTEN (April 1950)

I have my own world.
—Lyonel Feininger

Your sister Ruth, long after her college days were over, resumed her studies and earned a teaching credential, no small accomplishment at any age and a great one at forty. Not yet permanently assigned, she acted as a substitute wherever she was sent for the day, often to kindergartens in San Fernando Valley. One morning, from an elementary school in Sherman Oaks, she called to say that she wanted to see you, and shortly before three o'clock, you were walking across the yard toward her classroom.

It was a warm afternoon, and through the open windows, you heard the thin concert of children's voices, high in pitch and quick to dwindle, but always there were some on the air, always a shrilling as from a flock of birds, and in the sunlit room you could seem them, all those small and unstill birds. As you watched their labors at arrangement, at poising this thing on that thing, at moving the immovable, at nothing at all, your mind spun back to your own time in a similar place, your own bickering, your own small struggle with reluctant things. . . .

Colonora, he called it, and a teeming little round it was, nowhere to be found save inside his head. A place of tall people, he made it (all, or many, he), and fiddlers dressed in red played its deep and crooked streets. There in Colonora yachts were steepled, and cathedrals raced, and cardboard towns could be folded, it seemed, and stored away. Isosceles clouds were drawn on his skies, crowds hastened while standing still, buildings leaned, eavesdropping, and jaded locomotives slept on oval feet. No wars were fought in that realm, none but those he chose to wage, controlled disasters, really, shows of force that came to naught, nor were acts of God suffered to occur in his dominion, that kingdom contained in a sand-box, and only one child would die there—after eighty-five years of play.

To Ruth, just coming from a doorway, you said, "What did you want to see me about?"

And she said. . . .

SCENE 77

BLUES FOR *A MAN WITHOUT SHOES,* 6 (May 1950)

The book rode you. Where you went, it went too, and it couldn't be cast from your mind, left behind as you passed to something else. So constantly did you think of it that at times the thought seemed to become the real, and then it was the book itself that filled your head, a thing of weight and dimension. For five years now, you'd borne its failures, and you wondered how much longer you'd go before you said *enough. Enough!,* you'd say—but what then? Would the thought go away, the book, the weight, or would it stay to bear you down for the rest of your life? It rode you, it rode you like guilt.

In a sense, every book is autobiographical, even a biography of someone else, and *A Man Without Shoes* was no exception. Purporting to tell the story of a character named Daniel Johnson, in essence it was the story of Julian the Harlem-born Jew. Almost all of it fancied, still somewhere within the figment was the fact, somewhere within Daniel (your father's middle name) was the actual you. To some extent, you'd revealed yourself in each of your four preceding books, but the revelations had been indicative of personal views in the main, of the americanization of one particular Jew; only here, for the first time, had you shown your political bent. Of Sacco and Vanzetti while they lived, you'd known nothing, not even their names, and you'd grown so ashamed of your ignorance that you tried to live it down by inhabiting Dan Johnson and being as he was, informed, zealous, and, when the two Italians died, forlorn. In a small way, you atoned for the fact through the fiction—but of what worth was the quittance if it went unseen? Until the book saw the light, it was only a confession to yourself, and never, therefore, would you say *Enough!*

§

In the spring of 1947, after Reynal & Hitchcock's withdrawal from its contract to publish the book, your then agents Russell & Volkening had offered the manuscript to Little, Brown & Co., where the liberal Angus Cameron was editor-in-chief. By that time, you'd returned to California, and what you knew of the book's career, you learned from Henry Volkening through the mails. That correspondence no longer exists, but from the presentation you later made to Desmond Hall,* *it was touch-and-go at Little, Brown* — a near miss, you said, with Cameron apologizing for the way things had gone.

Thereafter, the book was rejected in succession by Harper, Scribner's, Houghton Mifflin, and Simon & Schuster. At the last of these, as you related to Hall, *it struck fire with Maria Leiper, Jack Goodman, and two other editors. The four of them carried the book to the top, Simon himself according to Maria,* but in the end, the rise was followed by a fall. It was Knopf's turn next, and then it was Dial's, and in March 1948, the book reached Random House, whose Saxe Commins wrote thus to Volkening:

> I am afraid that we cannot make you an offer for John Sanford's formidable and highly original novel. We cannot ignore the skills of this episodic and unrestrained book, but it strikes us as all virtuosity. Unfortunately, the general reader cares very little about such displays of versatility. I doubt very much that we could find a market for Mr. Sanford's book. That is why I must ask you to send your messenger for the manuscript.

You have no way of knowing whether a messenger was sent as demanded, but however retrieved, the book trudged from Random House to Appleton-Century, where, you told Hall, *Jane Lawson and Ted Purdy liked it a great deal, and so did a chap named Ted Jaeckel.* Still, as four had fared at Simon & Schuster, so fared three more here.

And then — once again Angus Cameron.

Ted Jaeckel had moved on to Little, Brown, taking with him his editorial report to Appleton-Century. In it, he'd said:

> I have waited to write my report on this 1073-page manuscript to see whether the initial enthusiasm would wear off. At present, I feel that it has the makings of a truly great American novel. The obvious comparisons are Farrell and Dos Passos, especially the latter, but there are differences which reflect well on Sanford.

He'd dwelt then on your central character, whom you'd outlined to John Woodburn at Harcourt several years before, and he'd recounted his story, which no one yet had troubled himself to do:

> The story is simple and direct. Dan Johnson is born in New York City in the first decade of the century, son of a hack-driver. He grows up sensitive to his surroundings and the people he meets, evaluating what he is taught or picks up, and develops a set of values which are pretty impressive. He is influenced by his uncle, a socialist.

---

* See Blues for *A Man Without Shoes*, 1

The story is interwoven, as *U.S.A.* was, though Sanford is more successful with the whole history of the times, with a feeling of movement and growth and a strong American heritage. It is extremely moving. The first 304 pages are an entity, and the best part of the book.

The close of the section marks Danny's transition into spiritual manhood. He has been working with a group of people on the Sacco-Vanzetti defense, and this section is the most moving I remember in any novel of this scope.

The author has intelligently climaxed this part of the novel with the execution of the two Italians, and Danny's first sexual experience (sensitively and unobjectionably handled), so that there ˙ no great welter of sentiment, but a true emotional experience.

Endorsed in such terms, why had the book been refused by Appleton? The praise may have been undeserved, but praise it was, and you thought then as you think now, that the ways of publishing are strange indeed. There was more to the report, and eventually Jaeckel recorded some *dis*praise:

The middle part of the book is a section covering Danny's two years on the bum, wandering the country and responding in his own idealistic way to scenes of historical events he had loved so well in books. This part becomes a gigantic paean of a big, young, strong country, poetic though written in the direct prose of working-people's speech. Danny learns from all he sees, rejects a few illusions, imagines himself in love with a bitch (this is not made real enough for me), returns home.

The last and longest section concerns Danny back in New York, pottering around at various jobs, maintaining his toughmindedness to the point of childish braggadocio. He falls in love with a girl and marries her, goes to night school to study economics, but stops to have an affair, finally resolving his conflicts for the first time decisively by signing up to go to Spain to fight.

Enlisting in the Lincoln Battalion was certainly in Dan's mind, and in some early version of the manuscript, he may have been shown doing so. The only copy extant, however, ends otherwise. It ends, in fact, showing him being dissuaded by his wife, who argues that in discharging his obligation to a democratic Spain, he'd be abandoning the same obligation to his native land; he can serve the one, she says, only by running away from the other.

Continuing his report, Jaeckel wrote:

There are these things to be said for this novel: for all its length, it is completely engrossing, which is more than I can say for Farrell;

unlike *U.S.A.*, it focuses its panorama on one man, giving the book a unity and tightness which makes it more interesting to read than Dos Passos' work; it is a completely 'American' novel in scene, style, and content, an oblique history of this century up to 1937, with an American character as the touchstone.

Dan Johnson is an average American and a fairly typical working-man, but not average as one of Sinclair Lewis' satirized characters. He is neither as ignorant as Studs Lonigan nor as over-sensitized as Danny O'Neill in Farrell's later quadrilogy; rather he is aware, eager, young, curious, and perplexed. His motivations are human and understandable.

The book is, on the whole, admirably presented, flatly narrated with a tension that arises from the inherent dramatic quality of the material and of this country. The author is compassionate and honest. He achieves usually a distinctive objectivity, allowing comment and opinion to grow out of the amazingly real dialogue of the characters. His understatement is clever, his sentiment touching, his characters understandable and sympathetic.

In the paragraph that followed, Jaeckel gave his reservations. They were serious ones, and it might've been wise to be governed by them. But being governed by another was never your way of writing, and while you may have listened, surely you did not hear.

My criticisms are these: the book falls down after the first section. Dan's final awareness takes a long time, and there are some slow parts which can be cut. Some of the descriptive reflection in the middle section is the author's rather than Dan's and should be trimmed down. The book is best when its characters are talking, less engrossing when the author is speaking, and fairly successful when the characters are reflecting. What is lacking dramatically is a larger climax in the closing chapters of the book. After the tremendous impact of the first section, something is needed to end the book more dynamically, and some of the other characters need to be brought a little closer, made consecutive and full.

The report concluded with Jaeckel's recommendation:

I have made a rough word-count of this book and estimate it to be 430,000 words long.*

If the author can heighten the middle and end to equal the first 300 pages, we should bring this out in three volumes a few months apart and issue them in one volume when it becomes feasible.

---

* An overestimate. As published, the book contained fewer than half that number.

It is an experience to read, rich with a deep warm wit and understanding, truly alive and vigorous. It is the closest thing to the great American novel that I have seen yet, a major contribution to our literature, and worthy of great respect for having achieved so many of its author's aims.

In the spring of 1946, on the strength of the Jaeckel report, Cameron asked for a resubmission of the book to Little, Brown.

§

Angus Cameron. . . .
Little appears when you try to recall him. Through the layering of years, you can't see his size, his looks, the color of his eyes—nor do you recognize the voice, if it's his that you hear. All that comes to mind is the sense that he conveys of being in a static state, a mass at rest. When you think back to his lack of resolution, you feel stopped by it still, and you seem to pace it, pace it, like something once wild in a cage.

On its second submission to Little, Brown, the book was under consideration from July to October, at which time Cameron acted by inertia, and again the book was refused.

§

Rinehart followed, its editor-in-chief John Selby writing to Volkening on the 10th of December:

> I am sorry (and I really mean sorry) that after a good many violent arguments and much soul-searching, we have decided we can't take on Mr. Sanford.
>
> Anybody would be an idiot to claim that he can't write or to deny that there is an enormous amount of good stuff in this book. Just the same, it would involve a complete re-write from about page 200 on, and that of course is most of the book. As it stands now, the chief character is exactly the same person from his birth to page 1070, and between there and page 1073, he suddenly comes alive and makes the first decision of his life. That makes no sense to me.
>
> I honestly think this book would take much of the time of one editor for nine months or more, provided Mr. Sanford were willing to cooperate fully, and I wonder if he would be that amenable. I am sure that eventually somebody will be unable to resist taking on such an obviously fine talent, but I am afraid we can't afford the chance.

And when Doubleday responded likewise, Volkening quit you, and the book was on its own. A lost child, it became, wandering from door to door, all of them closed. Duell's door was closed, and Farrar's, and Holt's, and doors tried before were closed, Harcourt's, Appleton's, Viking's, Dial's, and doors too that wore forgotten names. By the summer of 1950, the book had been turned away thirty times and more. . . .

And then Cameron, once again asking for the book.

§

"Don't send it," Maggie said, "Go there with it — and take *The Bandage* along."

And taking both books, you went.

SCENE 78

THE BIG CITY (June 1950)

On the Avenue

From the St. Regis, you turned southward on Fifth and went with the morning traffic through an arcade of sun and shade that misted away in the distance. The summer day was bright with glass-flash and flakes of color — flags, brass, costume display, a Monet in motion. To passersby, you might've seemed a part of it, one of the hinted figures, one of the glints, but you belonged there no more, and you knew it. Always the place would take you back to your beginning, always it would make the dead live again; but it was their home now, all those strangers you were going with or flowing past; and it was you, not they, who were strange.

Little, Brown & Co.

Through a window of the reception-room, you looked down at the granite lions crouched before the Library entrance. From where you stood, they were only chunks of stone now and then scored by a friction match. Between them, people stopped on the steps, spoke to others, and moved on; and people stopped when there was no one to speak to; and still more stopped as if they'd reached a missing stair. And as you watched, the scene changed to one you'd fancied, and you saw Dan Johnson in the come-and-go. He was holding a clip-board, from which dangled a pencil on a string, and he was crying *Sign here! Sign your petition for Sacco and Vanzetti. . . !*

159

"You may go in now, Mr. Sanford," the receptionist said.

Leaving Dan on the steps below, and yet bearing him with you in manuscript, you went to the indicated door. It wasn't Cameron who awaited you, though. It was John Woodburn, your one-time editor at Harcourt, and he said, "Hello, Hotspur."

Hotspur, he'd usually called you, for the rash-brain he thought you to be, but there was nothing in the word as he used it now, not even the warmth of a name. Wherefore all you said was, "Hello back."

At your last meeting, there'd been words hard and rasping over *A Man Without Shoes*. In his anger, he'd almost accused you of betrayal, as though, in having written the book as you did, you'd somehow broken your word. What word?, you'd often wondered. When first discussed with him, all that existed of Dan Johnson was idea. Nothing had been written, no story, no scene, and the only plan you had was the commemoration of an ordinary man. Before the writing began, you hadn't understood that there were no ordinary men, and therefore you couldn't've known that Dan would go where he did—to those steps between the lions, waving a petition for two (what had Judge Thayer called them?) *anarchistic bastards*.

"Surprised to find me here?" Woodburn said.

And you said, "I lost track of you after the bust-up at Harcourt."

"You could've written."

"Saying what—'Please'?"

"Saying, damn it, that maybe you were wrong! I'd sold you to Harcourt on the strength of *Johnson, Daniel*. Ordinary Dan, you said he'd be, one of the Forty Million, and what did you come up with? The Boy Lenin! Why, for Christ's sake, didn't you write the book you were supposed to?"

You remembered your first sight of him, across a table in the Bamboo Room of the Ritz. You remembered the rust-colored tweed he'd worn, rough as a rug, and you remembered too that it was a match for his complexion, as if he'd just come in from a walk in the wind.

"The opening sentence of *The People From Heaven*," you said. "You quoted it from memory. That pleases me yet."

He quoted it again, saying, " 'Daniel Hunter stood in the entry of the church, listening to the final bronze shimmers ripple from the bell-loft.' "

And you said, "I could improve that today: I'd get rid of *ripple*."

He'd faded since then, you thought. He was no longer a man with the bark on; he looked pale, as if peeled. Was he ailing?, you wondered, had his numbers gone wrong, his readings risen?

"I'll bet you forgot this, though," you said. "The way you opened your pitch for me to Harcourt."

"How did it go?"

"You said I was 'an important and powerful writer who has just now come upon the books he is destined to write.' "

"Did I really say that?"

"And when I handed you *Shoes,* you handed it back. *Destined,* I guess, was only so much spit."

"You're one hard-headed piece of suet, do you know that?"

"Everybody knows it."

"I don't suppose you've revised the book any."

"I may have moved it a little to the left."

"What's that other thing you've got there?"

"A new one."

"What's it called?"

"*The Land That Touches Mine.*"

"Does the title mean anything?"

"It's from a Lincoln story. Somebody called a man a land-hog, and the man said, 'I only want the land that touches mine.' "

"Sounds political."

"It *is* political."

Looking at you for a moment as if taking your measure, he said, "Aren't you going to ask what I do at Little, Brown?"

"What do you do at Little, Brown?"

"Stiffnecked and circumcized," he said. "I'm managing editor under Angus Cameron. He wants me to read the manuscript again."

"Does he know you slugged it at Harcourt?"

"I told him."

You placed the binder on his desk and moved it slightly toward him.

"And while I'm at it," he said, "I might as well read the other."

Stacking the two binders, you said, "I'm at the St. Regis."

On parting five years before, neither of you had offered his hand; neither of you did so now.

A Leave-taking at Town Hall

At corner-crossings of the Avenue, you could see a last layer of light over the Hudson. The street-lamps were not yet on, and in the confusion between night and day, you walked through colors that changed as you went. From a top story here and there, a building glared back at the going-down sun, and in the gloom below, you passed still-life windows and their spills of merchandise—furs, silverware, a torrent of shirting. Of the shop-names, many were now unfamiliar, but there'd been a time when you'd known nearly all, and you thought of that time, dwelling on long-gone evenings with long-gone girls, but though you made them live for a while, you could not give them words. You were on the site of an event that had happened—you—and hardly a trace remained. St. Thomas's was there, and two blocks down St. Patrick's, but where were the voices of the years that could never end? In your mind, you saw Emanu-El and Delmonico's, and you felt as though you were walking on their graves. At 43rd Street, the pedestrian drift was westward toward Town Hall, bright-lit against the now all-dark sky, and you entered the flow.

In the lobby, there were faces that you'd never seen before and faces that you knew; you nodded at those you recognized, but you kept to yourself in the merging crowd. Inside, you took a seat on an aisle some rows back from the platform, where a line of folding chairs faced the audience. You watched these fill with those of the Hollywood Ten due on the morrow to begin their prison sentences for contempt of Congress.* Last motions had been made in the Courts and last appeals denied, and they had this last free night to protest against their persecution. You cannot now recall who presided or who spoke or how many of The Ten were there for the farewell assembly. Of all that must've been said, no word returns, and you hear no cries from the gathering, no sound of applause, but you can still see shapes in that line of chairs, and you can still, as if you sat with them, see yourself below on the aisle. . . .

But you were *not* up there. Along with a thousand others, millions, you were watching the infliction of a wrong, saddened by the sight of it, but watching all the same. It troubled you that the wrong was being endured by The Ten in part that you might be spared, and you were troubled the more as the evening wore on. There was safety in being where and what you were, an unremarkable observer, an anonymous component of a crowd. You were as good as hidden, you told yourself, and therefore stay. . . . But you couldn't, you *couldn't* stay!, and during an intermission, you found a chair on the platform and sat in the open as if you were one of The Ten.

The King Cole Room

From a booth against the opposite wall, you gazed at the long mural behind the bar, a bright and precise illustration of the Merry Old Soul and his Fiddlers Three. Or could it be that you were looking at the pipe and bowl, the

---

* All were long-time associates of yours and, with one or two exceptions, much admired by you for their fidelity and courage. Now nationally known, they're given their real names here: John Howard Lawson, Samuel Ornitz, Alvah Bessie, Herbert Biberman, Lester Cole, Ring Lardner, Jr., Edward Dymytryk, Albert Maltz, Adrian Scott, and Dalton Trumbo. —J.S.

peacock sky, the clouds between the columns of a picture in your mind? You hardly heard the treble of colliding glass, the murmur of many voices, the laughter on the air: you were eyeing the facing wall—or was it a childhood book lying on the floor. . . ?

". . . wanted on the telephone, Mr. Sanford," someone was saying, and you watched the Captain of waiters plug in a hand-set.

The caller was Woodburn, who said, "What're you up to, Hotspur?"

"I'm with an old friend—Maxfield Parrish."

"The King Cole bar, eh? Well, that's as good a place as any for the news. Angus wants me to tell you we're going to do *Shoes*. . . ."

You glanced across the room at the King, the Fiddlers, the Cockaigne clouds—

"And after that, we'll do the other one. Drop in tomorrow, and Angus will tell you himself."

—or were the images those you recalled from the pages of a book?

Lafayette College Reunion

You said, "I saw the place last in 1923."

And Herb said. . . .*

When you registered for the two-day event—was it at Jenks Hall, or was it at McKeen?—you were given a great maroon-and-white button to flash from your lapel. Printed around a blank for your name was the advice to all who might seek it that you were a member of the Class of '25 and that you were there to attend its twenty-fifth reunion, there in Easton on College Hill. Sporting your buttons, the two of you paused on the steps of—Pardee, it could've been—and looked out over a sward at Dormitory Row, or where once the Row had stood.

"It doesn't seem so long ago," you said.

And Herb said. . . .

And then you said. . . .

But what more was there to say about those intervening years? Now that you'd lived them, they were measureless: time, you thought, the one thing in creation that burned without ash. Where did you go, then, you and he, where did you hunt for your eighteenth years? They weren't there on those pathways, in those vistas, or even on the air.

And you said, "We're wearing these buttons to show we're alive."

And he said. . . .

---

* Herbert Ortman, a classmate and later your law-partner.

At one of the downtown hotels that afternoon, there was a Beer Bust, and you remember a stranger peering at your button before saying *I'd know you anywhere!* And then someone announced that North Korea had just invaded South Korea.

And Herb said. . . .
And you said. . . .

Again, Little, Brown & Co.

"Mr. Cameron would like to see you," a voice said. "Can you be here at three this afternoon?"
And you said, "Yes."

It was the day after your return from the Lafayette weekend. The acceptance of your books had charged your blood and sent you off rejoicing, but the flow was flat now as you went down the Avenue, for you were thinking of Korea, thinking of it as a great mass that had somehow come free of the coast of Asia, and you walked without haste, as if to kill time before time killed you. Again it was Woodburn who received you, not Cameron, and when you saw your two manuscripts stacked exactly on his desk, you knew that Korea had reached the room.

"It was eight thousand miles away," you said. "How did it get here so soon?"
He touched one of the manuscripts, saying, "A book with Sacco and Vanzetti as the heroes," and then, touching the other, he said, "And a book with worse—a deserter. At a time like this, what can we do with things like that?"
"Publish them."
"God damn it, don't you read the papers? If you quit pipe-dreaming with Maxfield Parrish, you'd know that Truman just ordered our Air Force to South Korea."
"Somebody ought to speak out about that. Why not Little, Brown?"
"We're as anti-war as you are," he said. "But not while a war is on."
"That's not good enough. You've got to be anti all the time. If not, you never really are."
"You know something, Hotspur? You're crazy."
You took up the manuscripts, and again you parted without shaking hands.

From a Pullman Window

You watched the dumb show on the platform—the criss-cross of passengers, Red Caps, baggage-trucks, all, as on a silent screen, in soundless motion. Through the glass dome of the station, sunlight sprayed the tracks and trains, turning steel to silver and brass golden—and then the scene gave way to one in your mind, a scene due three days hence and a continent distant. It would take place on another platform at another station, and Maggie would be waiting there as you came down off the cars. She'd be eyeing you as you neared her, as though your absence had made you less familiar than before,

but she'd say *I'm glad you're home,*
and you'd say *Where's Juno?*
and she'd say *What happened back there?*
and in the car, with Juno between you, you'd say *Korea happened, and we're in for trouble. . . .*

The train was moving now, out from under the dome and into the open yards — and then you were in the tunnel, and all you could see was your image on the wall.

THE COLOR OF THE AIR, IX

THE STRIKE — 1892
HOMESTEAD, PENNSYLVANIA

> We will want three hundred guards for service at our mills
> as a measure of precaution against interference with our plan
> to start operation of the works.   —H. C. Frick

The party assembled at Ashtabula and went by train to Bellevue, where it boarded a tandem of barges. An hour or so after midnight, these were taken in tow by the tug *Little Bill*, and a start was made for the Carnegie docks thirty miles away up the Monongahela. There was no wind, and the stool-brown stream hardly broke the lights laid down from shore. A shag of mist scrimmed the Golden Triangle, and when the flotilla passed, Fort Duquesne could not be seen. But even if the time of day had not been night, even if the sun had brightly shown the old blockhouse, few aboard the scows would've known its history, and none of those few would've cared.

> *We anticipate some demonstration upon the part of those whose places*
> *have been filled.*   —H. C. Frick

What the Pinkertons foresaw was a round of cold-cocking, and that was about all. They were jailbirds in the main, or chaff at best, bruisers, roughraff, and sent against a caboodle of locked-out Hunkies, they meant to do some sapping for their five a day and found. Walled in by armorplate, they squatted on cases of Remingtons, or they sprawled in slumber on the decks. They were taking it quite easy, even the seven whose number was up.

We think absolute secrecy essential in the movement of these men.
—H. C. Frick

It was about as secret as a Bessemer in blow. The whole country was in on the cruise, and when it got to Homestead, a good four thousand met the Pinks at the pier. They met them without flowers and streamers, without speeches and music, without the city's keys. They met them with rifle-fire, rafts of burning oil, bombs made of blasting powder, and a cannon cast for the Civil War. They met the Pinks with death.

As soon as your men are upon the premises, we will notify the Sheriff and ask that they be deputized.   —H. C. Frick

The Sheriff got near enough to smell three hundred pairs of pants, but that left him a long way off, and if he swore in anything, it wasn't the Pinks; it was their shitten-britches. Bagfuls, they were, the hired sons-of-bitches, and for a day or more, they waddled around in those iron-clads, skidding in bilge, crap, and gore till five a day and found lost all its sweet for some (the seven dead ones) and some of it for all. Let Frick do it himself, the live-and-kicking said, and up went the white flag, the last clean shirt-tail left. The Hunkies agreed to let them land—if they first took off their hats.

When these works resume, it will be as non-union, and employees will have to apply as individuals.   —H. C. Frick

When the Pinks came down the planks, they had to pass through a crowd grown to twenty thousand, and if they were tough at the start, they soon enough got soft. Curses alone would've made the going bad, but stick and stone made it worse as the little parade went by. It was pissed on and smeared with dog-drop, and dead cats were swung and thrown, and a woman's umbrella poked out an eye. There were broken noses and noses broken twice, and one of the Pinks was two balls short when he got to the end of the hike. There were forty thousand hands in that Hunky gantlet, and those that ran it were lucky to live, except maybe that slob with blood on his fly.

The U.S.A. is a great and growing country. (This is confidential and not for publication unless name is omitted.) —H. C. Frick

Later, of course, the soldiers came.

SCENE 79

A FLIGHT OF STORMY PETRELS (July 1950)

From Riverside, the road ran toward Ontario along the right-of-way of the Union Pacific, and for a mile or more, neither you nor Maggie spoke. You knew without speech, though, that it was *trouble* that made you speechless. The word was in the car undiminished; in a continuous volley, it was still in play between you.

At some tree, some crossing, some telegraph pole, Maggie said, "Trouble of what kind?"

At a further tree, a further crossing, you said, "Remember how we jeered at Japan when people were jailed for 'dangerous thoughts'? Well, we jeered too soon, because we've done just that here."

"I've never been as wide-eyed as you about the nature of this country. You're always taken by surprise."

"The Ten are in jail for a legal belief. What's wide-eyed about expecting more than political persecution?"

She said, "You think Communism is legal because there's no law against it? The Ten know better, and so may you."

In the orange groves at either hand, the rows seemed to converge on a vanishing-point in the trembling distance. "I know it," you said. "I just hate to admit it."

"The trouble you meant, then, was trouble for us."

"The Ten were only the beginning," you said, and in your mind you saw a scud of soot-black birds skimming the crest of a wave.

SCENE 80

THE EARTH WAS WITHOUT FORM (July 1950)

> and darkness was upon
> the face of the deep

Through the doorway of the composing room, you watched Saul Marks at the keyboard of his typesetting machine. On a reading-rack at eye-level above it was a sheaf from the manuscript of *A Man Without Shoes,* and in a shivaree of gears and connecting rods, presto!, he was transforming sheets

167

of paper into sheets of lead that read in reverse. And when so conjured one day, another machine would change them back to paper, and reading from left to right as before, lo, they'd be a book! The Mover, aware of you even amid the racket he was making, turned to the doorway. . . .

Those who were merely acquaintances took him to be a mild sort of man, deferential, even, for he spoke softly, almost breathlessly, as if he feared to give offense. In truth, he was ever alert to take it, and he bated his tone to control his fire and not show that it was out. It was never out. A typographer of much distinction, and with more to come, he none the less bore himself as if all the world were leagued against him, as if in speech and thought it held him cheap. He well knew his worth, indeed he esteemed himself, but even so he seemed bound to find disesteem in others, though no other was of such mind. Within him ever the down-deep smolder, the simmer of anger, and none could foresee the word—or the silence—at which he'd start to blaze.

For a reason still unclear, he granted you permission to observe him at his work. It was a little, you thought, like leave to witness Genesis 1, and you quite understood that you had no voice there in the Void, nor might you question the order or the manner in which the Creation was being wrought. He was the Architect, he alone, and accepting that you had no say, you stood apart and marvelled at the art that grew from his hands.

The book, like the edifice he meant it to be, would build slowly, and when finished in the following year, it would be a proportioned object that would never fail to suit the eye. But by then, you'd have spoken the ill-considered word or neglected to speak when speech was called for, and you and Saul would be friends no more. You'd tell yourself that *A Man Without Shoes* was in being at last—but it would be a gain that did not restore what you'd lost.

SCENE 81

DR. GUSTAVE HOLMGREN, cont'd. (July 1950)

Between you on his desk lay a pack of Fatima cigarettes, its red and yellow wrapper touched off by the sun.

"What do you call these gaspers, Gus?" you said. "Fa-timas or Fat-imas?"
"Fa-timas," he said. "But I know better. I looked it up."
And you said, "So did I."

He tried to look at you steadily, but his tic was more ungovernable than ever that day, and again and again the spasm put his head to a quarter-turn before it yielded and died away.

"Did you?" he said. "When?"

"This morning. Right after you called me."

"You wanted to trip me, you bushwhacker. What a mean bunch you Lefties are! It'll serve you right when you get your come-uppance."

And you said, "How can anyone smoke a cigarette named after a daughter of Mohammed?"

"I didn't bring you in from Encino to display your recent knowledge," he said. "I had something to tell you."

How did you know what he was going to say? What was there about him that spoke before he did, that broke the news about to break? You'd always been aware of his quirk — how could you not have been? — but because you liked him, it had become as little remarkable to you as the pitch of his voice, his way of walking, his choice of cigarettes. You knew of those things, and they were things that went with the man, wherefore they stayed at the edge of your mind. Now, though, the seizure that wried his neck for once seemed to try your own.

"And what would that be, Gus?" you said.

"I've made arrangements to get rid of this God-damn twitch!"

The twitch, you thought, always the twitch. How often had you told him that none of his friends noticed it, and none would know it was gone? And how often had he said that it was his head, and *he* noticed it?

"At which hospital?" you said.

"The Good Sam."

"Who's going to do the work?"

"A neurosurgeon from St. Louis."

"St. Louis! Why not somebody from here?"

"I tried the top two, and they turned me down."

"What reason did they give?"

"Too risky, they said."

"Then, for Christ's sake, why go ahead with it?"

"Because I can't stand the way people look at me."

"The people who look at you are your friends. You're doing this for people who turn away."

"Vladimir Ilytch, you still don't understand. Only a hunchback knows how a hunchback feels."

"In one way or another, we're all deformed. It's the fool, though, that tries to get straightened out."

"Don't talk to me about fools. The risk you're running is as great as mine, so maybe we're both going to get it in the neck."

"A bum joke."

"I didn't mean it as a joke."

"I wish I could say something that would change your mind."

He managed to convey a shake of the head that was voluntary, saying, "Don't try."

"When do you go in?"

"Three days from now."

"I'll be there," you said.

And he said, "Stay away."

You can still see that pack of cigarettes, red and yellow, lying on his desk in the sun.

SCENE 82

WON HANDILY, SECOND AND THIRD DRIVING (July 18, 1950)

Messalina, unraced since the previous fall, was brought out at Hollywood Park in the Chapman Woods Purse for her first start of the summer season. Trained by C. T. Leavitt and ridden by apprentice Ray York, she "made the pace in hand," according to the Racing Form chart, "saved ground, and drew out in the last eighth, winning with something left" by nearly five lengths. Her time for the six furlongs was 1.10 2/5, only 4/5 of a second off the track record.

SCENE 83

DR. GUSTAVE HOLMGREN, concluded (Late in July 1950)

Your telephone calls to the Good Samaritan drew the same noncommittal response: *Dr. Holmgren is making the expected progress.* What was expected?, you wondered, and expected by whom? When you could learn nothing more on the wire, you went to the hospital to inquire in person. There, at the Nursing Station on Holmgren's floor, you were informed that other than the information you'd been given, none could be supplied, and, further, no visitors were permitted in the patient's room.

"But he's not a patient to me," you said. "He's my doctor. He's my friend."

"I'm sorry," the Charge Nurse said. "I can't help you."

"Can't you just say whether he's going to be all right?"

"No, sir. I cannot."

At the elevator bank, you stood staring at the *Up* and *Down* buttons as if trying to choose between them. In fact, though, you were stranded, and you watched doors open and doors close, and still you stood where you were, having no place you cared to go. Someone touched your arm, and you turned to find Dr. Bluestone, who years before had referred you to Holmgren.

"Bernie," you said. "What brings you to Good Sam?"

"I sometimes have a patient who prefers it to Cedars," he said. "Not too often."

After a pause, you said, "You're not asking what *I'm* doing here."

"I don't have to. I *know* what you're doing here."

"Well, God damn it, Bernie! How is Gus doing?"

He moved away to a window, where he gazed down at roofs, traffic, and small foreshortened figures in the street; when he spoke, it was as if to what he saw through the glass.

"It went sour," he said.

Sour, you thought. Green-gowned, those in the operating-room had been concerned only with one of the senses; they convened around a table to consider a matter of taste.

"Sour!" you said. "You mean somebody blundered!"

"It was a delicate thing, John. Gus must've told you that himself."

"Any operation is delicate, but a good surgeon brings it off. It doesn't go *sour!*"

"The man Gus had was one of the best. Do you think he'd let a second-rater touch him?"

"Then it shouldn't've gone sour," you said. "And if you say it was one of those things, I'm going to yell."

"What the hell are you—a pathologist?" he said. "You can't even *spell* anatomy, and here you are—an authority on surgery."

You spoke very quietly, saying, "It was bungled, wasn't it?"

"If you ever saw a man laid open, you're realize what a skinful he is. He's a sack of pipes and wiring, and to reach the right nerve, the right muscle, a surgeon has to work with his hands under blood. Well, with Gus he reached the wrong nerve, the wrong muscle—and it *was* one of those things! His respiration stopped, and a tracheotomy was mandatory. His breathing now is artificial."

"Will it ever. . . ?" you said, "will he. . . ?" but you couldn't finish.

He might've shrugged, he might've nodded, he might've shaken his head, but he did none of those things. Instead, he kept on looking through the window, and after a moment, you walked away.

To your back, he said, "If it'll make you feel any better, it *was* bungled."

SCENE 84

THOUGHTS ON THE ROAD TO DEL MAR (August 1950)

while you were passing Balboa, he was being spoken over at some church or mortuary or possibly in the parlor of his home, and as you left Laguna, Dana Point, Capistrano Beach, he was being lowered away in a park of stones, there to lie under one of his own that would recite his name and dates but make no mention of the twitch that had brought him to that place, for the twitch, rectified by death, would not be there to wring him more, and your friend would be done with anguish and as free as any other to face the other world, freer far than you, on your way to a racetrack to back a losing horse, and at Carlsbad, Encinitas, Solana, you'd hear someone say Good-bye, Gus. . . .

SCENE 85

TOVE CHRISTIANSEN, housekeeper* (August 1950)

What comes to mind before all else is her quiet—or the quiet that was her element as for others it was air. She came and went in silence, the little she spoke was low-pitched, and her rare laughter was a sound you hardly heard, for it was no more hearty than a sigh. She was capsuled in that stillness, but she showed no desire to break out of it; on the contrary, it seemed to secure her against a breaking in. Even her smile was slight, as if she feared it might lead to exposure—and yet now and then she did reveal herself, unwillingly, you thought, and out of pride, and you learned of her having lived long in

---

* After Ruth Borne had married and moved to Vallejo.

172

Japan, where her husband's fortunes had flourished, and she told you too of how the war had caused the loss of all.

When she wasn't occupied about the house, she'd retire to her room and read (or would she just sit and wait?, you'd wonder, and if so, wait for what?), and you'd not know she was there unless you called her name through the door. *Secretive*, though, wasn't the word for her; rather it was *sequestered*, as if to her, existence was bearable only in seclusion; and, remote at the start, she was remote to the end of her two-year stay. All the same, you admired the way she went about (*cloistered*, you'd think), and if she liked you, which she may have done, it was because you never trespassed.

Only once did she come outside herself and let you see her in the light. It was on the very day that she'd applied for employment, at the suggestion, she said, of her friend Mrs. Emil—and then she was in the open with a rush. . . .

. . . *I'm desperate, do you understand? My husband is no longer himself* (no longer himself, she said), *and I have two children to provide for, and no money is coming in. I must have this job. I'll work for whatever wages you're willing to pay. I'm desperate, Mr. Sanford. I'm.* . . .

. . . At the mention of your beloved Ingeborg Emil, the job had been hers, but it took you a moment to make her realize it and bring her to a stop, and even then her mouth was forming that final word—*desperate*, it was soundlessly saying.

Thereafter a week had passed, and you and Maggie were still awaiting an edible meal. Seven dinners had been served you, all of them ill-conceived and worse prepared, and as each was removed barely disturbed on the plate, there was a rise in your housekeeper's agitation and a further decline in her cuisine.

On a stroll to the barns after the latest failure, Maggie said, "She's scared stiff. She's so afraid of losing the job that she can't think."
"She can think," you said. "The trouble is, she thinks she's lost it."
"Has she?"
"Fire a friend of Mrs. Inge? Not me."
"I'm glad, because I wouldn't've let you. But something's got to be done."
"By whom?"
Maggie laughed. "By you, of course. But go easy with her."

In the morning, after Maggie had left for the studio, you took the housekeeper by the arm and ushered her to the parlor. There you motioned her to a chair, and drawing up another for yourself, you sat down almost knee to knee with her.

"Mrs. Christiansen," you said, "or Tove, if you'll allow me, I want you to tell me something. What in the world is the matter with you?"

She could say nothing, and all she could do, it appeared, was roll her apron down after rolling it up.

"If you won't tell me," you said, "I'll tell you. You're so fearful of failure that you can't even boil water. You haven't done one thing right in a week, and all because you're ready to fall down with fright. Maggie and I are unhappy about that. We don't want people to be afraid of us."

But she was.

"You're a fine woman," you said, "a responsible woman, and best of all, you're Scandinavian. In this household, we love Scandinavians, and we love no one more than your friend, the wonderful Mrs. Inge. Which means, my dear Tove, that this job is yours till you quit of your own accord."

By then, she was smiling one of those small smiles of hers. . . .

That evening, and then for two years, you and Maggie were regaled, regaled!

SCENE 86

MESSALINA MADE THE PACE IN HAND (August 7, 1950)

> was under vigorous handling in the last
> three-sixteenths, and stalled off Isle of Mist.
> —Racing Form chart

After the little ceremony in the winner's circle, you and Maggie followed the filly back to the barns to watch her cooling out. An unsociable sort, you sometimes thought her, disdainful, even, she fought first the groom who sponged her off and then the hot-walker on her circuits of the ring. She took nearly an hour to come down, and when, her blanket removed, she stood in the late afternoon light, she shone, and the shine rippled with her breathing like a stream.

"Well, you can go home now," Charlie Leavitt said. "She come out of it just fine."

"On that last go-around," you said. "Didn't she take a false step?"

"John, her only false step was letting you buy her. Go home."

The road to the north ran alongshore and rarely far from the head of the beach. The sun was low on your left, only a diameter or two above the horizon, and the shadows of trees lay like trees themselves, felled across the road. For no reason, you remember that day: you can still see Cardiff and Leucadia and

174

the long straight through Pendleton: you can still see the sun, almost resting on the water, and those fallen trees on the road.

Somewhere on the way, Maggie laughed and said, "*A false step.* You sounded like a real hardboot."

"I picked the filly out, remember, so maybe I do know a thing or two."

"That's why I laughed—because when you came from New York, you didn't know beans with the bag open. She's a first-class filly, and you did pick her."

"That Ray York gave her a damn good ride, or she'd've gotten nailed today. How will the chart read?, I wonder."

"*Won driving,*" Maggie said, but something in her tone told you that she was speaking to more than your question. "*Maggie Roberts broke well, saved ground, and held on to win in a hard drive.* I didn't realize it till the other day, but I'm *still* driving."

"I never noticed it," you said. "I thought you took your job in stride."

When she spoke again, it was as though she hadn't heard. "I was lying on my couch and looking up at that slaunchwise Manet, and I said to myself: *What am I doing here?* I like Metro, sure—they've been good to me—but they've been getting too much of my time, and John is getting too little."

You thought of the Paramount days fourteen years before, of your writing partner the dour Joe March and the footsteps you heard every morning through the door; you thought of meeting her at last in the elevator, of Oblath's Cafe, of the way she glowed when she sat against the sun. . . .

"My contract runs out in February," she was saying. "What I want next is a new one calling for six months on and six months off."

"I'll get it for you."

"No more driving."

"No more driving," you said.

"You don't object, then, to my being around?"

Where were you at that moment—at San Onofre, at Poche Siding, or were you passing an unnamed beach, a tidal lagoon, a dirt road leading away through a vale in the hills?

"When we first started going together," you said, "you never sat on your side of the car. You sat on my side, almost in my lap."

"That was fourteen years ago," she said as she slid across the seat.

SCENE 87

Seated with you at the breakfast table, Maggie held the morning paper open before her, informing herself, you thought, of the fires of the hour, the killings, the falls from heights. Idly you took in the heading, *Santa Barbara News-Press*, and idly too the day and the date on the line below, and you remembered *a sight across the Hudson from a window on the Drive—a sign that came on with night, a flow of lettering out of the darkness, saying THE TIME IS NOW, and then a flowing away, the moment flowing with it. All night long, the sign insisted that THE TIME IS NOW, and all night long, NOW fled away.* It was never now, you thought, not even in those newsprint columns that Maggie was scanning: the fires were out, the games had been played, and on the roads and the main, the acts of God had already been wrought.

"I'm writing about *then*," you said.

She lowered the paper a little, enough to show you the question in her eyes.

"*A Walk in the Fire* is about the past," you said, "and when I work on it, I live there."

"It's a good thing you're able to do that," she said. "How else could you make the scenes real?"

"The one I read you yesterday—did that one seem real?"

"It made the race happen all over again. That Eight Thirty filly was gaining on us from the quarter-pole to the wire, but Messy wouldn't let her by. She simply wouldn't quit."

"What else do you remember of that day?"

"All of it—the drive down to Del Mar, the race, the drive home."

"Do you remember the next day, and the day after that?"

"No reason to. They were just days. Why do you ask?"

"Because I'm in the summer of 1950, and I'm coming to a whole year so vague in my mind that I seem to be seeing it through frosted glass. What were we doing in that year, I wonder, what were we thinking and saying, and didn't we have any fear?"

"I'm not too clear myself about that period," she said. "Except for *A Man Without Shoes*, things were going well for us, and I guess we just lived the days one after another and enjoyed them all."

"But the country was well into the McCarthy era, and Hiss was in jail, and The Ten were in jail, and Nixon was riding high. Didn't that mean anything to us? Did we simply go on racing horses and fooling around with dogs?"

"McCarthy, Nixon, Hiss, the House Committee—they were a sickness, and some people don't talk about sickness. They keep it in the back of their minds."

"The back of their minds!" you said. "And what's up front?"

"In July 1951," she said, "we went to Kentucky and bought two more horses."

"We must've been crazy."

"On the contrary. We acted sane."

SCENE 88

PROSPECTUS (September 1950)

Leaving the print-shop on Manzanita, you drove out along Sunset, following the tracks of the Red Car line toward Hollywood. Now and then, on reaching a stop-light, you glanced down at the seat beside you, where a blue-covered batch of brochures lay. Each of these contained a 16-page signature of excerpts from *A Man Without Shoes,* the topmost, which was open, revealing a notice in the serene typography of Saul Marks:

A MAN

WITHOUT

SHOES

A Novel by JOHN SANFORD

On or about March 1, 1951, The Plantin Press will issue a limited edition of John Sanford's new novel, *A Man Without Shoes*. Given here are six selections from the work: the first three, "Father's Name," "Mother's Name," and "Date of Birth," constitute the actual opening of the book; the others, "Buckeye Johnny Appleseed," "Marse Linkum," and "Paul Bunyan and Friend," are random selections.

Here, you thought, near enough to be touched were six parts of a book long before begun as *Johnson, Daniel,* and without thinking, you did touch them, impelled, it may have been, by a feeling of affection. In your mind, the character was now almost indistinguishable from the book; with each of its thirty-some rejections, he'd become less a paper being and more a thing of substance, dimensioned like reality, and you weren't far from regarding him as sentient. It would've been no wonder that you felt for him affection.

A streetcar drew abreast of you, and you heard its gong and its sputtering trolley for much of the way to the junction at Vermont, where the Boulevard began. Johnson, Daniel, you thought—how different he was from what you'd intended! To John Woodburn at Harcourt Brace, you'd proposed a typical young American in whom many would be able to see themselves. He'd be the average of their abilities, their aims, their fortunes, their range of thought, but somewhere in the writing, he was no longer yours to direct. Instead, or so it seemed, *he'd* directed *you*; ordinary Dan had led you out of ordinary ways. It was as if he'd chosen a role for himself far more intense than the one assigned, and gone then the common Dan in whom all might perceive their kind.

The Boulevard cut across a corner of Barnsdall Park, and, straightening out, it made for Western. A few blocks more, you thought, and you'd turn off on Taft, the side-street on which your father lived, and you'd find him, as you usually did, in one of the chairs on the lawn. You'd stop a little way distant, and you'd watch him for a moment as he gazed at nothing of that time or place, unmindful even of his cigarette, half of which had burned to ash. What was he seeing, you'd wonder, what scene that only he remembered and only he could revive, what was he saying to someone, and how did that someone reply? But you'd never know, because you'd never ask.

"Hello, kid," he'd say as you neared him. "What brings you to town?"

And you'd say, "You and this," and you'd hand him one of the Plantin brochures. . . .

But that was as far as fancy took you, for you'd reached his building only to find the deck-chairs missing and no one on the lawn. Were you on the wrong street, you wondered, or had you stopped at the wrong number, and glancing at the gold-leaf legend above the doorway, you read *1720 N. Taft.* You were at the right number on the right street, you thought — and then stunningly you knew it was the time that was wrong: your father had moved away all of five years before. You tried to account for your mistake: was it force of habit that had brought you here? was it thoughtlessness?, was it an excess of thought about something else? — but none of these was acceptable, for all presumed that you'd had no reason. What *was* the reason?, you wondered, and you were still wondering as you drove off across Hollywood toward the Wilshire District, where your father now lived. Why?, you wondered. . . .

He was taking the sun in the courtyard where, above the pale pink flagstones, the heated air churned. "How goes it, Philly-boy?" you said.

"It goes like this — and then it gets worse," he said, and he laughed at his own rueful joke. "What've you got there, kid?" He opened the brochure to the title-page, and before him in red and black, your book proclaimed itself in a type-face known as Bembo. "An elegant thing," he said. "I suppose the book will be the same."

"The typographer is an elegant guy."

He gave you a Shapiro look, and he said, "I still know a thing or two, kid. *You're* the elegant guy. You always were, even when you lived out of my change-pocket."

"Well, what's wrong with making a good showing?"

"Nothing, but you never could pay for it." He allowed you time to speak, but you let the time pass. "A good showing comes high, Julian — but will it make the book better?"

Why were you not as reasonable as he? He always thought well, which meant he had forethought too, but however much you admired his way, you'd never been able to follow it. You were rash, as he'd told you early, and you were rash still. Even so, nothing you did could alienate him, nor could you ever feel less than pleasure at being less than he.

"Some people never buy a new book," you said. "Like Uncle Dave, they find what they want on those tables in bookstore doorways, dusty, rained-on, and almost always two bits each."

"If you know that," your father said, "why this flash? Is it because your wife is footing the bill?"

"She *is* paying, of course, but that's not the reason." What, you wondered, did you know of reasons?

"What is, then?"

"I love books, and I think they ought to be as good to look at as they are to read."

"Nothing water-caked for you, eh, kid? Not even *War and Peace.*"

You laughed, saying, "You used to say the apple never falls far from the tree. This one rolled."

"Tell me," he said. "How much is this venture going to cost you? Cost Maggie, I mean."

"Close to seven grand."

"Seven grand," he said, and you watched him do what you'd only fancied before: he gazed at sights that were far away. " 'That's Julian,' people will say. 'He always travels first-class.'"

"I once blew in my last six bucks on a necktie."

"I believe you, but it was *your* money. This seven thousand is Maggie's."

"How about this? It was Maggie who pushed me into publishing the book. I spend money, sure I do, and sometimes I spend it like a sailor—but never like a *drunken* sailor."

Gradually his gaze withdrew from those far-off things (what were they?), and he said, "You're one lucky guy, do you know that?"

He turned a page, and you watched him read:

A MAN WITHOUT SHOES

PART ONE

FATHER'S NAME

Late one night in the fall of 1908, a man emerged from a livery stable near Coenties Slip and walked south and then west toward Bowling Green. He was a hack-driver, operating a Pope-Hartford landau from a cab-rank at the Vesey Street exit of the Astor House, and between calls he had lounged with other drivers along the hotel walls, watching traffic change with the changing hour: the drays and runabouts of morning, the victorias of noon, the electric brough-ams of evening, and then, in the gas-lit dark, the drays again, their Belgians plodding the cobblestones on muffled horn.

A wind off the Bay, damp and salt and faintly iodine, struck the man as he passed the Custom House and headed for home, a two-room cold-water flat on the fourth floor of a tenement in an alley running uptown from Whitehall. There were distant places on the wind, and there were strange flavors, and the man deep-breathed as if to know them by knowing the migratory air, but the far came no nearer, and the nameless remained unnamed, and he spoke himself a soft prayer, saying, "Ah, God, to see it all! To see it all some day!"

He turned in at a street-level vestibule, and as he mounted a brass-knuckled flight of steps, a door opened above, and light lac-quered the spindles of the stair-well. A woman's voice made a mild question of his name, but he gave no reply in words: he churned chimes from a pocketful of coins. On the top landing, there was a long embrace, after which, handing the woman a purse, the man locked the door behind them. . .

SCENE 89

THALBERG BUILDING, THIRD FLOOR (October 1950)

"In my office this afternoon," Maggie said, "I got to thinking about how good I'd had it at Metro for—what is it now, a dozen years? Remember Charlie Leavitt's remark the time we were watching a mare roll around in the grass? *She's suffering with comfort,* he said. Well, *I* was suffering with com-fort, rolling in it—till all of a sudden I realized my contract had only three-four months to run. You'll never guess what I did. Never."

"Then you'd better tell me," you said.

"I wrote a note to Mr. Thau."

"That's not so out-of-the-way."

"I felt that my being at the studio was largely due to him, I said, and I wanted him to know I was grateful. But here's the part you'd never guess: I said it made me sad to think that when Spring came around, I'd be gone from the lot."

"With the snows of yesteryear," you said. "No, I'd not have guessed."

"I can't imagine what made me say that. Unless. . . ."

"Unless what?"

"Unless I was trying to stir up some action."

"Well, come Spring, you'll find out."

"Sooner. Ten minutes after getting the note, he called and said, 'Send John to see me tomorrow morning.' "

§

On the way to Culver City the next day, Maggie said, "I've been thinking about that note to Thau. There was even more behind it than feeling sad and wanting action."

And you said, "What?"

"Metro isn't the Metro it was, not since Schary* became executive assistant to Mr. Mayer."

"How is it different?"

"There's a different atmosphere. You can sense it whenever there's a mention of Schary's name. People seem uneasy."

"When you think about it, they have a right to be. They remember his speech to the Guild the night of the debate about what to do about The Ten. *Give them up,* he said, *and the rest of you will be safe!* What he meant was *Throw them to the wolves*—and, God damn it, that's just what the Guild went and did!"

"After that, he was Mayer's white-haired boy, but the old man will live to regret it.

§

Opening her door for her, you saw her boating scene, *The Seine at Argenteuil,* hanging askew as usual on the wall; righting it, you caused the stream to flow as it should instead of seeming to flow uphill. Then you kissed Maggie and went upstairs, where, in Thau's outer office, you were invited to sit while you waited. You chose to wait standing, and it may have been that you gazed at other prints, at their frames only, or, for all you remember, at nothing but wall. In thought, you may have been rerunning Maggie's twelve-year career on the floor below, knowing that you were welcome here only because she was welcome there, in Room 243. There it was that she performed, there in a space adorned by an off-balance Manet, she played a machine with the skill she'd acquired in a three-month course at Greeley Business College (tuition $45)—but where, you wondered, had she learned to compose ideas, whence the wit, the natural language, the quick and inventive turn of mind? Such things could not have come with those exercises in Gregg and those speed-runs on a Remington; they were gifts she must've gotten before she ever breathed.

And now perhaps you did see pictures, an album in motion, black and white photos browned and tanned by time: Maggie seated on a runningboard, her

---

* Dore Schary, protégé of Mayer and ultimately his successor as head of the studio.

182

feet a foot off the ground; Maggie in front of home, a tar-paper shack in the tules; Maggie in a classroom (back row, sixth from the left); Maggie and the four other girls of a basketball five. At all such times and all such places, you thought, she'd been making herself ready for the room on the floor below. . . .

"Mr. Thau will see you now, Mr. Roberts," the secretary said.

§

He was a close-mouthed man, guarded, even, and in his presence, you always felt the presence of a third, some overhearer from whom the word must be withheld. He'd speak through a slot he made of his lips, he'd glance across his shoulder as if at the listeners he feared, and at times his voice would scarcely reach your ear—he was a vigilant man, but watchful of what, you wondered, wary of whom?

He tapped an inter-office memo lying before him, saying, "Explain to me what Maggie means by this."

"If that's the note she sent you," you said, "I think she's blue about nearing the end of her connection with Metro."

"Where did she get that kind of an idea?"

"Well, her contract runs out in March, and so far nothing has been said. . . ."

"So what does she do? She sits down and writes—what *is* this, a farewell letter?"

"I'm sure she didn't mean to upset you, Mr. Thau."

"Not only me. Eddie Mannix too. Don't she know by now what we think of her on the Third Floor?"

"She did, when Mr. Mayer took an active part. She's not so sure now. Things are different, she says."

"Not with me. With me, she's what she was when she first came on the lot—a Company asset."

"She'll be happy to hear that."

"You know something? I took to her right away. She's a lady, you know what I mean? A decent person."

You were sitting with your left leg crossed over your right; you changed position, crossing the right over the left; but you said nothing.

"People like her don't have an easy time in this business. The men are pretty rough. Bums, some of them, and they don't stop being bums on account of a woman being around. But with Maggie, nobody ever took a liberty."

Again you recrossed your legs, and still you said nothing.

"A hundred times we must've met," Thau said, "and to this day, she never called me *Ben*."

183

His telephone rang, and, answering, he listened briefly. His reply was muted and staccato, as if he were giving the *Go* order in some secret undertaking.

He returned to you, saying, "She could've done that, called me Ben, but she don't take liberties either." He took up the memo, a blue sheet, three-quarter size, and he read aloud from it. " 'Dear Mr. Thau, I feel very sad when I think that in a few short months. . . .' " He put the memo down and said, "In a few short months, she's going to have a new contract. Now, what've you got in mind?"

What you had in mind was the Greeley Business College, a two-room outfit located above a bank, was it, a store, the Home Gas & Electric? — a school equipped with worn desks and worn chairs and old and worn machines, these for students of shorthand and forty-odd circular keys, among such learners Maggie. And in fancy, you were cruising the aisles of one of those rooms, finding there the grave face, the fine hands, the form you knew so well, and then from that time you were coming to this place, to where she was on the floor below. . . .

"I see you're shaking your head," Thau said. "You don't want a contract?"
"That isn't it, Mr. Thau," you said.
"You want a raise, then. A certain amount more could be negotiated."
"What Maggie wants is less."
"Less?"
"She works best when she feels she belongs. A term-contract would give her the continuity she likes. Three years, four years, whatever you say. . ."
"It's hers, no argument."
". . . but she wants to work only six months a year."
"What about the other six?"
"This'll sound peculiar, Mr. Thau, but she wants more time with me."

He seemed to require witnesses to what you'd said, and before responding, he sought them in the dimmer corners of the room.

"She wants to give up half her salary for that?" he said. "Sixty-five thousand dollars? Excuse me, but that isn't peculiar; it's crazy."
"All the same, Mr. Thau, that's what she wanted me to ask for. Is there any chance the studio would consent?"
"If we would agree to more, why not to less?"
"She'll be very pleased."
"Here's what I'll recommend — a five-year contract, no options, six months off every year, twenty-five hundred a week."
"Settled," you said, and you started to rise.
"But," he said, and you stopped. "If she wants to work the other six months, she works for us, nobody else."

You nodded, and your hand was on the doorknob when he stopped you again.

"She thinks the studio is different with Schary second in command?" he said. "What makes it different?"

You looked back at him, and for once his face was no barrier between you.

"She says Mr. Mayer is a man, and Schary's a marshmallow. Inside of Mr. Mayer, there's guts. Inside of Schary, there's only more marshmallow."

A smile touched his face, marred its surface for an instant, like a breath of air on water, and then it was gone, and now it was he who shook his head—not at you, but at Maggie Roberts on the floor below.

SCENE 90

SEVENTH RACE AT HOLLYWOOD PARK (November 9, 1950)

Called the Goose Girl Purse in the Condition Book, it was written for fillies and mares three years old and upward at three-quarters of a mile out of the chute. A stakes-class field of six was entered, among them two actual stakes-winners, Mrs. Rabbit and Mrs. Fuddy. Messalina carried 106 pounds and was ridden as usual by Ray York. According to the chart in the Racing Form,

> Messalina had speed from the beginning, raced Mrs. Rabbit into defeat inside the eighth pole, and outfinished Some Gal. The latter, steadied early, came out for the drive and got to almost even terms with the winner a sixteenth out, then hung. Mrs. Rabbit, hustled to the front soon after the start, dueled with Messalina for the lead until mid-stretch, then tired. . . .

Time, :22.1, :45.3, 1:10.1 Track fast

MARK TWAIN — 1893

GIVE A DOG A BAD NAME

> *Given under my hand this second day of January,*
> *1893, at the Villa Viviani, village of Settignano,*
> *three miles back of Florence, on the hills.*
> Mark Twain: *Pudd'nhead Wilson*

In the tale as told, two children were born on the same day to the Missouri household of a certain Percy Driscoll. The mother of one was black in a sixteenth part of her blood and therefore, under the laws of the state, black in all eight pints of it. Her son, got by a white father, was black only in a thirty-second part, not nearly enough to dinge his skin or kink his hair, but he was no less nigger than his mother and just as much a slave. *Valet de Chambre* was the name she gave him, after a phrase she'd heard above the stairs, but he answered to something lower-flown: *Chambers* would always fetch him.

The other child born that day came from the groin of Mistress Driscoll, and he was as white as God's laundry, the clouds in the sky; he was white from the outside-in and the inside-out, white from A to izzard and halfway back to A. His name, which his mother was allowed but a week to delight in, a week to speak before she died, was *Thomas à Becket,* a big handle for a little blade.

Chambers and Tom, infant slave and infant master, alike in age, place of birth, and actual color, which was the cameo-pink of canned salmon — both now were fostered by the mulatto woman. They sucked the same pair of tits, they cheesed up the same sour curds, they shiced themselves in the same brown carefree way. On many a spring and summer day, they sat face to face in a toy wagon, gumming bacon-rinds, reaching for sounds, smells, and flash until sleep sank them without warning. They were hard to tell apart. The elder Driscoll could distinguish them only when they were dressed: his own child wore ruffled muslin and a necklace of coral, the other one a tow shirt and no *bijouterie.*

Now to the Driscoll household, hard lines came. Thrice had small sums of money been stolen, the dollar bill, the odd coin, or thrice had they walked away, and on the fourth occasion, the slaves were summoned and told that unless the thief owned up, all would be sold downriver and no two to the same master. All, of course, confessed, the mother of Chambers along with the rest, and for the moment, Driscoll's hands seemed tied. But with danger past, she knew that danger remained. One more loss of loose change, or none, for no reason was needed, and her son might end in some far-south field, a hand, a man named Boy. No long-tether times for him then, no rafting or fishing, no soft touches won by foxing the whites, no slow-speed days, no skim off the *crème de la crème*—and in sudden dread, she switched the halves of the Driscoll whole. The muslin and coral went to Chambers, and the tow smock went to Tom, and together with the clothes went the names.

There were queer consequences. Before the switch, the children had been like as drops of rain; afterwards, strange to say, in no way at all were they the same. The great change took place in the new Thomas à Becket, the Valet de Chambre that was, almost as if magic resided in the unfamiliar name. If so, it was evil magic. No sooner did the little slave sit at the little master's end of the wagon than he became odious. Five months old, abruptly he turned spiteful, cranky, and base; a bully, a glutton, a crooked stick, he cried without cause, held his breath and blued, spilled food or threw it away, pounded, scratched, ruled with an iron hand no bigger than a doll's—a nigger doll's.

What did all that, you understand (and made for murder later on), was that dash of black blood, that taint, that tinker's damn, that metastatic fraction, that thirty-second part.

SCENE 91

JANUARY 29, 1988

"Are you doing this deliberately?" Maggie said. "In the three volumes published so far, you've yet to speak of the—I hate the expression—the creative process."

"Why do you hate it?" you said.

"It's fatuous. And when the creator himself uses it, he's pompous too."

"Lucky for me I don't use it."

"All the same, there *is* a creative process, and you *do* create."

"It must be like growing. I'm unaware of it."

"Well, *something* goes on while you're working. I know, because I've spoken to you, and you're a long time coming back from wherever you've been. Where is that, and what happens there?"

You were on one of those drives about the country that you took on some of your afternoons. That day, the route lay along Valley Road and up the steep slope of Toro Canyon into the oak-tree hills. Near the rise of Garrapata Creek, a gate barred the way, and there you turned and parked to view the chain of the Channel Islands. From an altitude of fifteen hundred feet, Santa Cruz looked much less than twenty miles away, but you were eighty-four, and your vision no longer permitted you to distinguish its coloring. You remembered a dapple of browns and greens, like camouflage, but all you could see now was a long low mass at the base of the sky.

"I can't answer that," you said. "But *you're* a writer too. Where do *you* go, and what do *you* do when you get there?"

"We work differently," she said. "I never write a scene or a sequence without knowing the end at the start. Not you. You have no idea where you're going, but somehow you manage to get there."

"Get *where*?" you said. "Even when I get back, I don't know where I've been."

"You've said many times—you even say it in these books—that you aren't much of a thinker. That can't be true. Books don't get written without thought."

"Henry James wrote outlines for his novels that were novels in themselves—novels about novels. Me, I can't see as far as the next page."

"And yet," she said, "there are the books, seventeen of them so far. They have purpose, all of them, they have progression, they have unity. If you can't think, how do such things come about?"

At the bottom of the gully, sycamores grew, smooth-skinned and straight, and through them, like part of their foliage, you could see acacias that were powdered with yellow blossom.

"Not supernaturally," you said. "I don't do the bidding of the voices, like those *creatores* we've been talking about. What posturing! The bastards posture even in their photographs—they're rapt, they're listening to the Muses! That's flim-flam. A man can only hear himself."

"Isn't that the—creative process?"

"Sometimes I look at the shelf where my seventeen books are, and I think, 'I wrote them. The words and phrases, the images, the rhythms, if they have rhythm—all of that came from some part of my brain, if I have a brain.' " And then you looked at her, saying, "But don't ask me how."

And she said, "How?"

"Somewhere in yourself, you store every stimulus, great or small, and all your life, whether you know it or not, you draw on it for the work at hand. Everyone has his own retrieval system. I've called on mine seventeen times, and seventeen times what I needed has flowed down my arm to the page.

You won't find that in photos of the deep thinkers, but that's all there is to the creative process."

"That ought to be in the book," Maggie said.

And you said, "I'll put it there."

And then, with a glance at Anacapa, you drove off down the hill.

SCENE 92

FIFTH RACE AT HOLLYWOOD PARK (December 9, 1950)

Messalina's final appearance of the year was in an allowance for three-year-old fillies at six furlongs. She carried top weight of 118 pounds and again was ridden by Ray York. There were nine in the field, and the start was good for all but Foxie Green, who dwelt in the gate and finished last. As the Racing Form reported,

> Messalina raced with the top flight from the start, was on the outside much of the way, rallied to strong handling on entering the stretch, and wore down Castle Hill inside the final sixteenth. The latter sprinted into a clear lead soon after the start, saved ground while being held in light restraint, was under pressure all through the final furlong, and while unable to resist the winner, appeared best of the others. Big Gert, never far back, raced very wide on the turn and held on fairly well. Miss Blue Lea was never a serious factor. Kinfolks was outrun. . . .

Time, :22.3, 45.3, 1:10.4 Track fast

SCENE 93

BACK, BRIEFLY, FROM THE DEAD (January 1951)

"At the studio today," Maggie said, "I got wind of the latest about Mary Chilton."

With the name came a memory of pain, the memory as pungent as the original. Ten years had not been enough to abate it, nor, you knew, would ten twice-told; it was not to be sedated by time. You saw again the house

189

in Toluca Lake, and the rain of that night was no less heard than before. Your friends of the Left, Jim and Mary Chilton, were your guests at a dinner prepared and served by your well-loved Danish housekeeper, Ingeborg Emil (to you, always, Mrs. Inge), and the board had been cleared, and a fire was going, and you were watching tobacco smoke, drawn by the draft, stream under the lintel and pour upward—pour upward, you thought. Of the talk, you remembered only the voices, a one-tone sound like the sound of the rain, and you felt yourself drifting with it until Mrs. Inge, dressed for the weather, passed through the room on her way to the door.

—You say *Wait. I'll drive you to the bus-stop.*
—And she says *Oh, no, Mr. Sonnfort. I go by mineself.*
—And Mary Chilton says *Jim, our car's blocking John's. You drive Mrs. Inge to the bus.*
—And Jim Chilton says *I don't drive servants.*

You remembered the pause, you remembered and suffered the pang of *servant,* you remembered ordering people from your home for the only time in your life, and you remembered that as they went, Mary said *God damn it, Jim! Why can't you keep your fuckin' mouth shut?*

Ten years back, that rainy night was.

"She's been on the town," Maggie said. "Ever since she split with Chilton."
"She's the better of the two. She's only a dirty-mouthed bum. He's trash."
"On the town, but not yet on the street. She works those bars on Santa Monica."
"She used to be a beaut. I wonder what she looks like now."
"A guy she tried to hustle turned out to be a plain-clothes cop, and he ran her in. It was her first time, and they let her off. She didn't learn much, though, because she's back in those bars."
You looked up from whatever you were doing to say, "Are you making a point?"
And she said, "Something ought to be done."
"Like what?"
"Seeing her. Talking to her. Showing her she still has friends."
"How would the talk go?"
"I don't know, Jabe, but we can't let her go down the drain. After all, she *is* on our side. Or she *was.*"
"It won't be easy to find her," you said. "After ten years. . . ."
And she said, "Try."

Those who'd known Mary Chilton either knew her no more or they gave you numbers that no longer were good. It was through the Casting Department at Metro that you finally reached her on the telephone.

"Mary," you said. "John Sanford."

"Well, for Christ's sake!" she said. "Twat do I owe the honor?"

"Maggie and I would like you to have dinner with us."

"Really? So soon after the last time?"

"It wasn't you that put us off. It was that coffee-houser you were married to. Will you join us at Chasen's?"

"When?"

"Tomorrow evening—at seven, say."

"On one condition."

"Agreed. Name it."

"That you never mention my ex-, the prick-fester!"

She wasn't there at seven, and halfway to eight, you said, "We might as well order. She isn't coming."

And Maggie said, "I wonder why she changed her mind."

"In her line, the hours are irregular."

"You're still uneasy with her kind, aren't you?"

"What do you mean—*still*?"

"You told me about a girl you met while you were living at that hotel in New York. The one Pep West used to manage."

"The Sutton. What *about* the girl?"

"You said you liked her."

"I did like her."

"What do you remember of her?"

You laughed, saying, "A million freckles."

"That's an odd thing to mention first."

"What should I have said?"

"That she was a call-girl."

She was twenty years gone, but you could still see her as you did, sunning herself on the Sutton roof, a Seurat in a bathing-suit.

"Once you found that out," Maggie said, "you stopped liking her, didn't you?"

You even remembered her name—Romaine—and you said, "Yes."

"Why?"

"She was a public place."

"And you're a private guy."

A voice said, "Who's a private guy?" and when you turned, there was Mary Chilton.

She looked done. Her contours and her coloring were there still—the figure that you recalled, the dark red shade of hair—but she seemed now to fill her skin too full, and her face wore a flush as from exposure to the cold. It was her speech, though, that told more than the rest, the thicker tones of a lowered pitch, as if some glandular numbers had undergone change.

191

Rising to greet her, you seated her between you and Maggie, saying, "It's been a long while."

And Maggie said, "Much too long."

Without a glance at the menu your waiter put before her, she said, "A Pernod."

"And what to follow, madame?" he said.

And she said, "Another Pernod."

"Order something," you said.

"I just did."

"Food, John means," Maggie said.

Mary shook her head, saying, "How long has it been—nine years, ten?"

And Maggie said, "It was a couple of wars ago."

"Why don't you say I haven't changed?"

"We've all changed."

Mary rotated her glass, making the absinthe swirl, and staring at the greenish liquor, she said, "I don't mind that so much, but the times have changed too. As someone has written, this is the time of the toad." Draining her glass, she beckoned to the waiter for the second to be served. "There are more toads in this town than there are in a swamp. And do you know where they are at this very pissin' moment?" Her eyes were fixed on far away, as if she could see the place she had in mind. "They're lined up at the Federal Building, waiting their turn to fink."

Her gaze now was on the absinthe emerald lying at the bottom of her glass, and as she twirled the stem, the gem seemed to move in its setting.

Maggie said, "You better have something to eat, Mary."

And Mary said, "Eating makes me crap. Drinking makes me happy," and she signaled for a third Pernod.

With it, her talk became unsequential, and she ceased to respond to anything said by you or Maggie. Rather did she seem to be conversing with herself, asking and answering as if she were twain. From time to time, you'd hear a reference to the Federal Building, and then she'd jeer as at someone going in or someone coming out, and once she said (to whom?) *You sell your friends, you son-of-a-bitch! I only sell myself.*

You learned her address from cards you found in her purse, and unwilling to let her drive her car, you and Maggie took her to where she lived, a small flat below the Strip in West Hollywood. She had to be helped up the stairs, and once inside, she stopped trying to stand and sprawled across the bed. Covering her with a throw, you and Maggie went away.

Neither of you spoke for miles. You were going up Coldwater Canyon toward the Valley before you could say, "The saddest thing was that douchebag hanging on the bathroom door."

"God, no," Maggie said. "The saddest thing was lying on the bed."

SCENE 94

DEFINITIONS (January 1951)

"Fink," Maggie said. "What kind of word is fink?"

And you said, "You've never heard it?"

"It's a new one on me."

"I'm surprised."

"Did you ever hear the word stringhalt?"

"No."

"Then we surprise each other," she said. "Now, what about fink?"

"Remember a film John Ford made, based on a novel by Liam O'Flaherty? It was about an Irishman who betrayed the Sinn Feiners for money. The Irishman was played by Victor McLaglen, and there's a scene where he comes to the British for his pay. It's lying on a table between him and an officer, but the officer won't touch it with his hands. Instead, he moves it across the table with the tip of his swagger-stick, and the Irishman picks it up."

"Well?" Maggie said.

"The Irishman was a fink."

"I see."

"What's stringhalt?" you said.

And she said, "Look it up, college-boy."

SCENE 95

PRETTY AS A LITTLE RED PAIR OF SHOES (February 1951)

In speaking to you of her mother and father, Maggie had said *The kids kept coming, seven that lived. There were twenty years between the first and the last, so Mama must've been what Daddy called her....*

Pretty as a little red pair of shoes, he'd said, but he was years gone now, and she, eighty-four and lying in a hospital bed, had all day been on the verge of following him, taking along what was left of the image, a still little but worn and faded pair of shoes. Three of her daughters stood beside her, striving to postpone her going by such useless stir as puffing her pillows and arranging her hair. She'd fallen that morning and broken her hip, and the shock had nearly put her through the door and sent her on her way. Her heart had stopped once, and, started again, its beat was slow and irregular. Every few moments, a nurse or an interne would enter, and there'd be pulse-counts and auscultations, quantities would be measured and tubes examined, and then there'd be entries on a chart and impassive departures.

Ranged along a wall with your brothers-in-law, you knew that in the end it would rest with the gray and aged occupant of the bed: she, not the daughters, not the white-dressed staff of medics, would decide whether she'd go or stay. It was late in the evening before she opened her eyes for the first time since her fall. She looked at the faces around her and lined along the wall. She seemed to consider you all, to weigh you against the worth of her husband, dead after a marriage of sixty-seven years, and from her expression it was clear that the living had lost.

"Next time," she said, "let me go."

SCENE 96

THALBERG BUILDING, ROOM 243 (February 1951)

Opening the door, you saw what you'd seen scores of times before—the couch, the typewriter stand, the listing Manet, and Maggie at her desk with a script in her hand. Familiar especially the last, an always-pleasing figure in the chair; that day, though, her mind seemed to be somewhere else. She hadn't turned to stare at traffic, trees, or space, but you felt that her gaze, which was fixed on you, saw through you to things not there in the room.

You said, "Aren't you going to ask how I fared with Mr. Thau?"
"Oh," she said. "Of course."
"The contract you want has been approved by the Company—five straight years at twenty-five hundred a week, six months off each year at your option."
But she'd strayed again, you thought, back to wherever she'd been before. "My first job was with Woolworth's in Greeley," she said. "I made a dollar a day."
"Thau doesn't want you to sign the contract, though, not till he makes sure the time off doesn't affect your rights under the Pension Plan. Very decent of him. It hadn't occurred to me."

"I worked in the Candy department," she said. "I sold peppermints, chocolate creams, and what we called carmels."

"He said he's sent the papers to Equitable in Texas for an interpretation."

She hadn't gone, as you'd thought; she'd been there all along. "That dollar had real value," she said. "It bought me what I needed. But the money we're talking about now will even buy what I *don't* need. It isn't money any more; it's a number."

"Maybe," you said. "But it's a number that measures your value to the Company."

"I started here at five hundred a week. Am I five times as good as I was?"

"You're not being overpaid *now*; you were underpaid *then*."

And now she did look away, saying as if to traffic, trees, and space, "When I wanted to take six months off every year, you went along with the idea. But you've never said what you think of it."

The moment was one you'd known was coming, bringing with it the question you'd hoped to avoid. She'd turned, thinking you might be reluctant to face her, but it was yourself that you were disinclined to face: you knew that you didn't know what you thought of the idea. *Why* didn't you know? Where she was more than satisfied, were you less, and where she was open-handed, were your hands closed? *Why* didn't you know—or did you know only too damned well. . . ?

You said, "You're more generous than I am."

"What makes you think so?"

"Your first impulse is to give; you have no second impulse. My first is to keep; I give on the second."

"Why do you change?"

"I'm ashamed, I guess."

"Don't be," she said. "What counts is that second impulse. Very few have it."

THE PLANTIN PRESS ANNOUNCES (March 1951)

The notice was printed on the four sides of a sheet folded once, the cover of which foreshadowed the title-page of the book:

The Plantin Press announces

A MAN

WITHOUT

SHOES

A Novel by JOHN SANFORD

The two inner pages had been written by you:

ON OR ABOUT MAY 1, 1951

THE PLANTIN PRESS WILL PUBLISH

A MAN WITHOUT SHOES

A NEW NOVEL BY JOHN SANFORD

Author of

THE WATER WHEEL	1933
THE OLD MAN'S PLACE	1935
SEVENTY TIMES SEVEN	1939
THE PEOPLE FROM HEAVEN	1943

APPROXIMATELY 500 pages in length, *A Man Without Shoes* will be issued in an edition limited to 2,000 signed and numbered copies, of which 1,975 will be for sale at $10.

The volume will be a large octavo (6½ x 9⅞″) in 12 on 14 point Ehrhardt type on specially made paper (the type and paper of this announcement) and bound in decorated paper-covered boards, with buckram back and printed label.

197

"I HAD NO SHOES AND COMPLAINED,

AND THEN I MET A MAN WITHOUT FEET."

VARYING *in phraseology, the quoted saying, to which* A Man Without Shoes *owes its title, is common to many languages. Its sermon, however arranged and whatever the tongue, remains standard: to rebuke the sin of discontent and inspire the virtue of resignation.*

A Man Without Shoes, *a novel concerned with an American attempting to discover the America of his time, covers the first three decades in the life of one Daniel Johnson—the period* 1909-1938. *More particularly, it treats of his struggle against and ultimate rejection of the doctrine that whatever is, is right—that this is the best of all possible worlds, so made, with its injustices and inequalities, and so to be endured without hope of change. The principal character, born to be one of the shoeless but ripening into defiance, states his own intention:* "*I mean to complain till I get my shoes or lose my feet.*"

There were two changes from the wording of the prospectus: the date of publication would be May 1 instead of March 1, and the type-face would be Ehrhardt instead of Bembo.

SCENE 98

THE HOUSE COMMITTEE HEARINGS IN WASHINGTON
(March–April 1951)

On looking back, you tell yourself that only the dead would not have known what was happening, and yet you seem to have been unaware of it until you saw and heard it on the air. Were you dead, then, or, as good as dead, dreaming, when the sound-waves reached you, the rays of light; were you in or out of life; were you in the haze between sleep and waking as those voices came through space and those faraway figures were seen? A place of execution, the stately room you were shown on the screen, its high ceiling a plaster sky above a table, center, that might've been a scaffold or a pyre, and there were crowds like those that gaped at a Tyburn jig or at dancing in a fire. You could almost hear the trapdoor fall, almost feel the flames. . . .

§

— You can't see the dais where the Committee sat, and if a flag standard stood against the wall, it too is past recall. But light finds each witness, fixes on him, it seems, binds him to his chair, and the faces arrayed behind him glow. . . .

"I was at Francis Cooke's," you said. "The two of us spent the afternoon staring at The Big Glass Eye. Every once in a while, the camera would stray from the witness and make a tour of the room — and then it was like watching people watching something die. I came near thinking they were enjoying themselves."

"Came near!" Maggie said. "You're simple, John, They *were* enjoying themselves."

"I can't believe that."

"Oh, dear," she said. "Whole families go to a hanging as if it were a picnic. You can get passes for an electrocution. And when some suicidal oaf is on a ledge ten flights up, the mob in the street hollers 'Jump!' That's the kind of world we're in — and you can't believe it!"

"I'd sooner stay simple."

"Don't stay long."

§

—Scene and sound found you on the instant, and you saw and heard them as though you were at the place of their occurrence instead of afar. In that distant chamber, day after day the faces of a crowd that, however much it changed, always seemed the same, and, like the crowd, witnesses too came and went, different only as to name. Of the Committee, nothing returns save its presence, a blur at the edge of vision, a clouding of the Eye, but clear still the faces of the crowd as the fire of fear in the victims grows. . . .

"Back in the lower grades," you said, "even in kindergarten, there was always some picknose kid who'd snitch. 'Miss Nolen, Alfred threw the chalk,' or 'Emily is making faces.' "

"And what did Miss Nolen say?" Maggie said.

"I don't recall that she said anything."

"Suppose the snitch had said, 'Julian threw the chalk.' "

"I'd've stood in the corner instead of Alfred."

"It's the snitch who should've stood in the corner," Maggie said. "But Miss Nolen let him grow up to snitch in Washington."

"Her full name was Mary Howe Nolen," you said. "Why do I remember that?"

"You always liked teachers. You must've liked her."

"I did, very much."

"Still, because of her, *you* may be standing in a corner some day."

"The Nolens aren't to blame for the snitches."

"Nothing starts with nothing," Maggie said. "*Something* is back of the snitches. In that piece you wrote about John Brown, he says *Nits grow to be lice.* Well, your Miss Nolen grew a nit."

§

—Again the doomful room in the dimful Eye, and again the torment at the table, center, and again you're watching the beholders more than the sight itself. Questions extract names, places, numbers, teeth rooted in conscience—out they come, roots and all, and the faces in the background mirror nothing, as if the image had been rejected by the glass. . . .

Your father said, "My friends in the cafeteria ask me questions about the Hearings."

"What do they want to know?" you said.

"They say, 'Why don't those Communists in Washington admit they're Communists?' "

"And what do you tell them?"

"They're laymen, Julian—olderly people, as Grandma Nevins used to say. Some of them came from the Old Country, and most of them never went

200

to school. They know nothing of the law. The law frightens them."

"Still, they *did* ask you to explain."

" 'This is an Inquisition,' I say, and they say, 'Inquisition! For a Jew, his whole life is an Inquisition!' "

"That should've made it easier for you."

"It didn't," he said. "To them, to their minds, persecution is limited to the Jews. They don't understand that it's used against *all* heresies. They think a witness can admit to being a Communist and then saunter from the room."

You took up his hand and studied its short fingers, saying, "You know a thing or two, counselor."

And he said, "I came from the Old Country too, but I happened to go to school."

§

—At that table, center, there's no bone, blood, or ash to show that there the lives of many ended, some of them brave and some craven, some defiant and some who went abegging—but all, you remember, proud or paltry, died. . . .

Maggie said, "Which of the snitches did you hate the most?"

And you said, "That hard-guy actor, the one who always plays a killer. He cried, the yellow bastard, while he gave them fourteen names!"

"I hated the one who said he was snitching for patriotic reasons."

The last refuge, you thought.

"Patriot!" she said. "The man who wouldn't drive Mrs. Inge to the bus!"

THE COLOR OF THE AIR, XI

THEODORE ROOSEVELT—1901

THE AMERICAN

> *Britain must be kept up to the mark.*
> —T. Roosevelt
> *Damn the Dutch.*
> —T. Roosevelt
> *Those Dagoes will have to behave.*
> —T. Roosevelt
> *Look at those damn Spanish dead.*
> —T. Roosevelt
> *I am alive to the danger from Japan.*
> —T. Roosevelt

When the telegram came, he was about to kill something in the Adirondack woods, a deer for its hatrack or a bear for its robe, or, lacking nobler game, he was taking aim at frogs, preening sparrows, fish asleep in pools, but whatever the prey, he was poised to slay it when the telegram came. As the wire ran, it was touch and go with McKinley, or touched and going, for Holy Willie had gangrene, and by dawn, it read between the lines, he might be dead and gone.

They hauled Teddy down off a mountain and hacked him fifty miles to the railhead, and then, by special train, they sped him west toward a bed in Buffalo. Long before light, though, he was merely bound for the White House by a roundabout way. They swore him in that afternoon, and he said *in spite of the terrible blow,* and he said *the honor of our beloved country,* and he said—but what was in his mind, not what did he say, what did he see behind his one good eye?

Was it a gun, a Remington he'd brought from Dakota, say, or a Krag from Kettle Hill, or was it the express he'd used on the Upper Nile, which? And was he watching the ninth of his nine lions twitch, the first of his five elephants, or any of his thirteen rhinos and seven hippogriffs? Was he kneeling near the wrecks of leopards, was his hat on right, did his belly-fat show, was the sun too bright on his specs? Or did he dwell on the Czolgosz pistol—and that reminded him! He moved into the Mansion before Mac's widow moved out with her fits, and he tried keys and chairs and Cleveland's wine, and he sneaked a few winks in Lincoln's bed. . . .

> *You must always remember that the President is about six.*
> —Cecil Spring-Rice

He was forty-and-change that day in Buffalo and half as much again when his brain blew up (*Remember the Maine!*) at Sagamore Hill, and, all of a piece, his days were less a life than a lifelong gasconade. He was a lover of livery and the livid phrase, a clap-sword and a double-dare-you, and they drew him as a four-eyed Buster Brown dragging a toy cannon in the street. Where he went, there a roar arose, as from a crowd, and he seemed to need more space than a place allowed him. He was always in motion, always *doing,* and always he'd paw and pound and mill around—Teddy, the one-man herd. He'd grin and bare his teeth, he'd wave his arms and crank the wind, he'd strike his palm, lay down the law, like the snot that owned the bat and ball.

He was smoke, steam, and fizz, and he seemed to hum, as if filled with bees, and where others strolled, he strode, and where they spoke, he screamed. He was all cut and shoot, and he entered a room as through a breach in the wall, and though brave enough at fisticuffs and twisting Chile's nose, the rich when they whistled could always make him heel. He was a skittish friend, a now-and-then liar, and a tin soldier to the end, when the little flag broke off and the paint wore thin. He was his world, and outside his skin, there was only applause. When it stopped, he died.

SCENE 99

SCHEHEREZADE (May 1951)

With evening coming on, you were waiting for Maggie to return from the studio. Seated on the steps of the porch, you gazed down the driveway, watching for her headlamps to ray through the trees. On the lawn before you, the dogs, dim masses in the growing dark, went their straying ways in the maze of scent they found on the air. From a near branch, a night-bird called, and you heard far sounds too, the constant undertone of traffic, the rounds of other lives in the course of being lived.

Which way home had she taken?, you wondered. Was she using the Glen or Benedict, and, if either, had she reached or passed Mulholland, where she could see through the dusk the Valley, a bed of broken glass? Was she driving with care, as she usually did, was she keeping the stripe on her left, was she staying well to the right on the curves—or was her mind a mix of many things, of other places and other times, of her parents, her pets, her script, and you? Was she going a little too fast, you wondered, was she crossing the middle line. . . ? And there, quickly, your thinking seemed to change down to a lower gear and slower motion, and you heard, long prolonged, the din of a collision, and you saw wheels on an endless spin in the air. . . .

And then her headlights made a sweep of the grounds and stopped when they found the driveway. You hastened toward the gate; the dogs, ahead of you, raced.

"Sepulveda Pass has the fewest curves," you said. "It's the widest too."
She seemed to be busy, standing off the dogs, but she heard all the same. "I'm careful, Jabe," she said.

§

"One of those story sessions in Mayer's office," Maggie said. "I was on the point of leaving when I got a call from his secretary, Ida Koverman. I'd been given a book to read, and the brass wanted to know what I thought of it."

"What book was it?"

"A biography of Simon Bolivar."

"Bolivar! Didn't they know what he was?"

"If not, I told them."

"Told who, by the way? Who was there?"

"Oh, Eddie Mannix, Mr. Thau, and Sam Katz, and McKenna the story editor, and of course Mr. Mayer. When I attend one of those things, I'm less a writer than an entertainer. It's like *The Arabian Nights*."

"Don't they ever read the material themselves?"

"Some of them do, not all."

"And what did you have to say about The Liberator?"

"Their notion was that, being upper crust, he was *safe*. He was a revolutionary, I told them, and his aim was to drive Spain out of South America."

"Why do they play around with stuff like that? They must know they'll never film it."

"It fascinates them," she said. "A few years ago, they owned a book on Zapata. It was by Edgcumb Pinchon, the man who wrote *Viva Villa!*, and it was a beaut. It fascinated me too, and I wrote to the Third Floor, asking for the assignment. For a wonder, I got it, but I wasn't on the script a month before they sold the property to 20th."

"Did they ever make anything you recommended?"

"No, and I begged them to buy *The African Queen*."

You watched her kneel to embrace Juno. The little Airedale, limp and half-asleep, licked her face once, and then the other half fell asleep.

You said, "You're some punkins, the way you speak up to those big boys. I'm proud of you."

"Do you mean that?"

You laughed. "You said the same thing when I asked you to marry me. Cinderella couldn't believe she had the smallest foot."

"I still don't believe it."

You left her bent over Juno and went to the door, where you turned to say, "When you come from the studio, do you have to drive through a pass?"

She looked up, saying, "Why?"

"Couldn't you use the Boulevard?" you said, and you left the room.

SCENE 100

ON THE ERIE* (May 1951)

". . . Governor," Maggie was saying, "Julian has been worrying about something."

"And what's that?" your father said.

You'd gone into the house for some now forgotten reason, and they were on the lawn beneath a window, where you could hear them through the screen.

"He's not the kind to fall all over people," she said. "It's his manner that shows them how he feels."

"So. . . ."

"So he worries about whether you know how much he cares for you."

They'd passed, and their voices had grown fainter.

"I've loved that kid since the day he was born," your father said.

"Oh, he knows how *you* feel about *him.*"

"Does he? I don't fall all over people either."

"He just knows," she said.

And he said, "So do I."

And then they were too far off to be heard.

SCENE 101

A MAN WITHOUT SHOES, the book (Late Spring 1951)

When printed and bound, the entire edition of two thousand was delivered to your home. It arrived in packages of five, and taking the first of these from the van-driver, you went with it to your room. There, whence the book had fared forth on its years of wandering, you broke open the wrapper and stood a copy endwise before you on the desk. The tones of the jacket warmed you, its buff paper, its title in turkey red, its brown ornaments, like the stamping on chocolate—and for all you can now recall, you may have spoken, saying *Johnson, Daniel,*† and in an unwitting echo of your father's *Julian, Julian!,* you may even have said *Dan, Dan, what a thorn you've been through the years!*

---

* A race-track expression for one overhearing "inside information."

† The principal character, also the early title.

You remembered his origin and the life you meant to show, and you remembered too the way the war had made him stray from your intention. Somewhere in the writing, he'd seemed to begin evolving on his own, to make the pen-hand his, and you felt that he was not of your doing, the Dan inside that jacket, the Dan who wore those clothes. And then, suddenly and finally, the notion left you that your own creation had shown you the road. It was over, the fancy that a character had begotten himself, and least of all this one, so nearly patterned on you. Like you, he'd begun by thinking his country revolutionary, and like you, he'd found that it would rebel only to keep a people enslaved. He'd been one of the many once, and so had you, but when you took to the Left, so did your Dan (*ton semblable, ton frère*), and then it was you, not he, that led the way.

By now, the books had been unloaded and stacked, and they almost blocked the hall, four hundred packages minus one, and as you stood in your doorway, staring at them, you thought of a saying of your Uncle Dave's:* *One horseshoe may bring you luck, but a load of horseshoes is junk.* Were these books junk?, you wondered, were they nothing but junk, after all?

SCENE 102

A LA RECHERCHE. . . . (March 8, 1988)

She said, when you finished reading her the scene you'd written the day before, "Once, when you began the autobiography, you meant to preface it with what you called *A Note on the Color of the Air*. Do you recall how it went?"

"Vaguely," you said. "I threw it away."

"Well, I saved it."

"You did? Why?"

"I thought you had a good idea. I still think so." She went to a drawer, rummaged up a pile of paper, and returned with a creased sheet of your testimony bond. "Would you like to hear what you said?"

"Read."

"It's a bit highflown at the start, but it gets better. 'An autobiography,' you wrote, 'is defined as an account of a life written by its subject, and it is usually produced by one of the *choice and master spirits of the age*. Admittedly, the life about to be detailed is not one of those: it is a tree in the forest crowd, and in this reading of my own annulations, nothing will be found

---

* Actually Elbert Hubbard's.

that is rare. There will be no years of flood and fire; there will only be the rings of ordinary years. . . .' "

"When does it get better?" you said.

"Now," she said. " 'My wife has often wondered why, with my middle-class background, I'm always opposed to the rich. I never worked in a mill or a mine, she says, nor have I ever known a single soul who did. I never sold my time for wages, and I never carried a picket-sign. Instead, dressed in the best, I ate in dining-cars and watched the hungry walk. I squandered four-month summers at the shore, she says, and I took my sabbaticals (from what?) in London, Paris, Madrid, and Rome. What am I doing on the Left?, she wants to know, how did I get so far from home? This book is an attempt to answer her questions—and, I might add, my own.' "

"I knew what I was doing when I threw that away."

"You think so?"

"By now, I've written *four* books, not one. Where are the answers?"

"You answered every question when you realized that ordinary Dan was ordinary you."

"How does that answer anything?"

"You're very slow," she said. "You've written four volumes of an autobiography to find out where and why you changed from nothing much to something more. But there never was a reason, because there never was a change. No voices came to you, as you tend to believe, none but your own, and when you took the road to the Left, it was only yourself that you heard."

"What you're saying, then, is that the four books went for Sweeney."

"If that means what I think, you're even slower than I thought. Those books tell ordinary people that they aren't ordinary at all. Once you understand that, you may begin to write Number Five.' "

SCENE 103

A MAN WITHOUT SHOES, Copy #1 (June 1951)

For my beloved wife
—inscription

Of those packages of books in the hallway, you would later write that it was as if the passage had been narrowed by a cord of wood. It was more than a light inconvenience, for anyone however small had to sidle to go by it, but you let it stay in the hope, even the expectation, that sales would soon diminish it. As always, you were fond. Subscriptions were slow in coming and scant when they came, and after half a year, fewer than two hundred copies had been disposed of. Long before that, though, you would yield to Maggie's mute appeal and consign the rest to a warehouse.*

Upright before you, as on a long-gone summer's day, is the first copy of the book that was found by your hand. You gaze at it, bound now in tawny morocco, but you feel no need to touch it, to open it, to study its letter-press printing, to read to yourself your words, nor need you seek the epigraph, a transcendent sentence of Paul Robeson's, spoken one night to the Friends of the Abraham Lincoln Battalion:

The people are a powerful source of power, he said.

SCENE 104

A MAN WITHOUT SHOES, as merchandise (June 1951)

Hoping for reviews, you sent copies to the *New Yorker,* the *San Francisco Chronicle,* the *Saturday Review,* the *New York Times,* and the *New York Herald Tribune.* Only the last responded—through Irita Van Doren, its literary editor—and then but to say, "We do not review publications of the Vanity Press." You didn't understand why self-publication was vain and commercial demure, but you understood with pain that your understanding wasn't required. The rule was rigid that a book generated as yours had been was beneath critical notice, and by not one word would that rule be broken during the year. Instead of a rain of orders, therefore, you received only the dew of a few: by year's end, one hundred and seventy-five copies would be gone from the hall.†

---

* There they would remain for some thirty years. In 1982, they would be taken over by Black Sparrow Press and re-issued.

† Through 1982, thirty-one years later, there would be two hundred and sixty-eight sales in all.

SCENE 105

A MAN WITHOUT SHOES, as a weapon (1951)

For want of reviews, the very existence of the book was concealed from all but a handful. That even they were aware of it was due to whatever word-of-mouth it was able to inspire, and scant enough it must've been, for only two expressions of opinion have endured, those of the writers Albert Maltz and Dalton Trumbo. Their letters lie before you, statements of the living once and now the permanent views of the dead. Both men had been known to you for years, at long range rather than intimately, but they were then, and they remain, on your lifelong list of the select. As members of the Hollywood Ten, each had taken his stand on principle when summoned before the House Committee in 1947, and each had been requited for his high-mindedness with a term in prison, and they had just been released when they read and wrote to you about *A Man Without Shoes.*

Maltz addressed you from his residence in Cuernavaca, Morelos:

> Dear John,
>
> Over the weekend I finished your novel. I do not believe that I know anyone writing today who writes with as much originality or freshness, with as much originally minted language as you do. Your prose contains poetry in the very best sense of that term. I doubt if there is a page in the book in which I was not struck at least once, and often more than once, by the original and unusual and rare quality of the writing.
>
> I found treasures of writing in very different types of scene. Writers like Gorki, for instance, have a poetic feeling for nature and are able to communicate nature scenes with beauty and evocative emotion. You have this, but you go beyond it. You communicate with freshness and originality the shifting patterns of all sensuous impression, whether it be nature or a city scene or a flat in a tenement. Only one other writer that I can summon to mind has so wide a range of sensory perception as I found in this book. That is Thomas Wolfe. However, he all too often buries his perceptions under his flood of language so that what emerges is music effective for the moment but quickly forgotten. Your art in this book is much more selective, much better disciplined, and of a superior order.
>
> Your novel has also a multitude of scenes that have truth, power,

humor, tenderness—or all of these in combination. Adding to this achievement, I cannot leave out a tremendous eloquence that comes into not a few of your scenes of dialogue or into your interspersed historical prose poems like the ones on Johnny Appleseed or Dred Scott or John Brown. I marvelled at the originality and pungency of language, the striking comment and the sheer eloquence.

I hope that by this time you know that I feel most sincerely that in reading your book I was in the presence of a very unusual, very fresh, and very big writing talent. At the moment I cannot think of another living writer who has equal abilities of this order.

I have been speaking of the bigness of your talent and your rareness as a writer, but I have not been speaking of this as a big novel, or as a fine novel, or as a great novel. Many parts are the proper product of your big talent. I do not feel that the novel as a whole is a proper product.

It is a critical bromide to speak of the stylistic heaviness of a man like Dreiser. Dreiser would be a more memorable figure in world literature if, in addition to the qualities he had, he had possessed a part of your writing talent. However, the fundamental need of the great novelist is the ability to present character. I believe with Stendhal when he says "Style is the secondary affair of the poet."

When I think of a book like *Crime and Punishment*, or *The Seven Who Were Hanged*, or *The Red Badge of Courage*, or *Anna Karenina*, I do not remember individual felicities of expression or the pace and rhythm of dialogue or anything particularly connected with style. In these books, or in any other, style is only a means of expression, and what is memorable is the portrait of people and the events through which they moved.

What does one remember about *Crime and Punishment*? It is the emotional life of a young man who has committed murder—his guilt, his anxiety, his seeking for retribution, his agony, his pursuit, his particular salvation. One remembers the man, his humanity, his ordeal. One remembers because the author has presented it in great fullness, with great persuasiveness, with great clarity.

Your choice of character, conflict, and theme was a real one and a deep one. Yet here for me was the failure of your book. I think it is a big failure. All through Dan's childhood I was held in deep absorption by the portrait of the father and mother and the portrait of the growing boy. I went along with you contentedly because I felt you were going somewhere. As the book lengthened, however, there were greater and greater blank spaces between the aspects of character that you permitted me to perceive. By the time of Danny's involvement in the Sacco-Vanzetti case, I was beginning to lose contact. I never felt (its) full effect upon the psyche of a growing boy. As a result, when Danny in a burst of emotion decides to leave home and see the United States, I found myself very surprised. Nothing in his past life was preparation for the conflict and disappointment which resulted in this act. The execution of Sacco and Vanzetti, with all that it meant to him, or the sexual episode with Miss Forrest and the revelations that came from it, did not explain Danny's act. Here was a highly intelligent and thinking young man, and yet I felt I knew him only on the surface.

Both the episode with Julia Davis and Dan's harsh experience in Florida are revealed vastly later in the book as having been of crucial importance in his life. Each was told in a very fascinating manner and I was deeply absorbed in them. Yet the *significance* of these sections, as you evidently intended it, did not come through to me at all. When Dan broke with Julia I understood it as the mature act of a man who liked a girl exceedingly well but who understood that she was so twisted in her soul that she would be very bad for him and that, therefore, he had to break with her. There was no agony of indecision, no loneliness, no emotional loss so keen that some years later he would be unfaithful to his wife because of his neurotic need to possess Julia in the person of another. You have dropped the very emotional and intellectual materials that were most indispensable.

The experience in Florida is an even better illustration. With Julia one at least knows that he made a return visit to her home and that even after time passed he sometimes thought he saw her in the walk of another girl. But the Florida affair you handled in a method so external that I had no comprehension it was to have a lasting effect upon Dan. One hundred and fifty pages later you tell me that this experience was catastrophic in its effect. In between you have given me a character in whom I become increasingly disinterested because I don't understand him. I don't know why Dan is so aimless. I don't know why he keeps speaking of himself as an ordinary man. You have omitted heart.

When we come to the end of the book, I can see in retrospect that after the episode in Florida Dan must have had a continuing inner life having to do with remembered terror, with fears of consequences if he should follow his principles into action; of self-disgust at what he took to be his lack of courage; of yearning to be an active political fighter. All of this must have been true of Dan in view of what you tell us at the end. Yet, you provide none of it in your book.

This is the period of the Depression and Dan is a class-conscious man, yet not until Spain comes along does he seem to dwell on whether he might join an organization fighting for Negro rights or the Scottsboro case or the social struggles of the period.

Another failing is that the dialogue in the latter portions of the book begins to seem untrue. I had the feeling of the author putting pungent speech and profound thought into the mouth of a character who didn't belong to such speech and thought. He is after all a young man of no great cultural background. Yet you have him talk with an emotional profundity of which you, John Sanford, are capable, but which doesn't seem true of him.

Your interspersed historical prose poems are quite wonderful in themselves. But what the hell they are doing in this book I don't know. It may be that you ought to set yourself the task of writing a book of prose poems on the history of the United States. Your sense of history is wonderfully keen and the imaginative freshness in these historical poetic interludes is very fine. I have never read anything better than your Paul Bunyan-John Henry tale, or your handling of Dred Scott, or the magnificent bite of your passage on John Brown, etc. An impressionistic history of the United States made up of pieces like this might well be a unique and lasting volume.*

I have written at this length out of my very great respect for your ability and my dismay at the central weakness in the book. There is not one line in all of Ibsen which contains the stylistic beauty on every other page in your novel. But my God what character comes out of his work. It may be that your writing ability, which is so big, is a curse. No living writer has more reason to regard himself seriously and with self-respect than you. Yet the failure of this book is of such a nature that you must review your literary method and your approach to the most fundamental of all literary problems, the presentation of character.

All best wishes
Albert

The Maltz letter as given here is an abridgment of the four-thousand-word original. It nonetheless renders his appraisal faithfully, omitting only collateral material and a variety of suggestions for future work. As written by him, and even as it stands, it's remarkable for the devotion it shows to the brotherhood of art; few are capable of his concern, and not you among them.

---

*Twenty years later, when the same suggestion was made by Maggie, it was acted on, resulting in *A More Goodly Country*, 1975.

How, then, did you respond to such generosity of spirit. Less generously, you fear, and certainly with heat. Why, you wonder, were you not milder in tone? Why does your reply seem to have been delivered in person — thrown?:

Dear Albert,

I have your long letter, and I'm grateful for the close study you've given *A Man Without Shoes*. No other writer has ever devoted so much time and thought to my work, and while I have to take issue with much that you say, I do it, I hope, in the spirit it was offered and in all respect.

You cite certain rules for greatness in a novel, and apart from not caring a great deal about rules of writing, I have little quarrel with them. With the conclusions you reach as those rules are made to apply to *A Man Without Shoes*, I disagree totally.

First, however, before taking up your main arguments, I want to stick my bill into that old pseudo-feud — style vs. content. There's no real antagonism. Stendhal or no Stendhal, style and content are of equal importance despite what you quote him for. I venture the guess that when he said style was secondary for the poet, he meant that to the poet style came so naturally that there was no need for dwelling on it, and that for others it was paramount because it had to be striven for.

He is the greatest writer whose ideas and characters are spoken the most eloquently. It's a fallacy that importance of subject lends importance to anything anyone may say about it. No belief could be worse for a writer — and no belief is responsible for more dull books. You pick four that you do not remember for *individual felicities of expression or pace and rhythm of dialogue or anything particularly connected with style*. You astonish me. *Anna Karenina* and *Crime and Punishment* might've been cited by me for style rather than by you for content, because while each is possibly the best writing-as-writing by its author, *War and Peace* and *The Brothers Karamazov* simply tower over them in value. As for *The Seven Who Were Hanged*, Andreyev is a second-rater alongside of Gogol, Chekhov, and Turgenev, all of whom you leave out in order to make your point — and any one of whom would have ruined it.

But it's the fourth example, *The Red Badge of Courage*, that really floored me. The others are from the Russian, and I have no way of knowing whether the translations limp. My own language I do know, and I think there can be little disputing that Crane is one of the three or four first-rate writers ever developed in America, a stylist above all else and a subject-matter man only deep down and thin when you get to it. His content is limited and his range short, but he is powered by one of the most original and poetic talents that ever worked in prose, and all before him (and much since) fades to drab.

It's Crane's fine craft that makes him dazzling, very little else, and when you say you don't remember him for *individual felicities,* you force me to wonder whether you remember him at all. Odd choices, the books you name, but this one is odd beyond belief. For my part, I recall no single character in the novel, not even the name of a character, not even a face, a place, a phrase: I remember only the emotion of fear presented so overwhelmingly as to evoke it in me. When you do that without ever having seen a battle, possibly without ever having experienced fear anywhere else, you do it with your art, with your *writing instrument,* as you call it, and not with your characterizations and subject-matter.

To get on to the specific relation of your rules to *A Man Without Shoes,* I have to quote again from your letter. You say *The fundamental need of the great novelist is the ability to present character,* and you dwell on the presentation of character, ascribing all the book's defects to my failure in that field. I said before that I disagreed with you; now I want to say why. Primarily, of course, I believe that in Dan Johnson I have a character of very considerable stature, built step by step and developed logically and with no little passion through his varied stages, the total coming to what I fatuously conceive as a complete man in a vital period. I might also say that I believe in Dan Johnson because you yourself show that you know him so well. You charge me with having omitted all dramatization of his emotional loss in Julia Davis and presenting him to you with a great hole in his face, yet in one bright sharp sentence you quash your own charge by saying *a loss so keen that some years later he would be unfaithful to his wife because of his neurotic need to possess someone like Julia in the person of another woman.*

How did you know that? Where did you get your material for that bright sharp sentence? From thin air? —or did you get it from the novel itself? from the defective characterizations? I put it to you that there was no void, first because you drew the full and only inference from Dan's affair with Emma James, and second because there was ample evidence on which to base that understanding. In other words, it was all in the book, and offhand I can support that with at least six explicit references that Dan made to Julia after walking out on her: they were in his actual return to Colorado Springs to look for her, in his impulse to hop a freight in the Hudson River piece, his futile scene at the telephone directory, and three conversations with his wife. Add to these his many low moods, all stemming plainly from his longing for a Julia as he desired her and culminating in his affair with an Emma as he found her, and you have what you so well summed up: *a loss so keen.* . . .

The heart wasn't left out of Dan, as you claim; it was all there, and you felt it beat. It would seem to be this, then: that you demand to know of an eighteen-year-old boy *the agony of indecision,* to quote you again, the pulling back and forth, the loneliness and weeping, the heartsickness, and that you demand to know it here and now and on the nose, as if anyone ever knew the full import of an experience at the time that he had it.

The next illustration that you give of my failure with Dan's character, a much more glaring one in your eyes, is my supposed withholding from the reader of the catastrophic effect of his beating and arrest in Florida. In your view, I went for suspense by concealing decisive information for 150 pages, only to suffer the penalty of being condemned to surprise, the effect of a moment. A man who understands the totality of the book as well as you do should not be so quick to forget its parts. You say *The thoughts you give your character are always a careful avoidance of what is evidently troubling him most deeply.* If something was *evidently* troubling Dan, then there must've been *evidence.* There *was* evidence.

The beating and arrest occur in a section of the book called PASCUA FLORIDA. Right there, Dan comes to an understanding of the almost irresistible forces he is up against; right there, lying on his cot in jail, he wilts under his fear of the Big Train, the Forty-eighter from Decatur. It was a long passage, the one dealing with that realization, and I can't account for your having overlooked it. Similarly, I can't account for the way in which you missed the many other passages that followed and elaborated on it. Most of these involved Dan's wife, and little by little he came to reveal to her his entire nightmare—but while Dan, in shame and self-disgust, could bring himself to tell her only a part of it at a time, the reader was left in doubt never; he knew what had ridden Dan from the start, and you knew it too. *Evidently,* you say.

I come now to what you call *contributing failures.* One such is mentioned in your rebuke of me for not having pitched Dan into the Scottsboro case. If you had written this book, you'd have found an obligation to plunge Dan into that fight. Your right to do that would've been absolute, on the theory that a writer is entitled to tell whatever story he may desire. You must allow me the same latitude. I simply was not writing about a man who was going to become involved in the Scottsboro case, but even if I had been, I think the Dan Johnson of *A Man Without Shoes* would've disqualified himself. He knew about it, of course (there are too many references to it in Tootsie's letters for you to doubt that), but after his disillusionment over the end that came to Sacco and Vanzetti, his escapist tour of the country, and his awakened fear, he was self-immobilized. A Dan Johnson who was *not* immobilized would've been a Dan Johnson founded on a different conception, and headed toward a different end. You seem to have the notion that because Dan was friendly with two Negroes, he must have become involved in every struggle for Negro rights. If there are no such hard-and-fast rules in life, why should there be any in art?

The high point of Dan's political life was reached in the Sacco-Vanzetti case, and although he remained class-conscious and vocal, he ceased for the time to be a participant. He was on the long plateau of knowledge-without-action, a common condition for all of us, and although troubled deeply about it, he managed to live a life that came finally to a promise of flowering. You were looking for a knight; with regret, I could only give you a man.

A word about Dan's dialogue, which you object to. You say *You have him talk with an emotional profundity of which you, John Sanford, are capable, but which doesn't seem true of him.* That's a tough one to knock over, but I think that any dialogue short of the clearly preposterous is acceptable. We don't tell Henry James that his characters, one and all, are capable of writing a treatise on grammar, nor do we tell Hemingway that people in emotion do more than grunt: we demand only that what they say be possible, and we make a literary assumption of educational backgrond, culture absorbed, and ideas digested, unless (which is not Dan's case) such an assumption is plainly unsupportable. We take it for granted that if a man expresses a thought, he knows something about it.

You say *I have always believed that the most important part of writing is the work that the writer does before he begins to write.* I don't. The most important part of writing is writing. The planning is of course sometimes reflected in the product, but more often than not it's a hindrance. In my case, it certainly is, for I've never prided myself on my ability to think. I'm quite a lousy thinker. But I don't think I'm a lousy writer—and therefore I have to doubt the invariable validity of your rule. A man can prepare and prepare, like Philip Quarles, and never get a line down worth a quarter. Or, if he doesn't hamstring himself altogether, he can plan with such rigidity that what comes out seems stamped from an inorganic block, from a blank, like a key. I happen to admire spontaneity, and it'll shock you, I suppose, to learn that *A Man Without Shoes* was written with no more preparation than rolling a sheet into this machine, that I didn't know where Dan was going, how he meant to get there, or why he was trying to — and you'll probably say (in fact, you do say) that it shows up in the finished product. Well, maybe it does, and maybe it doesn't, but the way of writing was *my* way, and it'd quite likely be the best way for many who plot and plan with literature as if it were only another system of weights and measures.

One more point, touching on the presence of the historical prose poems in *A Man Without Shoes.* The poems are not stray pieces of chamber music that I sought to inject into an defective symphony, as you put it. *Anything* belongs in a novel that in any way contributes to it. These poems, all representing an unconscious assimilation by Dan of his country's history and meaning, add much to his understanding, stature, direction, and sympathies, and they need no defense. Not if an opera needs no defense for having music.

To wind up, I want to thank you again for your extreme devotion. It's rare — but it's also Albert. Do write again. My best, as always, to you and Margaret.

Affectionately

John

The letter from Dalton, dated July 17, 1951, was written on the stationery of his Lazy T Ranch at Frazier Park. Only part of its first paragraph, complaining that you were hard to reach, has been omitted:

Dear John,

Paul gave me a copy of your book. I started to read it Saturday night, and stayed up all night and didn't go to bed until I'd finished it.

What do you say of a book you've liked? The letters I've received which go all out I've always disbelieved. Nothing, I say, can be *that* good. Of course I love such letters even if I don't quite swallow them (or didn't when I was getting them) but since writers are such a self-doubting tribe, they've never seemed quite as good as those which approached the problem of praise with restraint.

Well. I read the book. I think it's a fine novel, which is as much as you can ask of any novel, and more than you ever get these days. I think it may even be a great novel. When people say: the proletarian novel is dead, this proves they lie. The proletarian novel died of bad writing. And for you it never died at all and by God you've proved it.

It is so clean. It is so blunt. In parts it is so beautiful. It shows such tremendous growth on your part, and such fine command over yourself and the material. I read the chapter in which the boy comes home and discusses the fight at school with his father. I mean to say, I read this chapter aloud to Cleo and all three children and they howled with delight. Children are very important critics. You do what no one dares to do these days, and in such a simple, charming, self-evident manner that the reader simply cannot question it: namely, that a rich man is a thief. You say lots of other things too, all of them good, all of them true, and none of them ducking any question at any time. The delineation of the younger Danny from beginning to end is wonderful, his cheating, his pathetic failures, the things we've all done or thought of doing, yet the things which are never portrayed as part of a decent man, of a hero if you please. And much more, much, much more.

I think I have some idea of what you went through with it. I was in jail ten months and missed parole once and finally got out upon the expiration of the term. You must've been in jail with this for five years, and Paul tells me you missed parole 34 times, and finally had to buy your way out. What a disgrace, what a vomitous comment on American publishers, what a terrifying thing to all writers that you had to publish it yourself.

Well, that was the thing to do. It had to be published.

I have not too much liked your earlier books, although I recognized remarkable things in them, remarkable portions, that is. Perhaps I was crazy, or perhaps you have taken a great leap forward, perhaps quantity has changed to quality. In any event, for this book and for my money, you can piss on any author who has been published in this country in the last five years (how stupid that arbitrary figure of five years really is!), and if, in the process, you spatter your boots a little, send them to me and I'll clean them for you.

Affectionate regards to Maggie.

Dalton

THE COLOR OF THE AIR, XII

I.W.W. – 1914

NO ASHES FOR UTAH

It is only a hundred miles from here to Wyoming. Could you arrange to have my body hauled to the state line to be buried. I don't want to be found dead in Utah.

—Joe Hill to Bill Haywood

In January of that year, up to around half past nine of a certain cold night, a man name of John Morrison ran a grocery store in Salt Lake. From then on, his widow ran it, for he was on the floor, shot to hell by a pair of gunmen. A cop, he'd been once, and none so well loved, because twice before he died there in his bacon, spice, and dried picayunes, other gunmen had taken aim and missed him. The state of Utah said Joe Hill was one of those that put him down to stay.

Whether you believe that or not depends on this alone: how much do you own, a little or a lot? Withhold the sage and serious face, the frown, the rapt stare at blank space, the search for The Way on a wall; spare closed minds your pretense of candor, and stand or fall on your dollars and cents. How much do you own, mister, a little or a lot?

If you're rich, then you know Joe Hill was only a minstrel on the side. For his main holt, he was a stick-up man, a Wobbly stickup-man, and on that winter's night, he was one of the two that came to the store. And you know the rest, how he wore a mask, and how he prestoed out that .38, and how Morrison fell and where, and how his son shot the shooter and was shot to death himself, and, lastly, how two hours later and five miles away, a doctor treated Joe for a hole in the lung. You as good as saw it all happen—if you're rich.

If you're a different kind of stiff, though, if you're one of the hands, say (not a man, mind you, or even a worker, a toiler), if you break your ass for three a day and hide your card inside your shoe, then you know Joe Hill was no more in that store than you were. Those that swore they saw him lied, and no gun was seen in his clothes, and he threw no gun away, so God damn Doc Bird, and Doc McHugh the same. Joe was hit that night, and he never denied it, but when he said it was over a skirt, you took him at his word—if you were one of the hands, that is.

In Utah, mighty few others did, and when he refused to name the woman, he was headed for the door that opens once. As he went, he wrote more tunes for his sort to sing, and he sent Bill a second wire, saying *Don't mourn me—organize,* and then he drew a will in which he spoke a wish to become cinders and blown on the wind as food for flowers. And then a paper heart was pinned over a heart still full of blood, and when four shots drilled both, he was through the door and dead.

His friends came and carried him away, thirty thousand came, and he was burned in the fire he'd yearned for, and he was put in little packets, a pinch of him in each, and forty-seven states were made the richer by his dust. He was never found dead, though, in Utah.

SCENE 106

SIX MONTHS ON, SIX MONTHS OFF (July 1951)

Maggie's contracts, ten or twelve of them in pastel covers, were stacked before Thau on his desk, where they looked rather like the layers of a cake, so much so that when he touched the pile, your memory flashed, and the taste of frosting came and went.

"We just got them back from Texas," he said, "and Equitable approves."

"That's just wonderful," Maggie said.

"The six months off won't stop you being eligible for the Pension Plan. We have it in writing."

"You've been so protective of my interest, Mr. Thau. I don't know how to thank you."

"You want to know how?" he said. "Go sign the contracts."

He'd made a small joke, and, watching him, you thought you saw a smile to match. If so, it was of no duration, merely the passing disturbance of a still surface. And then up from nowhere in your mind came another thought, that you liked the man, not the one he showed you, but the one he tried to hide. What kind was that?, you wondered, what lay behind the company face? Gazing across his desk as across a great divide, you described him to yourself as nimble, furtive, nocturnal, on the *qui vive,* not the kind you'd ever taken to, but all the same you sensed a big-game quality in his quarry-size— and you liked him!

He was speaking to Maggie, saying, "Take these down the hall to the Legal Department—Mr. Hendrickson. You have to sign before a notary."

When Maggie rose, you rose with her, and you said, "I want to thank you too."

"You go, Maggie," he said. "I'll have a talk with John."

After she'd left, you remained standing, and for a moment he took your measure in silence, and in silence you let him step you off.

"I'm going to ask you a question," he said, "and I hope you wouldn't take it personally."

"There's no danger of that, Mr. Thau."

"People on the lot that know about this contract, they said, 'What has that guy got?' "

You stared at him, and then you laughed, saying, "Got? I've got nothing."

"They say, 'Here's a woman makes a hundred and thirty thousand a year, and she could make even more if she felt like. But she don't want more; she wants less. She wants to be with this guy John Sanford. What's he got?' "

"They ought to be saying, 'What's *Maggie* got?' "

"Sixty-five thousand a year, she gives up. No guy is worth that much."

"I agree."

"So?" he said. "Why are you letting her do it?"

"I don't *let* her, Mr. Thau, and she doesn't *let* me. We don't live by permission."

"I know what kind of a person she is, but you I don't know at all. Around here, nobody can figure you out. There's better-looking guys, smarter guys, richer guys, yes, and more likeable guys—but for you she gives up sixty-five thousand a year, and for what? To make your breakfast?"

Again you laughed. "*I* make *her* breakfast."

"Experienced people—you know what I mean, *experienced*?—they couldn't work a woman for carfare. They give; they don't get. But you. . . ," and he shook his head, "what's your secret?"

"I love her."

"That's the secret? That's why she buys you race-horses?"

Maggie was just entering, carrying the sheaf of contracts.

"Yes," you said to Thau.

SCENE 107

REPORT TO THE GOVERNOR (July 1951)

You went to see him on the following day, taking with you a copy of the new contract, and he listened in silence while you read him the paragraphs setting forth the modified conditions.

> ... such aggregate sum of Sixty-Five Thousand Dollars ($65,000) is hereinafter referred to as "the yearly minimum guaranteed compensation" of the author. . . .

Although your eyes were on the pages, the edge of your vision caught him holding one hand in the other and studying it as if there, in its color and conformation, was written the key to the clauses being read.

> ... the term of this agreement shall commence on January 1, 1952, and shall continue for a period of Five (5) Years. . . .

You thought, or you felt, that he was now regarding you, not his hands, and glancing up, you found that this was so, but he wore no expression that you could decipher, as he seemed to have deciphered you.

> ... during such parts of the year as the author is not rendering services hereunder, he will not render services for any person, firm, or corporation other than this company without its prior written consent. . . .

As you read on, a part of your mind detached itself to wonder what he was thinking. Did he note ambiguities that had escaped you, contingencies that you hadn't foreseen, did he approve or disapprove, or did he take no position at all?

> ... all further services rendered during the remaining balance of the year of the term shall be compensated at the weekly rate of Twenty-five Hundred Dollars ($2,500). . . .

You let the reading end there, and putting the document aside, you waited for comment.

It was slow in coming, and you said, "Well, what do you think?"
"Whose idea was that?" he said.
"Maggie's."
"Entirely?"
"From start to finish."

"And you never said a word?"

"It was something she wanted. What could I have said?"

"Some people would put up a hell of an argument over giving up sixty-five thousand a year."

"Would you want me to be one of them?"

He shook his head, saying, "I used to think Maggie was too good for you."

You reached out and smoothed his hair—how often had you done that?—and then you kissed his hand.

"Of course, I still do, kid," he said.

SCENE 108

AT THE FAR END OF EASY STREET (July–August 1951)

Eastbound on the City of Los Angeles*

At Ogden, you left your car to watch a helper engine attach itself to the train for the climb from Utah to the mile-higher plains of Wyoming. You stood beside the great double-header of 4-8-4s, and you listened to their breathing and the beating of their hearts: it was an old fancy of yours, that engines were alive; in a collision, you'd think, they'd bleed. And then you heard the *All Aboard* call, and you ran for the nearest vestibule.

As you entered your compartment, Maggie said, "I don't have to ask where you were, do I?"

"When I was a kid," you said, "I'd sit all day at the Long Branch station." The train was moving now, or—another old fancy—the world was going away. "Early in the morning, I'd see my father off to the city, and then I'd look for him on the first train back, even on a freight."

"What will you do when trains are gone? They'll go some day, you know. They're going now."

"I'll think of the names—the Monon, the Nickel Plate, the Wabash, the Grand Trunk. I'll think of the Pullmans. Pullman—whenever I use the word, one in particular comes to mind, the *Mendocino*. It was an observation-car, and it had a brass railing. It looked like a bulldog with gold teeth."

---

* Maggie's current assignment was a screenplay for Elizabeth Taylor and Robert Taylor. It would deal with the breeding and racing of thoroughbreds, and many of its scenes would take place in the Blue Grass country. To familiarize Maggie with the background, the studio had dispatched her to Kentucky.

Through your window, you could see the Uintas, a long range with a year-round hackle of snow, and for no reason you knew of, you thought then of a car you'd only read about—the *Superb*.

"The *Superb*," you said. "It was named the *Superb*, and nearly thirty years ago, it rolled over these very rails. It was coming from California with a coffin, and in the coffin was Warren Harding. . . ."

And after thirty years more, you'd write of that run:

> The story goes that his friends killed him, or that his wife did (the Duchess, he called her) to preserve his name. But whether he died from the outside-in or the inside-out, he went to hell or higher water from the city of San Francisco. Full of formaldehyde for the four-day ride back to the Mansion, he was put on view in a cutaway and a touch of rouge, and callers allowed that he looked alive—he seemed to be asleep, they said, and if so, he slept well, slept long. His train, streaming black and purple crape, ran all the way east to the Capital, and all the while he slumbered on.
>
> At trackside, there were millions from near, far, and further. They stood in ones and twos and strings and crowds, they covered every stack of ties, every gantry, they scared the crows from every cornfield, and in the last car some saw a casket pass, and some, with the sun behind them, saw only speeding panes of sky. A second or so, the blink of an eye, and the hot-shot hearse was there and gone. Not many missed the six gold letters of the word *Superb*, and those who were close told of the ghost of sour-mash whisky and, mixed with engine-smoke, the smoke of a Vuelta cigar, and though a nose or two caught a whiff of oil, it was thought to have come from the piston-rods.
>
> *I can take care of my enemies all right*, he'd said. *But my God damn friends. . . !*
>
> As yet, the door of that White House coat-closet was shut, and it still held its stew of smells—rubbers, umbrellas, chew-tobacco, an old man's sperm, and his dearie's perfume. But soon now, some-one would try the knob, a guard, a guest, maybe even the new tenant. . . .

Down Across the Prairie

At Chicago, you put up at the Blackstone for a night, and from there, instead of continuing by train, you rented a car for the four-hundred-mile journey to Lexington. Leaving the hotel soon after daylight, you headed south alongside the right-of-way of the Illinois Central.

Passing a small body of water near the outskirts of the city, you said, "That's Lake Calumet. Once it was part of a model town called Pullman, after the palace-car bastard."

"It looks more like a pond," Maggie said. "Why bastard?"

"He owned six square miles in here, and on them he built his God damn town—car-shops, blocks of flats, company stores, and all. He must've thought he was a feudal lord."

You tried to put your mind back to the vanished barony with its company strucutres on company earth, with its thralls drudging on the *Mendocino*, on a car to be called the *Superb*.

"He paid them $1.87 an hour," you said, "and when they struck for more, he locked them out and spent the summer on the Jersey shore. . . ."

> The town belonged first and last to George Mortimer Pullman. He owned it in bulk, and he owned it by the pound—the devil and all, he owned it. He owned every worm in it, every stone, every underground grain to the core of the world; he owned the air and the space above it to where space ended; and on the surface, he owned every brick, stick, and quill of grass, he owned the leaves on the trees and fallen leaves, he owned dust, snow, rain, birds while they lit and droppings when they'd flown away. He also owned the neat workmen he paid a wage.
>
> They hated him and, more than him, the town. They cared nothing for his tenements, lettered *A* through *J*, his one-tap flats, and the one-stool toilets that five flats shared, the pools and pleasances, the stores, and the Florence Hotel, where he fitted plutes and whores for private cars.
>
> One thing mattered to them, the thing they made—the gilt and walnut palaces, the inlaid domes they built on wheels. These they rode but once, on the shakedown runs, and on such occasions, they'd play at being their betters, feigning Cuban smoke from two-for-five cigars, fishing for fancied garters, dumping wheat, cornering gold. . . . And then they were back in their cold-water flats (*A* through *J*), and coup and killing went up the flue.
>
> A worker, a woman, said *We are born in a Pullman house, fed from a Pullman store, and taught in a Pullman school, and we'll be buried in a Pullman cemetery and go to a Pullman hell!*

The site of the town was far behind you, miles and miles, when you said, "After Pullman died, do you know who became president of the company? Lincoln's son Robert."

Coming into Lexington on the Leestown Pike, you reached your hotel, the Lafayette, at nightfall. The lobby, the diningroom, the bar, all were crowded, and there was talk on the air, smoke, laughter, the single smell of mingled food—and you were pleased, as if you hadn't known, as if you'd only now discovered, that the Breeders' Sales would open on the morrow in a pavilion on the race course at Keeneland.

And on the morrow, you and Maggie bid in two yearling fillies. One was by Messalina's sire Roman out of the Firethorn mare Falcon, a bay that you'd register with the Jockey Club as Little Italy. The other, also a bay, was by Eight Thirty out of Esteemed One, and her name would be chosen by Maggie: Early to Bed.

Scouting the Pikes

Pike, you learned, was short for turnpike, or toll-road, but there were stiles no more on the Frankfort Pike, the Paris, the Bryan Station, or the Russell Cave, and you drove them freely between white rail-fencing and laid stone walls, past long converges leading to a residence among the trees, past paddocks vast with grazing mares, with foals suddenly sprinting as if some blood-remembered barrier had just been sprung. . . .

Pilgrimage to Hodgenville

You wanted to see the log cabin of the stories, the smoked timbers, the sod floor, the fireplace Abe was said to have read by, the corner where his mother's bed of corn-shucks might've stood. You wanted to see where he began, as once, in the Peterson house, you'd seen where he ended with a high-caliber hole in the back of his head. . . .

And you'd write, a long long while after going to that place:

> He was born on a farm near Nolin Creek, he said, a lay of land known as Sinking Spring, or Cave Spring, as some called it, after a flow that came from a limestone rift. . . . But nothing was certain, not the day, the place, or the name. The past was blank time as black as space, and for all he could surely say, there was no cold sink in the rocks, or none he ever drank from, no chinked cabin, no farm he knew by any designation. He knew, if it was knowing, only what the dead had told him, and gone with them was his beginning.
>
> He must've wondered off and on whether he hadn't begun with

himself. There was no long continuation that led to him, no tether paying him out of yesterday's night. He was loose here in a small locale of light, a luminescence, it was, an emission, and he'd glow for a while and go out, and at the end, it may have seemed to him more of the void, as before he came.

In his lifetime, he never went back to Hardin County, never reviewed the road he'd come from Sinking Spring, or Cave Spring (or Rock Spring, as some few had it), but if he ever rose again, if his bones ever walked, he'd've found a cabin there, the very one he'd been born in, or so it'd be sworn to, and the grain of the wood, the knots, the nicks, the tallow-stain, all would've invited the recall of a single room, smoked and cured and candle-lit and a hundred years gone.

It was well he stayed away, for he'd not have remembered. There were paved paths instead of trodden grass, there were gardens where the corn-stubble stood, and the cabin no longer wore in the open air, in snow and sun and rain. It was a relic in a shrine, it was sixty steps up from the earth, behind festoons of chain. He'd not have known where he was when he saw the temple—Greek, was it, with that pillared porch?—nor could he have made his way unaided to the spring (Sinking? Cave? Rock?), and when at its rim, he stepped in someone's stool, he'd've been saddened by the living hatred and glad he died when he did.*

It was you there at the edge of that spring, and you said, "I wish I'd never come here."

And Maggie said, "It's time to go home."

SCENE 109

WHERE THE HEAVY GOING BEGINS (Late Summer 1951)

> subpoena, n. (fr.L. *sub* under + *poena* punishment. See PAIN)
> —Webster's International

Wednesday, August 8, 1951†

At about 11:30 a.m., a United States Marshal visited our home and stated that he wanted to serve us with subpoenas to appear before the House

---

* The sections on Harding, Pullman, and Lincoln are from *A More Goodly Country*.

† All dated material is from a record begun a few days later and running through November 21st.

Committee on Un-American Activities in Los Angeles on September 6.
There was little or no conversation. The subpoenas were accepted, after which
the Marshal left.

After some discussion between ourselves, we decided. . . .

Discussion — the word is there, the third in the second paragraph, and if it weren't
before you now, typed in pica and correctly spelled, nothing could make you
believe you'd used it. Discussion? Did you (a) *consider a question in open debate,*
or (b) *argue for the sake of arriving at truth?* What question? What truth? You
held in your hand, each of you, a single sheet of pink paper, and you read,
each of you, what the paper contained, the penalty, the punishment (See PAIN)
in store for them that longed for a Union more perfect than this perfect Union.

§

To U.S. Marshal James J. Doyle and/or William A. Wheeler:

You are hereby commanded to summon *John Sanford** to be and appear before the Committee on Un-American Activities in their
chamber in the city of Los Angeles on Thursday, Sept. 6, 1951, Room
518 Federal Bldg., at the hour of 10:00 a.m., then and there to testify
touching matters of inquiry committed to said Committee.

Herein fail not.

> Witness my hand
> John S. Wood
> Chairman

§

What were you doing when Doyle or Wheeler came? Were you writing
or reading or listening to *a jota Aragonese* (Glinka's?) on the gramophone,
or were you and Maggie talking, and if so, of what person or persons, what
places or things, what plans, what regrets, what premonitions? Or were you
somewhere on the grounds with guinea-hen chicks fleeing your feet, were
the kittens in a hay-rack merged in sleep, were your hands deep and cool
in a drum of oats, and were the portents there too, in the feed-room dust,
drifting through the air between a persimmon tree and a tangerine? What
were you saying or thinking, what were you up to when you saw a man
in the driveway, Doyle or Wheeler, moving unhindered toward the house,

---

* Save for the name, Maggie's subpoena was identical.

where only old Juno and the remains of her litter, two blind bitches and half-blind Jo-jo, were left to defend your four-acre world, and theirs?

There was little or no conversation. . . .
"Is your name Sanford?" Doyle or Wheeler said.
And you said, "Yes."
"John Sanford?"
"Yes."
"And are you Marguerite Roberts Sanford?"
And she said, "Yes."
"I hand you these subpoenas, then."
And then Doyle or Wheeler went away.
There was little or no conversation.

Were you in the house at the time and in which of its rooms, or were you out of doors walking a horse from a corral to a stall—but what does it matter? Wherever you may have been, you held in your hand a cataclysmic sheet of pink with a three-word nullification of the history that began at Plymouth Rock: *Herein fail not.*

§

That early, it was impossible to comprehend the extent of what had befallen you. There was no limit to it in time or space: no numbers could measure it, nor could fancy span its immensity. A moment before, you'd felt that you were part of an order, and however small the part, you'd known only the low-level alienation of the Jew everywhere; for the rest, you'd assumed that you belonged. That assumption could not now be made. It was then, perhaps, that you did begin to roam, through the house, it may have been, or through the aisles of the grove, hardly knowing where you were headed or aware of where you'd been. Of that wandering, all you recall is the clarity of small things, the shingled surface of a pine-cone (the imbrication, you thought), the fine thorns on a citrus twig.

After some discussion between ourselves, we decided to inform MGM im-mediately of the existence and service of the subpoenas, and accordingly. . . .

To Maggie, larger things were clear, and you can still hear, you'll always hear, what she said with such certainty as she gazed at the doom in pink that she held in her hand:

"John, my dear, my career just ended."

§

In the evening, you sat with her on the steps of the porch, staring through a filigree of foliage at the blackening blue of the sky. The yellow headlights of a cat—named Corporal for a pair of chevron markings—glowed for a moment as he flowed across the lawn. You heard a bird call in the darkness and a further bird reply.

"I wonder who the others are," you said.

And Maggie said, "Others? What others?"

"We can't be the only ones with these damn subpoenas. We aren't that important: I'm not in the picture-business, and you're not in the Party."

"No, but *I'm* in the picture-business, and *you're* in the Party. That makes us important."

"Us and nobody else?"

"Oh, we'll have company, never fear, but it'll make no difference. Remember the story I told you about a burning cattle-car? Forty head, it must've held, but when they died, they died alone."

It was night now, and the sky no longer showed through eyelets in the trees, black masses against the mass of black beyond them.

"You're an odd one, Jabe," she said.

"How so?"

"You think pain is easier to bear if others are in pain—as if there were just so much of it, and your share was small."

"I never said that Tom's headache was cured by Dick's and Harry's."

"Why wonder, then, about who else has a subpoena?"

"I want to find out what the hell is going on."

"But John, I *know* what's going on. They're after you for your politics and me for my job."

"I won't push it, Mag, but I still think there's something to be learned by asking around."

"Asking what? Asking whom?"

"We know a slew of people. Some may be in our boat."

Like what it denoted, the figure seemed to float, and you watched as though you could see it, buoyant on the air.

"*We're* in our boat, John," she said, "and they're in *theirs*. I know this town better than you do—I know people better too—and I tell you there's no help for us out there, not among your comrades and surely not among (what's the phrase?) the running dogs of capitalism."

"You have a right to be bitter," you said. "You've never had a wrong thought in your life, and here's the Government coming down on you harder than it ever did on a slave-driver. John Brown had it straight: *Had I so interfered in behalf of the rich. . . !*"

230

"I'm bitter," she said, "but only against myself."

Through the door-screen beside you, you heard Juno's collar-tags jingle. When you let her out, she inspected you and then Maggie, and in the safety between you, she coiled herself, sighed deeply, and closed her eyes.

"You're not to blame, Jabe," Maggie said, "and don't ever think so."
And you said, "I'll always think so."

Juno, in some dog-remembrance, raised her head and worked it into Maggie's hand.

You said, "She's dreaming of her old slipper-chair alongside your bed," and then you said, "Why do all our dogs turn to you?"
"I'm easier to know," Maggie said. "I'm more like a dog."
"I can do anything with them, but deep down they all belong to you."
"Look," she said. "Would you feel any better if we went hunting for those other headaches?"
And you said, "Yes. Yes, I would."

§

The man you chose for your inquiry was Jasper More, your fellow-teacher at the Little Red Schoolhouse several years before. His wife Ellen had been known to you even earlier through her work for the Russian War Relief, and acquaintance with both had matured to, or toward, friendship. You were close enough, at any rate, to look in on them without notice, and often had you done so through the years.

You were on the way, climbing the Laurel Canyon grade to Mulholland, when Maggie said, "Have you thought of what you'll say when we get there?"
"Prepare, you mean? What for? More and I are in similar positions. We're both novelists, and we both taught at the School—taught as a team, in fact. I figure he's as likely to have a subpoena as I am."
"What if he is? Maybe he won't be as ready to let on as you seem to be."
"He'd have nothing to gain by keeping mum."
"Oh, John," Maggie said. "Oh, John."

Night drew fragrance from the hillside, the sweet breath of broom, the astringence of sage, and in the damp curves, the earth itself exhaled.

"Oh, John," you said. "What does it mean this time?"
"That you expect so much. These people are just people, and like you and me, they're looking out for themselves. If they have subpoenas, they may have a reason for clamming up, comrade or no comrade."

You coursed Mulholland, glancing off at the great glitter of the Valley below, and then you started down the far side of Laurel.

"I don't think the Mores would do that with us," you said.
"No?" Maggie said. "Well, I *do*."

The Mores lived in the Wilshire district near La Cienega Boulevard. Their home was the upper floor of a two-family unit in a street-long row, all with the tile-and-stucco stamp of Spain. At either hand, trees lined the sidewalk (macadamias, More had told you, for he knew such things — the *macadamia ternifolia*, he'd said, the nut of Queensland). At intervals among them, a lamp-standard rose, its downthrow of light making tree-shaped shadows on the pavement, and in one of these you brought your car to a stop.

A curving corridor of rose bushes led to the staircase, and you were halfway up when Maggie said, "I want you to know something, Jabe."
"And what's that?" you said.
"I pretend you're a fool, but that's all it is — pretense. What you are is trusting, and if that's foolish, we're on a dying planet."
"You do me honor," you said.
"Ring the bell, you foolish man."
And you rang the bell.

On seeing you, the Mores made nothing of your not having called in advance; you were welcomed as though expected and led through the hall toward the livingroom. On the way, you passed a series of framed drawings in ink, each of them intricate and diagrammatic, like illustrations of a nervous system or the molecular structure of cells. They were More's work, and whenever you saw their filamentary lines, their minute formations, you'd wonder at his microcosmic mind. Once, you remembered, he'd shown you a single sheet of foolscap on which he'd written a three-act play.

The Mores indicated chairs for you and Maggie, and as they seated themselves, the wife said, "Well, Sanfords, tell us what brings you."
"We'll tell you standing," you said. "Today we were served with subpoenas to appear before the House Committee."
"Subpoenas?" Ellen More said, rising as she spoke. "You two got subpoenas?"
Only her husband was not now on his feet, and it was to him, delineator of mazes and involutes, that you said, "I thought, Jass, that you might have one too."
But it was his wife who said, "Why would he get one?"
"For the same reason that I did: he's a Party member."
"Not everybody knows that."

"Oh, come on, Ellen. He wrote a pamphlet on Servile Rebellions, he emptied people's pockets for the Lincoln Battalion, and he taught alongside me at the School. If I'm known, so is he."

She turned to her husband, saying, "If we don't get a move on, we'll be late."

And he said, "Late? Late for what?"

"Our appointment."

"With whom? What appointment?"

"I told you before. Don't you remember? Those people. . . ."

"Oh," he said, and now at last he rose.

"We're sorry," his wife said. "We have to go meet somebody."

"I understand perfectly," you said, and you took Maggie by the hand and walked her to the door. There you paused long enough to say to her, "Are you sure that car was following us?"

"I might've been mistaken," she said.

And then you were outside and going down the stairs.

Among the macadamias, the street-lamps made transparencies of light and shade, and through them, past an occasional vigilant window, you drove off toward La Cienega.

As you turned into the broad boulevard and headed northward, you said, "That son-of-a-bitch has a brain like a city dump—full of rags and orange rind. He even knows what La Cienega means."

"What else does he know?" Maggie said.

"A couple of years back, he was reading the Encyclopedia article by article."

"It only made him stupid. He's slower than his wife, and she's standing still."

You laughed, saying, "Not you, though. You picked right up on that business of being followed. We gave them a fit."

"Before this is over, Jabe, I'm afraid we'll give a lot of people fits."

"It's hard to believe, but they as good as threw us out."

"I never wanted to tell you this. For some peculiar reason, you liked them, and I didn't care to spoil things for you."

"They just did that for themselves."

"Remember the drive during the war to collect things for Russia—warm clothes, gloves, watches? Well, Ellen More was one of the collectors, and I handed over a Longines set with two little diamonds."

"And. . . ."

"When the war ended, I saw her wearing it."

You said nothing through a light-change, and at Sunset, you took a left turn and made for the Coldwater pass.

"I know what you're thinking, Jabe—that I should've spoken up before we went there."

"I sure as hell wouldn't've gone."

"That's what I figured—and you wouldn't've found them out for yourself."

"Christ, Mag, what *are* people, anyway?"

"You said it in one of your novels: People ain't such a much."

"A character said it."

"Whoever did, he knew what he was talking about."

"In the next book, I took it all back. I was in the Party, and Man looked good."

"You knew more when you were ignorant," she said. "By the way, what *does* La Cienega mean?"

"Swamp."

THE COLOR OF THE AIR, XIII

DIXIELAND—1918

THE BLACK AND THE BLUES

How then shall Pharaoh hear me, who am of uncircumcized lips?
—Exodus 6.12

They were stolen from the Portuguese, these people, or, if bought from some Bight of Benin chief, they were paid for in doorknobs worn as ornaments and pisspots used for hats, but, sold or crimped or simply sued from the beach, they were corded in a hold and sent to where that evening sun went down. They took nothing but themselves along, a skinful of black meat, not more than that, for no white weighed their sense of song. Some, though, it stayed through forty days in their own bilge, and one in every two lived to land. That was the beginning: ahead were three hundred years of the *Hat in Hand Blues* and the *Yessuh and Yessum Blues* and the *Beggarly Game Blues* and the *Blues for a Nigger on a Rope.*

And then came the Freedom War, and off went the Misters and the Masters to fight for their right to be pale snakes in dark grass, and fanfares played them down the one-way road. When found in some ditch or fished from a stream, they still had their Dixie cash, their Daguerreotypes, and their keys and knives and locks of hair, but, strange to say, no drum was ever seen, no wind-machine of wood or brass. Split, bent, and verdigreen, they were somewhere else and hidden, more highly prized than eyes, and soft on the air thereafter were the *Missy Screws for Vittles Blues* and the *Blues for Kike, Coon, and Pope* and the *Blues for the Blues* and that same old *Blues for a Nigger on a Rope.*

And now the courtly ones were gone, the better sort, the kind that wept when they let a nigger go: they were dead, without doubt, of the *Eeny Meeny Blues*. Back-door whites used the front door now, lesser lights than the nigger had been, counter-jumpers and mort-gagees, would-be gents and one-gutted all—these took the place of the cream of the cream, and another three centuries began, another coon's age, another blue moon to bend the knee. In cellars and similar caves, reeds quavered, drums were mauled, and the wind was wound with horns, and the sound was called the *Free When Hell Freezes Blues* and the *Never the Twain Blues* and the *Like it or Lump it Blues* and, as usual, those *Blues for a Nigger on a Rope*.

And now for street carnival they played, and for *carne vale* at the grave (O flesh, farewell!), and where the whores made hay, in Storyville, but they still weren't free, and it all went down the drain, down the brown river, it all flowed away with the New World trots—the *Blue Ointment Blues* and the *Blues for Junk and Booze* and the *Blues for that Created-equal Bunk* and of course the one about the nigger and the rope.

And then one day they wondered where that great spate came from, and someone said from Timbuktu, and someone said from the Dead Sea, and someone said from the God damn whites, and someone said let's go find out, and so they steamed a thousand miles and then a thousand more, and all they saw was the northern part of the south and a store of that rope, and they stopped looking for whatever it was they'd been after (who remembered any more?), and when some-one sighed out *Hope Deferred and Heartsick,* someone else said *Blues.*

SCENE 110

METRO CONFERENCE No. 1 (August 1951)

Thursday, August 9, 1951

The conference with Dore Schary took place in his office at MGM. . . .

For fifteen years, ever since the construction of the Thalberg Building, it had been the office of Louis Mayer. During her long employment by the Com-pany, Maggie had many times attended story-discussions there, but this was your first visit to the quarters, which embraced an entire wing of the third floor. The main room as you recall it was all of forty feet in length, carpeted with Orientals, and furnished with antiques and chairs and couches upholstered in leather. Your impression of whiteness may have arisen from an absence of impression: you have no memory of decoration on the walls. Behind a huge desk that seems now to have held nothing but a huge photograph* framed in silver, Louis Mayer's successor sat.

> *... We stated to Mr. Schary that the reason for our visit was to acquaint him with the fact that we had been served with subpoenas. The long relationship between the Studio and Miss Roberts seemed to call for the immediate communication of the information as a matter of honor, so that the Studio might take what action it saw fit. ...*

You'd known Schary in his screenwriting days, not well, but well enough to warrant the use of first names when you encountered each other at a gathering or as you passed in some public place. A quality you'd taken note of was his inability either to attract or repel, a lack of force, a neutrality. If a fire had ever burned in him, it had long since gone out, and what he'd faced the world with ever after was ash. He always recalled to you an old aversion of your father's: *Beware of the laugh with cold teeth,* he'd say; *beware of a man with a cold eye.* He'd've found no warmth in Dore.

SCHARY: Your motive in coming to me without delay is laudable. Not everyone would've been so scrupulous, Maggie. . . .

The pronunciation he affected was *Majjie.*

SCHARY: . . . But more important to the Company is the position you intend to take when you come before the Committee.

MAGGIE: We've given that some thought, but it's much too soon to say.

SANFORD: After all, Dore, our subpoenas are only one day old.

SCHARY: I was addressing Maggie.

SANFORD: When you address her, you address me. What do you take me for—her chauffeur?

MAGGIE: We're in this together. John speaks for both of us.

SCHARY: I only meant that I was addressing the studio employee. You're our sole concern.

SANFORD: And mine.

MAGGIE: I'm due before the Committee in a month's time. If the studio wishes it, I'll take a suspension without pay until then.

SCHARY: The offer does you credit, but I see no need for a suspension as of now. You've been working for Armand Deutsch, and I want you to continue—through the Hearings.

MAGGIE: I'll be glad to.

SCHARY: What I suggest now is that you confer with Eddie Mannix. He'll deal with the problem from this point on. . . .

---

* Of Schary's mother, you were told later by Maggie.

236

In your presence, he called Mannix, the executive vice-president of the Company, and arranged for an interview. On parting with you, he seemed to use his desk as a fortification, a work that immured him and thus prevented the shaking of hands. Had he supposed that you could bring yourself to make the proffer?, you wondered, and as you rose, your glance caught the photograph, and the word *impassive* (why *impassive?*) came to mind.

On your way to Mannix' office, in another wing of the third floor, you said, "Where does he get that *Majjie* stuff?"

"I detest it," she said, "but I can't very well tell him so."

"Anyone named Dore ought to be careful with names."

"One thing, Jabe. You got a little ruffled in there. That won't do us any good."

"He was down-the-nosing me. I won't take that."

"We don't need any quarrels. We've got fish to fry, so let's fry fish."

At 10:40 a.m. on the same day, we were shown in to Mr. Mannix, and our conversation with him lasted for approximately 25 minutes. . . .

Where Schary was precise, Mannix was rough-cut; where Schary was refined (meaning free from the coarse, the vulgar, the inelegant), Mannix was graceless, off-hand, hit-or-miss; and where Schary was nice (meaning affectedly fine, *délicat*), Mannix was a hard knot, a part of the populace, the riff and the general raff. Until then, Mannix had been a stranger to you, but you were no sooner before him than you seemed to hear your father saying *This one's all right, kid. Watch out for the other one.*

He stated that he had known of the subpoenas before being told by Mr. Schary and that he had arranged with the Marshal to have them served without publicity. . . .

MAGGIE: That was considerate, Mr. Mannix. We haven't told our families yet, and for them to read about it in the papers. . . .

MANNIX: Well, I was thinking about the Company too, you know.

MAGGIE: Even so.

MANNIX: The Marshal said he tried your place in Encino a couple times, but the gate was locked.

MAGGIE: I'm doing a script for Armand Deutsch that deals with thoroughbreds—breeding, racing, sales. We were in Kentucky getting some background.

SANFORD: And not knowing about the subpoenas, we also got some horses.

MANNIX: Not the kind of article you can take back.

MAGGIE: Like the subpoenas.

MANNIX: Dore, I guess, went into the matter of how you're going to testify.

MAGGIE: He did, but at this stage, as you can imagine, we're still in a spin.

MANNIX: My advice would be to get a lawyer.

MAGGIE: John's a lawyer, Mr. Mannix.

MANNIX: So I'm told, but it wouldn't be a good idea to be represented by your husband. Being he's involved.

SANFORD: Mr. Mannix has a point, Mag.

MANNIX: Also, it wouldn't be a good thing to use the studio lawyers. But I could send you to a law firm that I know, high class people, whenever you say the word.

SANFORD: That would still make it a studio connection, wouldn't it?

MANNIX: Somebody needs a lawyer, we recommend a lawyer. Where's the harm?

SANFORD: The studio would be tied to any course we followed, and we don't want that any more than you do. In coming to a decision, we have to be free to choose.

MANNIX: I'm not sure what you're trying to say.

SANFORD: Did you happen to watch the Hearings in Washington earlier in the year?

MANNIX: Around here, we all watched.

SANFORD: Then you must know what we're up against — something we wouldn't have to face if we were charged with murder. We have to prove we're innocent.

MAGGIE: The minute it gets out that we got subpoenas, every Tom, Dick and crazy-ike will think we're guilty.

MANNIX: So go downtown and tell them different. Tell them the truth.

SANFORD: The only truth these days is what Joe McCarthy says is the truth. He raves, and the people rave with him. You can't reason with that kind. Their heads are filled with you-know-what.

MANNIX: So what does it boil down to?

SANFORD: When we go before the Committee, we're going to take the position that affords us the most protection. The studio may not approve of that position.

MANNIX: What would it be, for instance?

SANFORD: We really haven't had time to decide, Mr. Mannix. We've hardly talked it over between ourselves.

MANNIX: Nobody's rushing you. But the *Company* might get rushed — you know, by the Legion, organizations like that — and we would have to know where you stand.

MAGGIE: You'll know as soon as we do.

MANNIX: Fair enough. So go on for now, working on what you're working on. . . .

§

From Culver City, you drove across Overland through Palms to reach one of the passes that led to the Valley. Before you for much of the way, the spine of the Santa Monicas lay in your line of sight, a thousand-foot ridge of brown and green.

"How do you feel, Mag?" you said.

"Wrung out—and this is only the beginning."

"I wish there was something I could do to make it easier."

"I know you do, Jabe, and I know you'd do it."

"That Schary—how tall do you suppose he is?"

"Six foot or thereabouts. Why?"

"He seems small."

"He is small."

"I hope we don't have to treat with him too often. Sooner or later, I'd tangle with him. I'd get to thinking about what he said to the Guild about The Ten: 'Throw 'em to the wolves, and the rest of you will be safe.' "

"Retaining a lawyer, then, makes good sense."

"You'd better understand this, though: we have no absolute right to counsel at the Hearing. He'll be there because the Committee allows him to be there. No witnesses will be called, so he can't cross-examine, and he can't object or interfere in any way."

"What rights *do* we have?" she said.

"Damn few. A Congressional committee has power, and against people like us, it's going to use it."

"What can it make us do?"

"Just about anything except testify against ourselves."

"How would we be doing that?"

"By giving answers that show we committed a crime."

"Crime! *What* crime!"

"The crime of being a Communist."

"There's no law against that!"

"Not yet. But if the Committee has its way, there will be—and that's the danger the Fifth Amendment protects us from. We can't be forced to tell whether we're Communists—in other words, they can't make us incriminate ourselves."

"Us and the hoods! Us and the Al Capones! What a disgrace!"

There was a silence then that lasted until you were in Sepulveda Pass, winding with it past chaparral and cactus on the sun-dried slopes and oaks and sycamores in the shade, and in the end, it was Maggie who broke it.

"I didn't mean that *we're* disgraced," she said. "I meant the country." And you said, "I know that, Mag."

Miss Roberts returned home and continued work on her current assignment, "The Girl Who Had Everything," a first-draft screenplay for Armand Deutsch, producer. . . .

Your housekeeper, Mrs. Christiansen, had a fifteen-year-old son named Karl (Don't try to pronounce it, Mr. Sanford—unless you're Danish.), and in the evenings, she would always go home. No presence less intrusive than hers was imaginable; still, it *was* a presence, and however little you were made to feel it, to that extent at least it restrained you. Once she'd left, though, the place became your domain again, a four-acre realm that you and Maggie were free to make use of as you pleased.

"Let's go and see the horses," she said.

You waded through a shallow of cats on the kitchen steps, and followed by the outdoor dogs, you walked the gravel roadway toward the barn. In the half-light, you could see a head outthrust from each stall, a trophy, it seemed, mounted on the wall—but they were trophies that spoke as you neared them, demanding the pellets you held in your hand. Satisfying them, you turned to find Maggie leaning against a paddock rail and gazing into the dim alleys of the grove beyond.

Into the cave of evening, she said, "From the first time we came here, I never wanted anything better. There could only be more, and for me more wasn't better. I had a job I was good at, and I could take care of everybody I loved. I had a decent house, dogs, horses, health. . . ," and there she stopped as though watching all those things take leave.

"I'm not on that list," you said.

"You? You're what made me enjoy the rest."

You kissed her, saying, "And what've I done but take the rest away?"

"It isn't your fault, Jabe. I keep telling you that."

"If you hadn't met me, you'd've had clear sailing all your life."

"And what would you have had?"

"Sometimes I think of that," you said. "I think: I didn't hear her footsteps in the Paramount hallway; we didn't meet through Joe March; we never met at all, and we didn't have these fifteen years. And do you know what always happens? I feel as if I've been trying to realize what Nothing means."

Friday, August 10, 1951

Miss Roberts continued work at home on the script of "The Girl Who Had Everything". . . .

"Mag," you said, "I think it'd be a good idea to keep some kind of record of these days. A record of events, talks, meetings, since we got the subpoenas."

"Why?"

"Without it, we'd never be able to remember where we were, what we said and to whom—that kind of thing."

"Is all that stuff important?"

"Who knows? It might turn out to be."

"All right, then, if you think it's worth the trouble."

"It won't take long to do—a couple of minutes a day—and under each report, we'll each sign our names."

Saturday, August 11, 1951

Worked on script of "Girl Who Had Everything". . . .

After both of you had initialed the entry, Maggie said, "This could be important, you told me. Just exactly why?"

"You were a secretary once. Did you take dictation or rely on your memory?"

"There's more to this than remembering, though, isn't there?"

"Yes."

"What?"

"You followed the Hiss case, everybody did, and you know he went to prison because he said one thing and Chambers another, and the jury believed Chambers. They believed Hiss knew him, they believed he passed classified information, they believed that bullshit about secret papers in a pumpkin. I don't know whether Hiss was a liar or not, but at best he had one damn bad memory. That's not going to be the case with us."

"This is beginning to sound dire."

"I don't mean to frighten you, but we've been informed against by some bastard we used to trust—*still* trust, maybe—and I intend to be sure of our sayings and doings between now and the Hearings."

Sunday, August 12, 1951

Worked on script of "Girl Who Had Everything." Finished first rough draft during afternoon. . . .

"About Congressional hearings," Maggie said. "Have you ever gone to one of them?"

"No," you said, "but they came up in a course or two at Law School, and also I've read about them. There was a hearing after the Teapot Dome thing, the Chivington Massacre, the Brownsville Affray—there've been dozens."

"You come from a family of lawyers. The law doesn't feaze you; you're at home with it. But *my* family—none of us has ever been in a courtroom, and I'm the only one who's been sued. The law terrifies them. It terrifies *me*."

"I'd be stupid if I said there's nothing to be scared of—even Alger Hiss knows better. But the truth is always a hell of a good defense—if you can prove it. . . . Who sued you?"

" 'Way back, when I was a reader at Fox-Hills, another girl and I wrote an original screenplay and sold it to the Studio. After the picture was made— "Sailor's Luck," it was called—somebody claimed we'd swiped his idea and sued Fox for a million dollars and named us as co-defendants. I was fool enough to mention it to my Mama, and she said, 'But, Great Sakes, Marg, how will you ever pay?' "

You laughed, saying, "How *did* you pay?"

"The guy never showed up for the trial."

Monday, August 13, 1951

Looked over material on "Girl Who Had Everything," then delivered same to Miss Farrell* at the Studio. Left note for Armand Deutsch informing him of progress and telling him I was at his disposal. Came home to await his call. . . .

You were in your room and at your desk, but you weren't writing, nor had you written for several days. What you *were* doing, though, is now hard to say. You may have been studying a jar of pencils, trays of clips and rubberbands, the Geodetic Survey maps you'd used to paper the walls; or you may have been simply sitting there, void of thought, within sight of many things and yet seeing not a one; or were you listening for what you finally heard— Maggie in the hallway and coming toward the door?

"It isn't only the legal part of this that upsets me," she said. "For the first time in my life, I'm being discriminated against. I thought I knew how Jews felt, Negroes, Mexicans, but I see now that I never really got inside their skin."

Juno had trailed her from the bedroom, and after fixing the location of your chairs, she retired to her cushion of cedar shavings on the floor.

---

* Head of the Stenographic Dept.

"Where I was born—Clarks, Nebraska—there was only one black man. Everybody called him Nigger Bob, but not out of prejudice; it was just their way of indicating the Bob they had in mind. And there was one Jewish family, the Bordys, but you wouldn't've known it if you saw them at the oyster-bar in my sister Pearl's café. And no one was rich in that town, and no one really poor, and I didn't see hate till a long while later, and even then it wasn't aimed at me. My brother-in-law Tom Schank is a Catholic, and when he moved to Kersey, over in Colorado, a bunch of country cut-ups burned a cross on his lawn. When I heard about it, I was angry, but what could my anger have been compared to his? . . . And now I'm where he was, where you are, and it's a hard thing to bear, the suspicion, the cold stare, the feeling you get that you don't belong."

Tuesday, August 14, 1951

Reported to Armand Deutsch at MGM. Conferred for one hour, at which time he said I could work at home if I wished. I did so wish and arranged to call him when I had the first ten pages revised. . . .

Through the grove, a pathway shaded by carobs ran, and sometimes you and Maggie would walk there, stepping with care among the pods, leather-brown and curving, that had fallen to the ground. These were a favored food of squirrels, many of whom lost their lives to cats when they ventured from the trees. You remembered seeing one escape once, but with some nerve fiber torn, only to bound crazylegged away and die a little closer to the sky.

"You spoke of truth being the best defense," Maggie said. "What could the Committee ask that a person would lie about?"

"The big question," you said, "the one they ask every damn time: *Are you now or have you ever been a Communist?*"

"I could answer part of that without lying. *I am not now,* I could say."

"They wouldn't let you stop there. They'd try to get you to say *I've never been,* and if you ever did, you'd wind up with Alger Hiss."

"What would happen if a witness—you, for instance—came right out and said *I have nothing to hide: I'm a Communist?*"

"They'd say *Fine. Now tell us the name of every Communist you know.*"

"Suppose you refused. Suppose you said *I'm willing to tell you anything you like about myself, but nothing doing about anyone else.* Could they make you talk?"

"No, but they'd sure as hell lock me up."

"I don't see why. You answered their big question."

"The law says I don't even have to tell them my age. If I want to be sullen, I can sit there with my trap shut. That's the protection I get from the Fifth Amendment. But once I admit I'm a Communist, I lose that protection, and I have to cough up those names—or pay the penalty."

"They don't give us much room, do they? Hardly enough to breathe."

There were evenings when you'd go for a drive, and with Juno as always on the seat between you, you'd cruise the back roads of the Valley through the syrup air of citrus groves. Where you went, you'd pass few cars, and often the only sound you'd hear was the piston-pound of your motor.

"Sooner or later," you said, "the folks will have to be told."

"I can't ever tell Mama," Maggie said, "and that worries me. There's a neighbor cattycorner across the street who dotes on scandal, and if she spots my name in the papers, she'll rush over with the news."

"All the more reason to tell your sisters. One of them is always there to stave her off, and most of the time it's Pearl and Midge both."

"You don't know this hank of hair. She's a dumpy little slob, and she runs off at the mouth. God, if she ever lets on to Mama about this, she'll wish she hadn't. I'll snatch her bald!"

"I never knew you to be so fierce."

"Only about my family. Nobody can hurt my family. You're good to them; you guard them like your own. . . . But what about the Governor? How do you think he'll take it?"

"He'll grieve for us," you said, "the way he did for a client in trouble. I always admired him for that; he didn't practice law for the fees."

"Would you want me to be there when you break it?"

"I'll do it myself. You'll be there even if you're away."

Wednesday, August 15, 1951

In afternoon, delivered to Milton Beecher's office an itemized account of expenses on trip to Lexington made for Studio, this following instructions of Kenneth McKenna to John Sanford. . . .

You found your father at the Ontra, the cafeteria where, for his knowledge of the law (for his sense of right, really), he was regarded by a group of *older-ly* men as their intervener, their referee. On this day, however, they'd not yet come, or else they'd come and gone, and he sat alone near a window, gazing through it at things he clearly saw though none of them was there. He turned as you touched his shoulder, and, joyful at the sight of you, he tried to kiss your hand.

"None of that," you said. "The son kisses the father's hand, not the other way around."

"Sit, kid," he said, "and tell me what brings you to town."

"The Studio wanted an expense-report on the Lexington trip, and I stopped here to make believe I care about you."

"Maggie didn't come along?"

There could've been only the briefest pause, but however short, it was enough for him to note it. In all your years, not often had you sought to fob him off, to mislead him with specious words, with the answer in avoidance, but whenever you did, you'd failed. He was undeceived now.

"What's on your mind?" he said.

"Maggie and I are in trouble."

"With each other?"

"Never that," you said. "Political trouble."

He shook his head a little and again looked away at some invisible commotion in the street, a parade, a part of history being replayed outside.

"I've been afraid of that, Julian," he said. "I've been afraid for a long time."

"The House Committee will be sitting in L.A. a couple of weeks from now. We've both been subpoenaed."

"Did you inform Metro?"

"The next day. But they knew about it before we did and arranged for the papers to be served without fanfare."

"That's less good than it sounds. It means Metro and the Committee are hand-in-glove."

"That didn't occur to me. I took it to be a favor to the Company."

"You're not much of a schemer, kid."

"You didn't teach me to be."

"I was never out to teach you anything. I didn't think I had the right to lay out your life for you. You've pretty much done as you pleased, and you seem to be a happy man."

"At the moment, unhappy. My politics have injured Maggie."

"Aren't they hers?"

"Not any more. Not for years."

"But they were once?"

"Yes. But she got involved only because she thought she was pleasing me."

"Why didn't you stop her?"

"She says I couldn't've stopped her."

"Did you try?"

"No."

"And she feels no resentment?"

"No."

"How does Metro feel?"

"They didn't commit themselves. They're waiting to see how she testifies."

"And how will she testify?"

"I tell you what we told them: We haven't made up our minds. We also said we might have to take a stand they wouldn't approve of."

"What were you doing—baiting them?"

"Not at all. But we're in a tight spot, and it's only right to let them know we mean to get out of it in the way that's best for us."

"Do you talk over these moves with Maggie?"

"All of them."

"And how did Metro respond to that one?"

"They just listened. But they value Maggie, and I get the feeling they'd like to split us."

Once more he watched the passing show that only he could see through the window, and you waited, wondering what part of the past he was bringing to life, but you could not intrude, you could not ask.

"Julian," he said, "you're nearly fifty, and though I still call you kid and always will, you're a kid no more. You've done things I'd never do, but that doesn't make me better or you worse. You're what you were at the start, someone with a mind of his own, and it's gotten you where you find yourself right now. This'll sound strange, kid, because I took a different road and got to the same place. I'm with you."

Thursday, August 16, 1951

Worked on revisions. During afternoon Deutsch telephoned to tell me that he liked the ending of the script (which he had read and re-read) a great deal. . . .

Informing Maggie's sisters of the fix you both were in was a very different thing from informing your father, and the two of you knew it. His vast legal experience had made him judicious rather than judicial, one who would not rush to judgment but seek to understand. Not nearly so broad were the sisters' horizons. Upcountry still and innocent, they were largely unaware of what lay beyond the hill, and being instinctively patriotic, they'd miss the drift of the Hearings toward patriotism compelled. They were like almost everyone they'd ever known, unsatisfied but acceptant, needful often but never beggarly, and now and then sour but seldom all day long: they were American, unrebellious though their heritage had been dissent. They would *not* understand. Even so, Maggie sent you to see them at her mother's while she remained at home. . . .

"When I got there," you said on returning, "the girls were gussying up your Mama. She was in her wheel chair, smoking her corncob, and by gollies, she made no attempt to hide it. After fifteen years, I figured I must be in the family. . . ."

"You've always been in the family," Maggie said.

". . . So I said, 'Mama, how about if I change my name to Smith?' You know what she said? 'I declare, you change your name more than you do your shirt.' The girls laughed."

246

"I wish they could get her to walking. They've tried and tried, but she simply won't. She's afraid the hip will break again. . . . Well, how did it go with Pearl Arizona and Bijou Arissa?"

"I waited till they'd put Mama down for her afternoon nap, and then I took them to the back bedroom, your old room, and said I had something important to say, something that spelled trouble for us, but I didn't want them to worry, because we'd come out of it with bruises, maybe, but no broken bones. Pearl said, 'Stop beating around the bush, John. We're grown people.' "

"That Pearl," Maggie said. "She likes things barefoot."

" 'You've probably been reading about the House Committee,' I said. 'Used to be the Dies Committee, and what it does is snoop into your political beliefs, especially if it thinks they're Communist beliefs. It stages hearings with cameras and the press all over the place, and it puts on a big show to prove that Communists are just about ready to take over the country.' Pearl said, 'Well, they took over Russia.' "

"What about Midge?" Maggie said. "What did she put in?"

"Only that Ed used to hear the carpenters talking on the sets at Republic, at Warners', but not after he was made foreman."

"I wish we could've kept all this a secret. I wish we could've left our families out of it."

" 'The thing to remember,' I said to the girls, 'is that this is a free country. We can have any religion or no religion, we can go where we please, and we can think as we please. This isn't Japan, where they used to jail people for *dangerous thoughts*. . . .' "

"That might've been a little hard to follow," Maggie said.

"Guess again. Little Pearlie Arizona said, 'Isn't Communism a dangerous thought?' "

Maggie laughed, saying, "How did you answer?"

"I said, 'Not in this country. There's no law that makes Communism a crime,' and she said, 'What're you fixing to tell us, John—that you and Marg are Communists. . . ?' "

THE COLOR OF THE AIR, XIV

LOUIS SULLIVAN, MASTER BUILDER — 1924
A LOYAL LITTLE HENNA-HAIRED MILLINER

A democracy should not let its dreamers perish.
— Louis Sullivan

Not much is known about the woman: the few who knew her drew
the shade, and what remains of her is hardly more than those three
of Frank Lloyd Wright's adjectives and a noun that ticks off her trade.
Loyal, little, and henna-haired was the way he described her, and
in some loft in the Loop, she made toques of satin and picture-hats
with plumes. When free, she'd come to stay with Sullivan, and she'd
sit out the day in his stale suite at the Warner, or she'd steady his
frailty as they traipsed the street. They'd do no harm to his aneurysm,
she supposed, those strolls to the corner on Cottage Grove or across
Thirty-third to the beach — how could they, when he merely inched
his way and stopped each yard for breath?

Enlargement of the heart would be his death, the doctor said, but
some die without dissolution, and Sullivan was already dead. He'd
died at the Fair of '93, and what killed him there was all those Par-
thenons for belly-dancers, all the dollar-billed shrines. The Midway
had been a-throng with plaster temples, Doric and democratic, and
when the dreamer stood among them, though his ticker kept on running, he no longer cared about time.

So they slowpoked around, he and the little milliner, or they sat
and spoke, or she poured him a drink, or she received his gray desire,
but often they moved not at all except in the mind, she to some
parade of fashion, he to the prairie city lined up at the foot of the
sky. In fancy once, he may have seen his Getty tomb (a requiem,
Wright had called it), and once the tower he'd built on Congress,
the corbeled and machicolated tower, and with it may have come
his partner's peculiar name — *Dankmar,* he may have thought on one
of those days. *Bitter thanks,* it meant, and he may have said it to his
loyal little henna-haired milliner — *Dankmar* — just before he closed his
eyes.

SCENE 111

A WOMAN WITH A COLD EYE (August 1951)

Friday, August 17, 1951

Deutsch called shortly before one. He was most agreeable and we made an appointment for 10 o'clock Monday morning, at which time I would deliver the first thirty pages of revisions. . . .

In the evening, you and Maggie drove through Beverly Glen on your way to the home of Francis Eaton in Bel Air. He was a Los Angeles attorney who'd been recommended to you by more than one of those from whom you'd sought advice. His name was not unfamiliar, for it had frequently appeared in connection with progressive causes, but he was not, so far as you knew, in the Left Wing himself. Though you'd never met him, nor had you ever watched his work in a courtroom, you'd heard that he was plain-spoken, persuasive, and always well-prepared. You could go further, you thought, and fare worse.

Looking out into the cool darkness of the twisting canyon, Maggie said, "Did I ever tell you that I know his wife? Sarah, her name is, and she writes."

"Writes what?" you said.

"She was on the Metro lot one day last year—she'd gotten a pass somehow—and she came to my room to show me a story she had."

"Why show you? Why not the Story Department?"

"She said a friend had steered her, and I guess she took me to be one of Metro's stable of junior writers."

"You should've set her straight."

"Spread my feathers? Not me. I let her go on—one novice to another—and I promised to read the story and let her know what I thought of it. And here's the odd part—it wasn't bad. Light but amusing. I took it to my producer, Steve Ames, and told him it had possibilities."

"Mag," you said, "you're a one."

"It was the right thing to do."

"As Dan would've said, you never done a wrong thing."

"Anyway, Ames read the story and agreed with me, but it wasn't the sort of thing he cared to do, he said. Trivial, he called it, but I left that out when I sent the story back."

"What did she say?"

"I never heard from her."

The Eaton house was a long way into Stone Canyon from the Bel Air gate and high above the campus of the university and the lights of Westwood roundabout. In the driveway, your lamps picked out a hillside of buggy-whip cactus and agave, against which a pillared Colonial reared as from a bank in the Tidewater. Received by both of the Eatons, you were shown to the library, where the conference began when you produced the subpoenas and handed them to the attorney.

"We'd like you to represent us at the Hearing," you said.
"I can understand why you preferred to meet at my home."
"Metro has kept things quiet so far, and we have too."
Eaton put a few preliminary questions to you, noting your replies on a tablet lying before him—your names, your ages, your places of birth—and then he said, "I always feel uncomfortable about this, but in order to fix a fee, I'll have to know your earnings."
"I'm a novelist," you said, "and I make nothing. Maggie is a screenwriter and her salary is twenty-five hundred a week."
Staring, Sarah Eaton spoke for the first time. "Twenty-five hundred a week!" she said.
Maggie turned to look at her—or, rather, to look in her direction, for, seeming to see nothing, she soon turned away.
"Twenty-five hundred a week! Well, you'll never make that kind of money again in this town. . . !"
And there the conference, just begun, ended.

As you headed down the canyon toward the gate, Maggie said, "We must have them to dinner some evening."

SCENE 112

A NOTE ON RETAINING COUNSEL (August 1951)

After your experience with the Eatons, you were inclined to put aside the suggestion of Eddie Mannix and appear for Maggie yourself. She persuaded you, though, to make another try, this time with a Sidney Cohn, a New York attorney who'd represented a witness at a recent sitting of the Committee and who was therefore no stranger to its procedure.

Having been told where you might reach him, you telephoned to acquaint him with the state of things and to propose that he put in an appearance for you and Maggie.
"When's the Hearing set for?" he said.

"September 6th."

"The 6th," he said, and you tried to see, through three thousand miles of your mind, a calendar, a diary, a newspaper dateline, and he said, "That's a Thursday. I can make it," and then he paused, as if to arrive at a number that went with you.

"I'm a lawyer myself," you said. "I know the agony of fixing a fee."

What did he look like?, you wondered, what expression did he wear, what clothes, what manner, and what was the color of his eyes and hair?

"Let's see, now," he said. "To be there for the 6th, I'd have to leave here on the 4th, and I couldn't leave *there* till the 7th, a Friday. That would kill the week."

"What do you charge for killing a week?"

"I'd have to get twenty thousand."

"In that case," you said, "let *me* counsel *you*: stay in New York."

"What figure are you thinking of?"

"What a week is worth to my wife — twenty-five hundred."

"I'd take that."

"Why did you ask for twenty thousand, then?"

"Oh, I don't know. You might've paid it."

And now you *could* see him, quite as plainly as if he were there in the room.

SCENE 113

SUNDAY, AUGUST 19, 1951

"Maggie and I have some news for you," you said.

It was to your sister Ruth that you'd spoken. She'd come out from Hollywood to spend the day, and the three of you were reclining in chairs on the flagstone deck of the pool. In the pink shade of each of these, a sprawled dog lay. It was a still day, but now and then a sigh of air would skim the water and fly away.

"You're too late," Ruth said. "The Governor told me."

"We hated to upset him," Maggie said, "but there was no way out of it."

"How's he taking it?" you said.

"Well, you know how he is," Ruth said. "What happens to the family happens to him."

"It could also happen to you."

"To me?"

251

"You teach in the L.A. School System. It may not like your connection with us."

"You're my brother. That's the only connection."

"But a pretty damn close one. My politics could rub off on you. The phrase for it is 'Guilt by association.' "

"That would be the unfairest thing."

"We're talking about Communism, Ruth—the Devil of the day. Forget fairness."

"I can't go around denying that you're my brother."

"I hope not. Just don't go around claiming that I *am*."

"Or that I'm your sister-in-law," Maggie said.

"Does that mean I ought to stay away from here?"

"Yes," you said. "At least until after the Hearings."

"A fine how-do-you-do," Ruth said.

You glanced around your four-acre empire of citrus and walnut, broken here and there by a flowering plum, a stone pine, a pear, and below the hemline of the trees, you could see Barred Rocks in the henyard, and in one of the paddocks, a mare dozed with her foal, and distant sound came through the stillness, the stamping of a hoof, a humming from the hives—and now, you thought, all had been invaded, and it was being overrun.

"Indeed it is," you said. "A fine how-do-you-do."

SCENE 114

DAY OF REST (August 19, 1951)

Morning

The foal in the paddock, a bay filly by Radiotherapy* out of September Child, was registered with the Jockey Club as Thirty Days. She was three months old now and taking on size, but always you seemed to be seeing through her to the small-scale thing she'd been on her first day alive. The mare had dropped her during the night, and you found her at side and sucking when you opened the stall in the morning. For an instant, you'd had the illusion of viewing the same object at different ranges, one close and the other long.

---

* An imported stallion belonging to the Merryman Farm of Ann and Tom Peppers.

"I just stood there, gaping," you said. "I thought I was seeing double."

Maggie, with her arms on the paddock gate, was watching the foal move, head down to lip at leaves left from a flake of alfalfa. "She's a pretty one," she said.

"And you gave her a pretty name: Thirty Days hath September Child. The next one ought to be September Morn."

Still looking away from you, she said, "If there *is* a next one."

In profile, she showed nothing, but you said, "You're sure, then, that your career is over."

"Aren't you?" And then, as if she knew the answer you'd give, she said, "You're wishful, Jabe. It's never dark for you; it's always day."

"My father would say, 'That's not a bad way to be.' "

"Most of the time, no. It's right to think the sun is shining—when it is. But when it isn't. . . ." She put a hand out to touch you and went on speaking. "You're many things to me, many *good* things, but you're the kind that only sees what you want to be there."

"What am I missing?"

With her free hand, she waved at the horses, the grounds, the house half-hidden by the trees, and she said, "This is our home. But did it ever occur to you that I had another?"

"Metro?"

"Metro."

"I didn't realize you thought of it that way."

"I'm not sure I did, either, not till that Marshal came. It was strange, but at first I felt nothing, as if I'd just been saved from some accident. I wasn't numb for long, though. I soon knew that I hadn't avoided the accident; I was having it."

"You're in no danger, Mag."

"No physical danger, no legal danger, but there's another kind—the one that's in the mind. Metro's going to show me the door, Jabe, and when it does, I know how I'll feel—as if my own family had thrown me out."

The mare had idled across the paddock to try you for a handout, and the little filly had tagged along. She let you stroke her muzzle, a thing of the finest silk, and then she let you wool her ear.

"You've had dealings with Metro," Maggie said. "You've seen how they treat me when it comes to money, but money's only a part of it, and maybe the smaller part. It's the way I'm treated personally that I prize, the way they act when I'm called to their offices for a conference or when they pass me in the hall. I'm welcome in the Thalberg Building. Room 243 is mine. It's been mine for a dozen years. It's the one room I could've furnished with more than my pair of figurines."

"They're not going to kick you out. They'd have a battle over it."

"You're going to fight Metro?"

"You have a contract with them."

"My David," she said. "What was it the Governor would say when you were outrageous?"

" 'Julian! Julian!' "

She nodded, saying, "That's it. . . ."

Afternoon

The grape arbor was on an arc of the turnaround at the rear of the house, and under a roof of vines stood a redwood bench. Within reach as you sat there, Concords hung in livid clusters among silver leaves, and the sun cast their patterns at your feet. Here was the precinct of the cats, and all four were somewhere near, three in a shallow of sleep and the other grooming itself in slow motion.

"This New York lawyer," you said. "When he gets here, we'll have to tell him the stand we mean to take before the Committee."

"I thought *he* was supposed to advise *us*."

"I don't know this guy, but he could be Daniel Webster, and he still couldn't make our decisions. We do that ourselves."

"What do we need him for, then?"

"To keep an eye out for the legal rocks. To see that we don't run aground."

"We told Eddie Mannix that Metro mightn't approve the position we took at the Hearings, but between you and me, we've never said what positions there are."

"I can lay out several, but you won't be satisfied with any of them."

"We can't wait much longer. We've got to hit on something."

You hefted a nearby bunch of grapes, purple-black, like a contusion. You tore one loose and rubbed its skin free of dust, and then it had depth, and it shone.

"I hope I won't sound like a lawyer," you said, "but then, why the hell not? I *am* a lawyer, and we might as well get some good out of it. If I say some things you know, it'll be because I want to be *sure* that you know."

You gazed at the dark little globe you were holding, and you thought of its sweet fluid and its citric center. You'd never swallowed the whole of a Concord, only the skin and the fluid; the pulp you'd spat away.

"When they call us to testify," you said, "we'll be sworn. After that, whatever we tell the Committee must be the truth. If it isn't, we can be indicted for perjury, and if we're convicted, which we surely would be, we'll sit in some clink for years. So, once you're on the stand, the truth. Is that clear?"

"Of course."

"All right. Now, the first choice we have is to go before the Committee and spill the beans. To fink."

You held the grape to a shaft of light, as if it were a gemstone, an amethyst, and you hoped you might see inside.

"That's unthinkable!" Maggie said.

"It was thinkable to the bastards who turned us in."

"Are we bastards?"

"We don't know yet. We have to think about the unthinkable. The bastards have jobs. They're respectable. They're washed clean and saved."

"Saved! What kind of person would sink someone to save himself?"

"I thought you were the realist here. *Any* kind of person, if it meant saving himself instead of you. . . . I met an English publisher once. He always came over on a French ship, he said: 'Lashings of caviar, and women and children last.' "

"It would be a bad way to live, knowing what I'd done. There wouldn't be a soul I could face. I couldn't even face myself."

"You owe something to your dependents—your mother, my father, your husband. You owe to Metro and to your country right or wrong."

"I also owe to me. I owe a decent life, and I can't have that by being indecent."

"I had to ask," you said. "I had to find out."

"You knew *without* asking."

"No one knows till he answers. We're talking about choices, and finking is certainly one of them, whether we pick it or not. There's nothing wrong with bringing it out and poking it around. We might find we're not above it after all. We'll never know unless it's there, and we deliberately pick against it. So—are we above it or below?"

"Above, damn it," she said. "Give me some other choices."

"One of them was used by the Hollywood Ten. When they were asked about their political affiliation, they refused to answer—or evaded answering—on the ground that the question violated their Constitutional rights."

"Rights such as. . . ?"

"Freedom of religion, freedom of speech, freedom of the press—the whole First Amendment. But there's no specific guarantee of *political* freedom. At best, it's only implied. It's thin ice, and it wouldn't hold them. It won't hold us, either, and we'll go to prison just as they did."

"I'm not honing for that," she said. "What else is there?"

"We can avail ourselves of the Fifth Amendment—or, as the Committee would say, we can hide behind it. When we're questioned, we give our names, and that's all. Anything further is making us testify against ourselves. We have no Star Chamber here—not yet, anyway."

"We touched on this the other day."

"I'm touching on it again. You may not like it, lining up with thugs, thieves, and Wall Street finaglers, but once you say *I decline to answer on the ground that I might degrade or incriminate myself,* you're in the clear."

"In the clear!" she said. "After smearing myself with, excuse me, shit!"

"If you don't do it, they'll do it for you. The purpose of the Committee, the only purpose, is to leave people smeared. There's no law making Communism a crime, and the Committee is never going to propose one, because it knows full well that the courts would strike it down. But to the bonehead public, it *is* a crime, and that's enough for Chairman John S. Woods. He asks his patriotic questions, and one way or another, we're covered with shit."

"My God, how can people be criminals if they've never broken the law!"

"You'll find out on September 6th."

You considered the evening-colored ball between your thumb and forefinger. Pressed, you thought, it would extrude a translucent sac, a pale green caul containing a pair of seeds or three, but you did not press it.

"I'm thinking of something you said the other day," you said. "It stuck in my mind."

And she said, "What was that?"

"You said you'd have no trouble answering part of their question: *Are you now or have you ever been?* You said, 'I can honestly say I am not now.' "

"But you said they wouldn't let me stop there."

"That's right. But you'd have something in the record that you'd like to see there: that you're not a Communist."

"Not *now.*"

"Don't worry about that. As of the moment you testify, you're able to say you're not a Communist, and no one can challenge that, not even the son-of-a-bitch who squealed on you."

"Suppose they ask me what I was last year, last month, last week."

"That's where you draw the line, even if they ask what you were when you got up that morning."

"I'm beginning to like it," Maggie said. "I feel comfortable with it."

"You can feel safe too. It won't break out from under you."

"I'd not have to lie. I'd be making the point that I'm not a Communist, which'll sit well with Metro. And the Fifth would stop them from asking me for names. I definitely like it, Jabe."

"Let's try it out," you said. " 'Miss Roberts, I remind you that you're under oath. Are you now or have you ever been a Communist?' "

" 'I am not now, Mr. Chairman.' "

" 'Of course, but what were you yesterday?' "

" 'I decline to answer, and so forth.' "

" 'What were you five minutes ago?' "

" 'I decline.' "

"You've got it, Mag."

"And I like it!" she said.

"One thing more," you said. "Forget the word *now*. Your answer will be: 'I am not a Communist. . . .' "

Why, you wonder, can't you recall what you did with the grape? Did you eat it whole for once or in part as before, or did you throw it away?

Evening

Maggie and you were seated on one of the two small couches in the livingroom, and between you old Juno had managed to insert herself for a spell of sleep. Something in the Spanish idiom swayed through the hallway from the record-player—the last of Ibert's *Escales,* was it, or a dance from *The Three-Cornered Hat?*

"This *I-am-not* thing," Maggie. "Did you work it out yourself?"
And you said, "It started with you."*
"Well, wherever it came from, it seems to sit better all the time."
You glanced down at the beloved black and tan lying beside you, and you thought *daughter of Lionheart Coldsteel out of Ginger of Royal Irish,* and then you said, "Runt of the litter, are you now or have you ever been an Airedale?"

SCENE 117

A STAINED-GLASS WINDOW (August–September 1951)

Monday, August 20, 1951

Went to studio. Returned portable typewriter to office of August Spadafore. Kept appointment with Deutsch and turned over first thirty pages to him. Discussed next scene and then came home to work on it. . . .

You'd watch her sometimes, but only when she hadn't seen you or known that you were near. She was able to work anywhere, at a desk, of course, but just as well, just as intensely, while propped against a porch-post or folded in a chair. You'd stand somewhere, watching her pencil cross and cross and cross a page, and you'd see, as though you were right behind her, the speeches it was making, the kind of shot, the points of view. When thought flowed fast, she'd catch it with the Gregg she'd brought from Greeley, and when the

---

* So far as you can learn, Maggie's was the first use of this defense. Later used widely, it became known as the Diminished Fifth.

run slowed, she'd slow too, go back to a longhand unchanged since first you'd known her. It was artless still, it was the original formation, without flourish and unadorned. In anything she'd written—a letter, a memorandum, a signature, even a shopping-list—there was a reading of her nature: what she was resided in those tracings, all meant for revealing and not a one for show.

Worked on script, revised, conferred—day by day, the record grew, and as the date of the Hearings came on, all the more did you wonder at her ability to put it from her mind, *worked, revised, conferred,* as though time were standing still. But it wasn't, and you knew it, and she knew it too.

§

Tuesday, August 21, 1951

Finished revisions up to page 40. Telephoned Deutsch to so report and made appointment for Wednesday morning. . . .

The two fillies you'd bought in Kentucky came off the train that morning at the Inglewood freight-station, where they were met by a van from the Merryman Farm and by Willis Reavis, the farm manager. They'd shipped well from Lexington, but after days in a car-stall, they needed walking before being vanned to Riverside. You watched Willis and his driver lead them round and round an oval, watering them often but always briefly along the way. It took half an hour to leg them, after which they were ragged off, and they stood before you gleaming as they stirred in the sunlight.

"Nice stuff, John," Willis said.

He rode with the fillies in the van, and you followed in your car. It was a two-hour run to the farm.

§

Wednesday, August 22, 1951

Kept appointment with Deutsch. Went over first 28 pages and turned over to Script Department for mimeographing. . . .

You'd driven Maggie to Culver City for the meeting, and after seeing her to Deutsch's office, you went to her room at the other end of the hall. There you busied yourself. . . . Busied? At what, if true, and if not, how indeed did you pass the time, or did you sit there doing nothing and let time pass you? Did you stare at her only possessions, the pair of dancer figurines? Did you open a drawer on a box of Parliaments, gold and gray and holding sixteen cigarettes? Did you count her pencils too, her paper-clips and rubber bands? Did you find a handkerchief, a rolled ribbon, a single glove that seemed still to hold her hand? Did you make one more try at aligning the Manet, did you touch her hooded Royal as if you were saying goodbye. . . ?

When the noon hour came, you thought of the huge cream-colored commissary, of the hum of two hundred voices, the knocking of crockery, the silver tongue of silver plate, and you left the room and went there, and, entering, you inhaled the exhalations of the food. On your way to a table, you saw Bill Latham, the agent who once had tried to persuade you to dispose of Maggie's horses. You were about to pass him when he spoke.

"They say you got a ticket to the Hearings," he said.
"Who are *they?*"
"Jack Langmore, for one."
"Langmore a client of yours?"
"When I can place him."
"He talks a lot. It's a shame he has no talent."
"But is it true, what I hear?"
"Why're you so interested?"
"A Party matter is a Party matter."
"It's true," you said, "and *you* talk a lot too," and you moved on.

Seated at another table, you gave your order to a waitress and then leaned back to take in the roundabout to-do, the sound and motion in the savory air. High-held trays sailed by, trailing well-nigh visible streamers of flavor, and amid the comings and goings, your eye recorded Latham as he went.

"Who was that guy?" someone said.
Looking up, you saw beside you the writer Howard Emmett Rogers, and you thought *one of those three-name names that Pep used to jeer at,* and you said, "What guy?"
"The one you stopped to talk to."
"Oh. He's an agent. Name of Bill Latham."
"I thought so."
"Then why did you ask?"
"I wanted to make sure."

Rogers returned then to his table, the long one that crossed almost the entire width of the room. There perched only the rare birds of the studio — the producers, the directors, the Gables and Tracys, the migratory playwright dropping down for a feast. Rogers was none of these. In fact, he was a journeyman at best, a jay among the songsters, but for reasons unknown to you, he was suffered all the same. You watched him resume his place, and you watched too as he privily related—what?, you wondered, what he'd just now learned from you? And you wondered further—why had he wanted to know?—and, rising, you went to his table, where suddenly his story broke off, and he and his listeners turned their attention to you.

Rogers said, "What's on your mind, Sanford?"
"Why did you ask me about Latham?"
"I told you—to make sure."
"Of what?"
"That Reds infest this lot."
"How is that your business?"
"It's every American's business," he said, and taking out a pocket notebook, he slapped it, saying, "I've got him right here, in my little black book!"
"You can take your little black book and shove it up your lily-white ass."
"I've got you in here too, Sanford. You're in trouble."
"In that case, so are you."
"What kind of trouble can *you* make for *me*?"
And you said, "Physical trouble, you son-of-a-bitch."

No one spoke, and you walked away.

§

Thursday, August 23, 1951

Deutsch telephoned to express excitement about story as it is developing. Told Deutsch would have pages 29–40 ready by late afternoon. He said to bring stuff in Friday morning. . . .

You went out of doors to watch the tractor-man crisscross the grove with his disc. He was being followed through the rows by his five-year-old boy, who stopped here and there to stoop for a leaf, a stone, a fallen walnut, nothing at all. Jo-jo, one of your Airedales, was out there too, tracking down the source of a scent, and after a long slow meander, he found it on the little boy's leg. Cocking one of his own, he pissed his singularity on a shoe and stocking, and then he turned to other things.

At the rear of the house, under the Placentia that shaded the turnaround, Jo-jo's sister Minnie lay dozing in the gravel. Using her as a cushion, a cat slept on the sleeping dog.

§

Friday, August 24, 1951

Turned in pages 20–40. Deutsch okayed. Further discussion Monday August 27. . . .

Elias Story was a labor organizer for the Screen Office Employees Guild. His lines and yours, therefore, had seldom lain together, but whenever you did meet, he pleased you with his radiant nature. A slight man, gaunt, insubstantial, still he gave off a glow as from a spirit ignited once and for all. Frail, restrained, unimposing, he had more force than the clamorous who flailed. Contriving to pass the medical examination, he'd fought in Spain with the Abraham Lincoln Brigade, and though he'd survived its defeats, yet another awaited his return to the States: an affection of the heart, caused by exhaustion and exposure, that would kill him years before the Hearings.

His best friend, a writer named Henry Sampson, was also known to you. In your files, two of his letters remain, along with copies of your replies:

Dear Sanfords—
Happy Holidays!*—and let's hope for a less ironic year. I'm almighty tired of it. Hope to do something drastic—it seems absurd to strike a heroic pose for a principle now become meaningless or worse.
Hank

Hank:
If your letter means what it seems to, you've lost Eli's address: he's in Spain. He'd've died before doing what you announce, and die is just what he did. One request: don't name Eli when you spill. Name me, and let him dream on about Madrid. Por favor.
John

Dear John—
I haven't done a damn thing so far except mutter aloud. I still fail to find any solution to the blacklist problem. It's high time, humbling and painful though it be, to bring a little cold logic to bear.
Hank

Hank:
There is no solution to the blacklist problem. Finking is a solution to something else—how to get rich. Why the rush to buy yourself a permanent place below the salt? Regards from Eli.
John

§

---

* Meaning the Jewish High Holidays.

10 o'clock. Discussed next section of script with Deutsch, also all rest of script in a general manner. Went home to work....

Francis Cooke had called, asking you to meet with him that morning at his home in Hollywood. As you drove toward town, the name of his street rose and fell as on a groundswell in your mind: Cheremoya, you thought, Indian for *round cold fruit.* Why did the word appeal to you, why did you like to think it, why, you wondered, was any word more appealing than another, and why had this one sent you to the books? Could you not enjoy the tree unless you knew the meaning of its name? What did you add when you learned that to the Quechuan Indian, its round cold fruit was the Cheremoya. . . ?

There were two houses on the lot, and Cooke occupied the smaller, the one near the property fence at the rear. He was waiting for you in a porch chair, but there was no exchange of greetings as you came from the driveway and took a seat on the steps. Gazing at the shimmered air above your car, you saw through it to greenery that seemed to writhe, like weed in a stream.

Cooke said, "You're not an easy one to talk to."

"You think so?"

"Everybody does."

"Still, you're about to try."

"I have to; I was picked. After all, they told me, I recruited you."

"You didn't. I was recruited by R. Palme Dutt and his *Labour Monthly.* You just happened to know that the R. stood for Rajani."

"Well, that ought to count for something."

"What, for instance?"

"We know that you and Marguerite have been subpoenaed. And you might as well know that subpoenas have been served on a dozen others, more than a dozen."

When he paused there, you said, "And you're counting on us for what?"

"The leadership wants a united front at the Hearings."

"The kind it wanted from the Hollywood Ten? The kind that made them wind up in the pen?"

"A united front," he said, "only in being represented by the same lawyer."

And you said, "For my part, I don't care one way or the other, but it's a different story for Maggie. I wouldn't toss her in with a dozen Communists for anything in the world. She's been out of it for years, and out she stays."

"This is a pretty good bunch. Four or five are people you respect."

"They could all be John Reeds, and I still wouldn't let Maggie join them."

"That means, I suppose, that you'll stay out with her."

"I belong with her."

"I wish I could make you see that you both belong with us."

The car was beginning to cool, and from time to time you heard it tick as expanded metal returned to size.

"Francis," you said, "I don't think you meant that, about me being hard to talk to. You could always talk to me, and you did from the start—you and five or six others. The rest I don't care for a pinch of snake-shit."

"Why have you got such a down on them?"

"Before I came out here, I was dead broke, but I never drew a breath for the underdog. After '36, though, I was in the money, and, for Christ's sake, I turned up on the side of the insulted and injured! The cause got into me, don't ask how, and it imbues me yet. But these guys wise on the *People's World*, they're the biggest disappointment of my life: the cause has had no effect on them. It hasn't raised them up; in fact, they've pulled it down. We wanted numbers, and we let numbers in, trusted them, put our lives in their hands. Look what they've done, the bastards—they've saved themselves and given us away."

"Even so, you haven't quit the cause."

"And I never will. But I sure as hell can quit the personnel."

Little heat came from the car now, and, beyond it, a hedge no longer seemed to be flowing up through the air.

"That tree," you said. "You know what it is?"

"A cheremoya," Cooke said.

"Ever eat the fruit?"

"I'd sooner eat a paperhanger's paste."

SCENE 116

WESTERN UNION (August 1951)

Tuesday, August 28, 1951

Worked on next section. . . .

In the early afternoon, two Day Letters were delivered (DON'T PHONE— sender's request) to your home in Encino. One was addressed to Marguerite and one to you. They were otherwise identical:

THIS IS TO ADVISE THAT YOUR APPEARANCE BEFORE THE COMMITTEE ON UN-AMERICAN ACTIVITIES HAS BEEN POSTPONED IN ACCORDANCE WITH THE SUBPOENA WITH WHICH YOU HAVE BEEN SERVED YOU ARE HEREBY DIRECTED TO APPEAR BEFORE THE COMMITTEE ON UN-AMERICAN ACTIVITIES ON SEPTEMBER 20 1951 AT 9:30 A M ROOM 518 FEDERAL BLDG LOS ANGELES CALIFORNIA
JOHN S WOODS CHAIRMAN

THE COLOR OF THE AIR, XV

ELLA MAY WIGGINS, c.1900–29
THE GASTONIA STRIKE

> *The mill owners here have been mighty good to their folks.*
> —a North Carolina preacher

It wasn't much of a strike. It only took a couple of days before the flush wore off, and the rush of blood became a walk, only two-three days till the millhands tired of commonist talk and honed for the sound of spindles, the pound of power looms. A day or two in the open air, and back they tracked, and they didn't seem to care that the strike had been lost—what did it matter? For a while, they'd made a noise out there in the road, and they'd heard some jaw about a union, but never having seen one in the Smokies, where they came from, they took it to be a bullshevik word with no ptickler meaning. All they could swear to was that they drew no pay on the picket-lines. There was no cash-money in carrying signs, or making a fist, or singing such things as

> The boss man sleeps in a big fine bed
> And dreams of his silver and gold.
> The worker sleeps in an old straw bed
> And shivers from the cold.

It was true enough, God knew, but it didn't quit the rent, so back they went for their two bits an hour: the men, that is—the women and children got somewhat less. A day or two or maybe three, and there wasn't much left of the strike—a tore-up sign, a picket-line pore as a snake, mostly yankee jews, and there was your strike, lost in the whirring of the spindles, the stomping of the looms.

Not for Ella May, though. She was still there outside the fence, still churning away with a stick and a square of cardboard, still shaking a fist at the windows of the mill, still singing about the boss man and the bossed, as if she'd never heard that the strike was lost. Ella May—who the hell was Ella May? A nobody, you'd have to say, a scrub come down from some farm in the hills, her past left behind with the trash of the seasons, blackened stubble and the dust of leaves, rags, tins, flakes of paper ash. No great shakes was Ella May, a chunked little woman of nine-and-twenty with one fine feature, eyes. Apart from such, she wasn't much to behold; in fact, after nine babies without a breather, she looked a little shrunk and not a little old. There's no telling what her tits must've been with all that sucking—like pockets, maybe, pockets pulled inside out—but her face was plain to see, and there were shrivels in it, as though she'd left her teeth at home. *I'm the mother of nine,* she said, *but four of them died with the whooping cough. All four at once,* she said, and in a few more weeks, she was dead herself. For Ella May, only then was the mill strike over—over, yes, but it was never lost.

She hadn't ever made more than nine dollars a week, she said, and with a family of nine, that came to about a dollar a kid, God damn it!, one God damn dollar to do for a kid!, and when those four came down with the cough, she asked the super to let her off nights and put her on days, but he wouldn't switch her, the son-of-a-bitch—a sorry man, she called him, *the sorriest man alive*—and four children coughed till they coughed themselves away.

Ella May! When others cast their signs aside, she was an army vast with banners, and where she marched she was many. She never gave up—*We all got to stand for the union,* she said, *so's we can do better for our children, and they won't have lives like we got.* Ella May! She was on her way to a meeting when five company gunmen shot her. Fifty people saw it, swore to it with a Bible oath, but a jury found the guilty innocent, let the guilty go.

If the mill officials get it in for you, they will get rid of you.
—a Gastonia minister

Well, they got rid of Ella May, yet when they go through the gates of the mill, there are some who say they can still hear her singing *Let's stand together, workers, and have a union here.*

SCENE 117

AGAIN, THE STAINED-GLASS WINDOW (August–September 1951)

Wednesday, August 29, 1951

Called Deutsch. Worked on pages 40–47. . . .

It must've been some concurrence of thought that made both of you stop what you were doing—what *were* you doing?—and turn, she to you and you to her, to learn the other's mind. If so, it would've been no remarkable thing: as in any such long association, often there was correspondence without an exchange of words. This time, though, assumption would not do for either of you: you had to know, and so did she.

You said, "I've been sitting here trying to remember the past three weeks."
"Since we got the subpoenas?" she said. "The thing I wonder about is whether I think at all."
"You work on that script for hours every day. But what about the other hours?"
"I feel like saying, 'What other hours?' I try to see back to that U.S. Marshal, but it's as if he wiped the slate clean."
"It seems that way," you said. "But we must've been thinking, whether we knew it or not."
"I tell myself to think, but ten minutes later, I have to tell myself again."
"What goes on in the head? The way we go through the days, no one would ever guess there was nothing underneath us. We're performing on air."
"But all the while feeling we're heading for a fall," she said. "That's not a thought, though, is it?"

§

Thursday, August 30, 1951

Steve Ames called. Asked me to write foreword for The Man In the Cloak *(his picture) and said Dore Schary wished it. Called Deutsch and informed him of assignment. He said okay. . . .*

The acreage to your north was vacant when you moved to Encino, but soon afterward it was acquired and built on by a man named Borden. No more than civility ever developed between you, and you'd merely wave to each other in passing or speak of something paltry if within the speaking range.

266

It was a relationship established by title deeds, a thing of metes and bounds, and through the years, if nothing had distanced you further, nothing else had brought you near.

What courtesies did exist were largely owing to his young son Peter, to whom you were known as *Mr. Saniford*. Often when you were out of doors, he'd come to watch you through the diamonds of the woven-wire fence. To the wide-eyed little boy, it was as if all the wonders of the world lay on your side of it, and never would he tire of asking questions about the horses, the dogs and cats, the guinea fowl that streamed like smoke across the grounds. They'd be hard questions, as a child's always are, and because you knew that what you said might become a permanent part of his mind, you'd try to be careful in reply.

He was there now, watching through the fence, but on that day, the wonders on view seemed to have no interest for him — or, since he was staring only at you, were you the only wonder?

"How about saying hello?" you said.
And he said, "I'm not suppose to talk to you."
"No? What *are* you supposed to do?"
"I'm suppose to *not* talk."
"Why?"
"My father said so."
"I thought we were friends."
"I'm not suppose to be friends."
"I thought we liked each other."
"I don't like you any more. My father said you was a bad man."
"Peter!"

You looked up and saw Borden approaching through his yard. There was nothing civil about him now, no half-salute as usual, no casual remark. There was only anger unconcealed.

"Go back to the house!" he said to his son, and without a word, the boy went.
"What's gotten into you?" you said.
"I want you to stay away from my boy."
"Stay away? I talk to him through a fence."
"Well, I want that to stop."
"As you say. But would you mind telling me why?"
"I don't have to tell you a damn thing."
"But I like the boy, and he likes me. Why did you tell him I'm a bad man?"
"Because that's what you are," he said. "I know all about you, *Mr. Saniford*."
"How? *I* don't know all about me."

"I've had visitors. A certain agency. . . ."

You understood at last, and you said, "A certain agency? If you mean F.B.I., say F.B.I."

"All right, F.B.I."

"And because the F.B.I. told you about my politics, you filled your son's mind with hate. He's going to be a shithead, Borden, just like you. . . ."

§

Friday, August 31, 1951

Went to studio at 10 o'clock, turned in two versions of foreword to Steve Ames, who said he was pleased and that would be all that was necessary. Left word with Deutsch's secretary that I would resume work as of then. Came home. . . .

"Somebody ought to write a paper," you said. "About how it feels to be a snitch."

And Maggie said, "I don't see any snitches coming forward."

"It wouldn't take a snitch to do it. *Crime and Punishment* wasn't written by a murderer. If you know about people, you can write about the things that people do. Snitching is one of them."

"It's easier to write about a murderer than it is about a snitch. At one time or another, everybody's felt like killing someone—we're not so long out of the cave—but show me another animal that snitches."

"Snitching is killing," you said. "Animals kill to eat, and so do snitches."

"It's a lot more complicated than that. The snitches—they're not hungry; they're scared. You watched those Hearings in Washington. You saw that hard-guy actor when they had him on the stand—a snake-eyed gunman in all his movies, and up there he was just Cry-baby Cripsey as he puked up the names. People like that—they don't get written by every pencil."

"All the same," you said, "when we find out who named us, it won't be much of a surprise."

"You swing back and forth," she said. "You don't know yet whether people are big or small."

"I still say, somebody ought to write that paper."

"You write it."

"Some day maybe I will."

§

Worked on GIRL WHO HAD EVERYTHING. . . .

Your yardman always had the weekend off, and on both of those days, it was you who cared for the horses stabled at home at the time. There were four paddocks to hold them. One was the demesne of the stud America Smith, whose stall opened directly into it; the other three, half leafed over by walnut trees, were for a yearling if you had one on the place, for the pensioner Willie Klein, now nineteen, and for the mare September Child and her foal of the current year.

The work of the morning was done. The horses had been turned out and fed, their bedding had been sifted and left to dry against the walls, and you were watching heads dive into feed-buckets or tossing a flake of hay—and Maggie in turn was watching you.

You knew of her presence only when she spoke, saying, "The first time you came out to meet the folks, you were all gussied up as if you were going to Carnegie Hall. I thought, 'My, but that sure is a tied-up boy.' "

"You and those folks of yours. Look what you did to me."

"I only said to take the pin out of your collar. How was I to know you'd fall apart?"

Your eye was on the small but constant motion of the horses, on their hearkening ears, on their sheen as they twitched in the sun, and you said, "I hate to think back to this, but up to the time I came to California, I'd never owned an animal. Everybody else had something—a dog, a cat. Christ, even a goldfish! Everybody, but not me."

With a wave of her hand, Maggie gathered the paddocks, an Airedale at a gopher-hole, a cat studying a turkey poult, and she said, "Well, you're making up for lost time."

A hind hoof cocked, Willie Klein stood dozing in a shaded corner, his tail slowly lashing him as though on its own. "That old bone-bag," you said. "He puts me in mind of Pep West."

"How so?"

"Pep used to stand like that. And come to think of it, he was built like a horse."

And then Maggie said, "You like all this stuff, don't you? The horses, the mutts, even the dirty work around the barn."

"I love it."

"I've always loved it," she said. "I never wanted anything better than we've got right here. It'll be hard to give up."

"Give up? What do you mean—give up?"

She walked away a step or two and turned. "The time's coming, Jabe," she said. "We'll have to give *something* up. . . ."

Sunday, September 2, 1951

Worked on next section of GIRL WHO HAD EVERYTHING. . . .

You were at your desk that morning, writing something or typing on your portable Royal, when Maggie came to the room, saying, "I just had a call from Steve Ames."

"Ames? What's he doing at the studio on a Sunday?"

"He was calling from home, and you'll never guess what for. He said he knew the Hearings would be coming up soon, and he wanted to know if he could be there with me—sort of, lend me his support."

"I'll be damned. How did you leave it?"

"I refused, of course, but I sure as hell thanked him."

"The other producers at Metro," you said. "How many know about the subpoena, do you think?"

"All. That kind of thing gets around."

"How many do you think will call? Like Ames."

"None."

"Not even Pan?"

"Berman's in England."

"What if he were here? You worked for the guy for nine straight years."

"He wouldn't do what Ames did if he knew it would keep me from going to the stake."

"All right, that's Berman. But there are twenty others over there. They can't all be Bermans."

"You're a dreamer, Jabe, and so is Ames. He wants to stick his neck out, the way you did at that sendoff for The Ten. That's two of you in a world of Bermans."

Did you speak then, or did she go on?

"I never had any illusions about Pan, not after the first time I saw him eat."

"What's eating got to do with it?"

"Nothing, maybe. But it didn't seem to be eating. It was more like feeding."

"What does that tell you?"

"Well, if you ate like that, I'd make you move to the barn."

"Let's go out there now and play with Seppy's foal. . . ."

Monday, September 3, 1951

Worked on next section GIRL WHO HAD EVERYTHING. . . .

"How do you pronounce p-a-r-i-a-h?" she said—or was it you?

"With a long *i*," you said—or was it she?

And was it she or you who said, "Long *i* or short *i*, that's what we are—outcasts"?

"There's a name for us in the Bible—Ishmael," which was something she might well have said.

And probably, because sometimes you were a showoff, you were the one who said, "The first three words of *Moby Dick* are 'Call me Ishmael. . . .' "

§

Tuesday, September 4, 1951

Worked on next section GIRL WHO HAD EVERYTHING. . . .

On Ventura Boulevard, about a mile from where you lived, was the scatter of buildings called Encino—an adobe that had once been a coaching-stop, a small post office, a gas-station, and a few stores for the convenience of the local residents. One of these was Sale's, a wine and fine-food shop, and you'd stopped there that day for a bottle of something—Irish, it may have been, or was it sherry? When you entered, another customer was being waited on, and you stood before a counter confronting the tapestry of labels behind it. The more you eyed them, the more they tended to merge—brand-names, trade marks, colors—until all of them blurred into one great hanging for the wall.

When you were outside again a few moments later, Maggie said, "Did you notice the man ahead of us in there?"

"Not particularly," you said. "Why?"

"That was John Lee Mahin."

"The screenwriter? I only know him by name."

"I know him a lot better than that—and he knows me. We worked together once on a Gable script for Sam Zimbalist."

"So?"

"He stood four feet away from me, and he looked right through me as if I wasn't there."

"Well, piss on him. Who cares about John Lee Mahin?"

"I do. I'm not used to being cut by anybody, let alone a flag-waver like Mahin. I'm as good an American as he ever was in his best hour."

"I wouldn't've thought his kind could get to you."

"I'm not sore at the Mahins, really," she said. "What galls me is the way they think. You can have a different religion, and you're all right. You can have a different color, and you're still all right. But just have different politics, and you're all wrong, and to hell with you, where you belong."

"Lenin is Old Scratch," you said. "Didn't you know that?"

She laughed. "I never told you this, but I was in a story conference once with Mahin and the director Vic Fleming. They spent half an hour talking about my ankles. They didn't notice I had cloven hoofs."

"Only half an hour?" you said.

§

Wednesday, September 5, 1951

Worked on next section GIRL WHO HAD EVERYTHING. . . .

"The other day," you said, "we were talking about giving up some things. What things—the horses?"

"Daddy put me up on a horse before I knew how to walk, and I've messed with horses ever since. When Metro fires me, horses will have to go, and you have no idea how I hate the thought. But, Jabe, we'll need the money they cost us."

Where were you at the time? Were you in the house, and if so, in which room and doing what? Or were you on the grounds, and what part of the grounds, the pool area, the corner where the barn was, or simply walking around?

She said, "Just how much do we have, Jabe?"

"Well, there's this place. With what we've done to it, it must be worth double what we paid for it. And then there are the bonds you bought all through the war."

"I let Metro take out for a $500 bond every week," she said. "And I'm the un-American!"

"I wonder how many bonds John Lee Mahin has."

"Damn few, I'll bet. It was a sucker bond, and the wise guys knew it. All the same, I bought one a week for four years—and I never thought I was a sucker."

"You've also got half a dozen Federal Savings accounts, and of course there's the checking account."

"What's it all come to, do you think?"

"Couple of hundred grand, about."

"Sounds like a lot, doesn't it?"

"It *is* a lot," you said.

"Sure, for you and me. But with my folks and your folks to look after, it won't go as far as you think. Not unless we pinch everybody, and it'd kill me to do that."

"Listen. We can go five-six years easy, on just what we have. And we won't exactly be sitting on our ass."

"No? what *will* we be doing—exactly?"

"Trying to make some dough."

"At what? And where?"

"Writing. And if they won't let us do that here, in some other country. They make pictures everywhere, and I'm told they print books."

"Would you want to leave your country?"

"No. But if I'm on its blacklist, it's on mine. I don't have to love what doesn't love me."

"Well," she said, "on September 20th, we'll find out who loves who."

""Whom," the showoff said.

§

Thursday, September 6, 1951

Worked on next section GIRL WHO HAD EVERYTHING. . . .

"*Informer*," you said. "What a tiptoe name for the son-of-a-bitch! As if he were merely giving directions or telling someone the time."

"Back in grade school," Maggie said, "we called him a *tattletale*."

"We did too—in school. But when we caught him in the street, he was a *squealer,* and he got what was coming to him. The Committee, though, treats him like a friend of Man. You'll never see this in the papers: 'The Government's witness, a *stool pigeon* known as Slippery Dick.' No, *sir*! He has the nation's respect. He's trusted. The very snake that just rattled!"

"Do you ever wonder who named us?"

"I wouldn't put it past anybody. . . . No, that's wrong. Otherwise nobody would put it past us."

"When I try to guess," Maggie said, "I always light on the people I like least."

"That can't be so, either, because it doesn't explain The Ten. A couple of those guys, the last thing I'd've looked for was fidelity—and they turned out to be as loyal as the rest."

"What *is* the test, then? What should the Party have been watching for in a recruit?"

"The obvious things, I suppose. Drunkenness, whoring around, stupidity. Beyond those, how could the Party have known who'd crack and who wouldn't? What're the signs of a weak character? There's no telling, really. Sometimes a drunk has honor, sometimes a teetotaler has none."

"I think it's more than a matter of chance," Maggie said. "I think you *can* tell."

"How someone will act when the chips are down? Why, we didn't know that about *ourselves*."

She shook her head, saying, "But we did, Jabe. What a person was once he still is. If he was a sneak, he's a sneak now. If he was a thief, he'll always be a thief. And a liar just keeps on lying. Nobody changes just because he read *Capital.* A grownup tattletale is a fink."

"We're far afield. We're talking about what makes an informer, if you'll allow the word. But we started by wondering who the guy is."

"Why say guy? It might be a guy's wife."

There was a pause, after which you said, "How come that never occurred to me?"

"You like women. You like them too much."

"I'm the one who named a horse Messalina."

"There are many Messalinas. Only one of them is a horse."

§

Friday, September 7, 1951

Finished section GIRL WHO HAD EVERYTHING. Turned over 68 pages to Deutsch and discussed points in next section. Also talked to Steve Ames re SHERIFF OF SISKIYOU and LETTER TO THE PRESIDENT. . . .

The main bedroom, designed by the previous owner, was the most spacious area in the house. Fully twenty feet square, it had a floor of pegged hardwood, and its walls, paneled to the ceiling in pine, offered a fine background for your posters. From time to time, the combination would change, but always on display was one or another of your arrangements of Bonnard and Lautrec, of Steinlen and Manet. You'd grown so accustomed to all these that you seldom regarded them directly: you could see them at will in your mind, their colors and lettering, their figures in clothes like those your mother had worn. You could see, therefore, the age they kept alive, and often, as now, you saw it in the dark, and as you lay in your bed, you tried to recall . . . what?, since it was all a long time lost.

Maggie spoke from across the room, saying, "Are you awake, Jabe?" And you said, "Yes."

"You'd be welcome in my bed."

"I know that, but it wouldn't do much good."

"Why?"

"This trouble we're in. . . . The trouble you're in because of me."

"Another time, then," she said. "But I wish you'd stop thinking that way. I'm in it because of myself."

The past, too, was another time, and you saw, as if the light were on, Bonnard's *Salon des Cent* in old rose and blue. . . .

There are no entries for Saturday and Sunday. The 8th and 9th of September do not exist: Friday's end is Monday's beginning, and no time intervenes.

Monday, September 10, 1951

Went to studio. Saw Armand Deutsch at 10:15. Went over pages 40 to 68. Came home to make changes. . . .

Through the window of your room, you heard tires grind the gravel of the turnaround, and then you heard the sound of a car-door closing, and then you listened through a silence for footsteps in the hallway. You don't know why you supposed she was heading for you—when you were at work, she seldom disturbed you—but you *weren't* working, and you may have sensed that she sensed it. Before you lay the manuscript of *The Land That Touches Mine,* and all you'd done that day was turn a few pages without purpose— because pages could be turned without thought. The manuscript had been there for a month, and for a month, you'd had no thought: it was as if the story and its components were immutable, as if the characters could say only what they'd already said and there were no other end than the one they'd reached. You were not working!

From the doorway, Maggie said, "Same thing as last night, Jabe?" And without looking at her, you said, "Yes."

Tuesday, September 11, 1951

Took changes to studio, went over them with Deutsch. Then took pages 40 to 68 to Script Department to be mimeographed. Discussed next ten pages with Deutsch. Went home. . . .

You were in the courtyard of the Smith home in North Hollywood. The summer day was warm, but a later season lay just beneath its surface, as if the air were water, cool down deep where sunlight ended. The flagstones were covered with leaves cast by the apricot trees, a red and yellow herd that a breeze stirred from place to place. It was fifteen years since you'd first been there, but little seemed to have changed. Still under the sunshade were the iron chairs and the circular table, and still standing against a wall was the glider from which, your hand trailing, you touched a sleeping dog on every to-and-fro, and still, you thought, you were gazing at what had brought and kept you there—Maggie.

You'd driven her to the studio that day, and on the way home, you'd stopped to call on her mother. It was in her (the olderly woman, your grandma would've said) that change was shown. She'd never walked since her fall earlier in the year, and seated now in a wheelchair, she appeared to have shrunk from small to smaller, and her hair was whiter, wilder than before, and her hands, never idle in her life, endlessly plucked at her sleeves. You could see her through a doorway, but though she was looking in your direction, she could not have been looking at you. There were great distances behind you and long flows of time, and somewhere at the end of them stood the man she'd begun to care for nearly seventy years gone: there was nothing in between.

§

Wednesday, September 12, 1951

Worked on (camping trip) GIRL WHO HAD EVERYTHING. Deutsch telephoned to inquire about number of pages in section I am working on and probable length of entire script....

Your father lived in a ground-floor apartment on Burnside a little way south of Wilshire. Through a French window, his livingroom gave on a forecourt and the street outside the wall. He was sitting there now, sideways to the light as if to read by it, but he held no book, no newspaper, and any reading he was doing could only have been from a writing in his mind. His gaze was on nothing outward and yet on nothing near, and quite like Maggie's mother, you thought, he was seeing faces and hearing voices that no one else could see and hear. At what point, you wondered, would you too begin to replay the past. He looked up when you tapped on a pane, and you saw him make a swift return to now.

After kissing his hand, you kept on holding it, and you said, "What were you thinking of just now?"

"Many things, kid," he said. "Many things."

His hand was thin-skinned, smooth, cool. "You were far away. Where?"

"Forget it. You never lived there." And then he said, "I called you to town to talk about the Hearings. You've been avoiding me—and avoiding the subject."

"I didn't want to upset you."

276

"How foolish! Once I heard about the subpoenas, I've had nothing else on my mind."

"I meant, upset you *more*."

"You think your silence is sparing me? It's making things worse."

"What do you want to know?"

"The actual situation. I can't get that from my friends at the cafeteria. I can only get it from you."

"Situation," you said. "There are dozens of words for it, but situation isn't one of them. We're in a hell of a fix, Gov, and there's no good way out of it."

"Fix, then," he said. "Lay it out for me."

"We don't know who they are, but witnesses must've testified before the Committee that Maggie and I are members of the Communist Party. We're now being called on to admit it or deny it. If we admit it—you know the law—we'll have to go further and name any members that *we* know. In other words, *we* have to become informers, and if we refuse, we'll go to jail for contempt. On the other hand, if we deny membership, we're bound to be indicted for perjury, and the Government will damn well see to it that we go to the pen, like Alger Hiss. That's not a situation, counselor; that's a fix."

"You say there's no *good* way out. Is there *any* way?"

"We've worked something out, Mag and I, and we won't be prosecuted, but that's the most I can say for it. In any case, it's better than singing our way out, like the yellow-bellies who named us."

"You know, I've never asked whether the two of you are Communists."

"Are you asking now?"

"No."

"Also, you've never asked why we don't do as others have done—betray our friends."

"I knew what you'd say," he said. "But there *is* a question I *will* ask. If you refuse to cooperate with the Committee—how's it put? become friendly witnesses?—what will the studio do?"

"That depends. If the Legion uses pressure, the Legion and the rest of the Know-nothings. . . ."

"Then what?"

"Maggie will be fired."

"That's bad."

"Very," and after a moment, you said, "When I came in, what *were* you thinking about?"

"Better days, kid."

And when you left him and waved a goodbye through the window, he didn't see you. He was back in better days.

§

Thursday, September 13, 1951

Worked on next ten pages GIRL WHO HAD EVERYTHING. . . .

Coming in off the grounds, you closed the door quietly, and you were conscious of the care you took, for you'd always chosen silence over sound. It wasn't that you were stealthy, you told yourself: you'd never sneaked, never peeped but once, never tried to overhear. Even when near enough, you were usually out of earshot, for it was your way of going—but why?, you wondered, and you wished you knew. The house was quiet too, and you passed through the hall to the bedroom, where you found Maggie viewing herself in a full-length mirror.

Without turning to the doorway, she said, "I know you're there, and I wish you'd go away."
"I came like the yellow fog of Prufrock. I didn't make a sound."
"I know all the same. I always do."
"What're you all dressed up for? Where are we going?"
"To the Hearings."
"Aren't you a little early? They're seven days off."
"I'm trying to decide what to wear."
Entering the room, you saw that both beds were overlaid with selections from her wardrobe. "All this stuff is too damn good for the Committee. Wear a sweater and skirt."
"The Committee," she said. "I dress for two people—you and me."
"I'm going to watch, then."
"Watch—but no remarks unless I call for them."
And you did watch, and as always, you watched with pleasure.

She was—what? forty-six now?—but her form was the one you'd known in the early days. Dressed or undressed, it hadn't lost its hollows and rounds; her waist was still concavo-concave, still remindful of her desk-top figurines, and arched still were her size-3 feet in their high-heeled shoes, the feet you'd heard fifteen years before as they walked the Paramount corridor. How strange, you thought, to be caught for life by a small pair of feet!

"What do you think of this one?" she said, still looking at the mirror.

§

Friday, September 14, 1951

Worked on next section of GIRL WHO HAD EVERYTHING. Decided to include a few more pages and a new scene. So advised Deutsch and told him would deliver new pages on Monday. . . .

On being notified that the Hearings had been postponed from the 6th to the 20th of September, you'd called your attorney in New York to acquaint him with the change. He was a member of the law firm of Boudin, Cohn, and Glickstein, with offices at 1776 Broadway, and as you spoke to him through the perforations in a piece of vulcanized rubber, you wondered where those offices were. You'd almost forgotten the numeration along Broaday, but some recall seemed to place 1776 at or near 57th Street, within sight of Carnegie Hall. Along with your words, you'd felt that you were somehow transmitting yourself, and that you, like the man you were speaking to, were enjoying the view from his room. There, down below you, were the apple-green coaches that crossed the town to and from Fifth, and you saw currents and eddies on the sidewalks, and you could almost hear the sound of engine-pound, auto-horns, voices, and you could almost tell the smell of smoke—and only one block distant, the Hall! But though fancy had flown you to Cohn's presence, you couldn't then—and you cannot now—see his face. He makes no image for your eye, and possibly not even for his own. When he stands before a looking-glass, does the glass look back, you wonder, or is he peering at a vacant room. . . ?

And now he was calling you to say, "I'm flying to the Coast tomorrow. You'll hear from me. . . ."

§

Saturday, September 15, 1951

Worked on changes of GIRL WHO HAD EVERYTHING. . . .

"All work and no play," you said to Maggie. "Let's go for a drive."

With Juno on the seat between you, you made one of your favorite runs—out along Ventura to the Triunfo Ranch and then into the hills to Lake Sherwood. It had been a year of light rains, and the water-level was low enough to strand the boat-landings and leave a broad beach of crazed mud on which the docks stood, it seemed, with their skirts raised.

You said, "They look as if they were told not to go near the water."

Beyond the lake, there were more hills, and you wound around them to the horse-farms on the floor of Hidden Valley. There all signs of drought ended. Pasture was still green, still deep, and mares and their foals stood in it seemingly short-legged, as though they were bovine. A black suckling, deviling its dam for the tit, tracked her through the grass, and in the shade of a roadside oak, you stopped the car to watch.

"What do we say to this guy when he comes?" Maggie said. "Do we tell him about the Party?"

"No reason not to."

"I hate the idea. It's our secret."

"It was never our secret, Mag. Three hundred others are in on it."

"I meant a secret from outsiders."

"It's a bad thing, holding out on your lawyer."

"You're my lawyer."

"Not for the record, and I'm glad of it. We have a purpose beyond these Hearings, you know—protecting your Metro contract. That'll be better served by this Cohn from 1776 Broadway."

"What if he doesn't ask?"

"Then we'll tell him."

To avoid the foal, the mare trotted off across the field, but the foal, whinnying at being denied, pursued her.

§

Sunday, September 16, 1951

Finished changes. Delivered pages 67–83 to studio to be delivered to Deutsch on Monday morning. Note attached. . . .

It was early afternoon when Cohn arrived at Encino. You went down to the gate to unlock it for his car and then followed on foot to the stone pine at the head of the driveway, where Maggie stood awaiting him. You can still see her there, still see the clothes she wore and the ribbon in her hair (it was green), and you can see Cohn's car and its kind and color, but as if it had come by itself, no likeness of its driver returns to mind.

You hear a voice, though, a disembodied sound, as from a recording, and it says, "Sidney Cohn."

And you say, "John Sanford—and this is my Maggie."

When you try to replay the conference, parts of it seem to have been erased, and it begins after the beginning and breaks off before the end.

". . . named Tavenner is counsel for the Committee," Cohn is saying. "At some stage of the proceedings, he'll put this question to the witness: *Are you now or have you ever been a member of the Communist Party?* There are several ways in which the witness may. . . ."

And you say, "Forgive me, Mr. Cohn, but this is where I cut in. I hope you'll take no offense when I tell you that you weren't brought out here to guide us through the Hearings. We know the perils well, and we also know what we're going to say on the stand. It'll get us past the Committee without harm, and it has this further virtue—that it won't make us look like yellow dogs."

Among your chairs on the lawn, four Airedales sleep as if shot. "Why not yellow people?" Maggie says. "No dog was ever a fink."

"True enough," you say, and you return to Cohn. "Also, we know this, that the Committee, four or five individual sons-of-bitches, is actually Congress and entitled to respect. I might add that we know how to behave in public, and we know how to dress. . . ."

Cohn says, "May I interpose a question?"

"Certainly," you say.

"There's a Sholom Aleichem story that ends something like this: *Why did we bring the horse?* That's my question. Why *did* we bring the horse?"

You laugh, saying, "I know the story, and it's a peach. We brought the horse, counselor, because of a circumstance I am about to relate. A little while back, Metro signed Maggie to a straight five-year contract. It's due to start on the first of January, and it guarantees her a minimum of three hundred and twenty-five thousand dollars for only six months' work each year. At her option, she may work longer and double her earnings. You're here to protect that contract."

"How?"

"With your presence. That alone will put Metro on notice that her rights are being looked after."

"Why don't *you* do that—with *your* presence?"

"My defense is going to differ from Maggie's, and in every other possible way, we mean to put distance between us. If I sat beside her at the Hearings, it would be thought that I was coaching her, that her testimony was designed to shield *me*. It isn't; it's designed to shield *her*."

"And so," Cohn says, "you brought the horse."

"Sholom Aleichem," you say.

And he says, "Peace unto *you*."

§

Monday, September 17, 1951

Had conference with Armand Deutsch on pages turned in, got his ideas on changes, went home. . . .

You'd accompanied Maggie to the studio, and while she conferred with her producer, you marked time in her room. For twelve years, you thought, that was what it had been: *her room*. Save for her two figurines, she owned no part of it that she could touch, nothing that she could weigh in her hand, none of the fixtures or furniture, not even the Manet aslant on the wall. But she did own a cube of space and therefore, you felt, what contained it—the room. It was hers, and her name was on the door. How much longer would it remain there?, you wondered. . . , and then the door was opened by a man you'd never seen before.

"Oh," he said. "I was looking for Maggie Roberts."

He was small and compact, about fifty years of age, low-spoken, and not a little remindful of Ben Thau. "I'm her husband," you said. "John Sanford."

"My name is Ames."

"Ames? Steve Ames?"

"Right."

And you said, "Come on in. I want to shake your hand." After inviting him to a seat, you said, "Maggie told me about your offer to go downtown with her when she appears before the House Committee. That was one hell of a gesture."

"It was more than that," he said. "I really would like to help."

"I've been in this town for fifteen years, and Maggie for more than twenty. We've known many people in that time, Mr. Ames, but no one else has done what you did."

"I have great respect for Maggie, and what they're doing to her is shameful."

"It would be even more shameful if they did the same to you."

"I don't know what you mean."

"We've been called Communists. In this country, very little worse can happen to you. It's a disease, and it's catching."

"I don't know what Maggie's politics are," Ames said, "and even if I did, it would make no difference—I'd still go downtown with her. Somebody has to show that we mean what we say when we call this a free country."

"It isn't," you said. "If you stand up for us, there'll be nobody behind you except pursuers, and you'll get what we're getting."

"You don't want my support, then?"

"It'll hurt you, and it won't help us. We're in for it, and we'll take our licking."

Again the door opened, and now Maggie came in. "Why, Steve. . . !" she said.

§

Tuesday, September 18, 1951

Worked on changes. . . .

282

"Anything you want me to do today?" you said.

Her script outspread, Maggie was seated at a card-table in the bedroom. The pages were slatted by the bay-window blinds, and in the slits of light, dust danced in suspension.

"That woman across the street from Mama," she said.
"What about her?"
"I'm still worried about what she'll do when she reads the news. She might rush in and tell Mama."
"The hell she will. The girls'll keep her out."
"You don't know this bitch. She's as hard to keep out as a bad smell. She *is* a bad smell."
"What's her name?"
"I never saw it spelled out. It sounds like Rondo."
"Suppose I give her a call?"
"How, if we don't know the spelling?"
"All right. Suppose I go and see her."
"Would you do that for me. . . ?"

At the Smith home in North Hollywood, you found Maggie's sisters in attendance on their mother. Telling them what you were about to do, you crossed the road on a diagonal to the neighbor's yard. A short, stout, keg-shaped woman watched your approach.

"Are you Mrs. Rondo?" you said.
"It's Ron*deau*," she said. "What if I am?"
"My name is Sanford. I'm a son-in-law of Mrs. Smith's."
"I know that. I seen you come and go."
"I'm here to ask a great favor of you."
"A favor? What kind of a favor?"
"A few days from now, you may be reading about my wife and me in the papers."
"I read about her before. She writes for the movies."
"This'll be different, Mrs. Rondeau. It'll be about things we want to keep from Mrs. Smith."
"You mean you done bad things?"
"*She* would think so."
"And what are you—ashamed?"
"Not at all. But we think an old lady like Mrs. Smith ought not to be agitated."
"What've I got to do with agitated?"
"You visit with Mrs. Smith sometimes. All I ask is that you make no mention of anything you may read about Marguerite and me."

"You got your nerve, Mr. Whoever-you'are. Coming on my property and telling me not to gossip!"

From the doorway behind her, a man said, "Get in here!"

The woman turned to him, saying, "He's got his gall. . . !"

"Get in here, I said!" And as the woman entered the house, the man spoke to you. "She won't say nothing, take my word."

And you said, "Thanks. . . ."

§

Wednesday, September 19, 1951

Finished changes. Delivered late in evening to Thalberg Building, instructing officer on desk to deliver to Deutsch first thing Thursday morning. . . .

When you turned into Wilshire and headed west, your father said, "Where are you taking me, kid?"

"To the Beverly Derby."

"Why such a high-class place?"

"You're a high-class guy."

"Not so very. There's a lot you don't know about the man in this suit."

"People don't know much about anybody, I guess, but I'd bet my life on you and Maggie."

"I don't know how she does it—working day after day right up to the Hearings."

"It's what a pro does, she says."

"She makes too little of herself."

"Her father used to say he didn't see much good in people it took two men to hold their hat on."

You parked your car behind the Derby and walked around the Rodeo corner to the Bar entrance on Wilshire. "I like it in here," you said. Your booth faced a doorway leading to the diningroom, from which as though borne by the polyphony of talk, laughter, china on china, came a stew of savor, the single smell of many foods. "Reminds me of the old Astor House," you said.

"You mean the *Hotel* Astor," your father said.

"The Astor *House*."

"But they tore that down in 1915."

"You took me there *before* 1915."

"How can you remember anything that far back?"

"We all remember food: it leaves a mark. You remember your mother's; I remember mine. One of my earliest memories is the beef tea she made for me when I was sick. And I've never forgotten the Puree Jackson at the Astor House. . . . Who was Jackson?, I've sometimes wondered."

"You're pretty calm," your father said, "considering that tomorrow is the 20th of September."

"It's just a day, counselor, like any other day. What will you have?"

After you'd given the waiter your orders, your father was silent for a moment, and then he said, "Do you know how old you were when your mother made that beef tea?"

"Five."

"Six," he said.

SCENE 118

THE HOUSE COMMITTEE HEARINGS IN LOS ANGELES
(September 1951)

Thursday, September 20, 1951

Appeared before Committee at 2 o'clock. On stand about twenty minutes. John on stand about five minutes.

When she moved to lay out her clothes, you left the room: you always did, though you'd known her long. Never through the years had she lost her reserve; she was as shy now as she'd been at the beginning, and again and again she'd make you think you were seeing her for the first time. Knowing that she'd proceed only after you'd gone, you went outside and waited for her in the shade of the grape arbor. It was still cool there, and the cats lay near you on a carpet of leaf-shadows. What would she be wearing?, you wondered. . . , and then she was coming toward you across the driveway.

Aware of your gaze, she tried to make herself smaller, as though hoping to iris from sight. Against her jacket, she was holding a purse of dark brown suede that matched the suede of her shoes. Her shantung suit was the color of milk chocolate, and it told in silk the tale of her curves.

What're you looking at?" she said.
And you said, "You, without the suit."

§

You were some way toward the city when she said, "How do you feel, Jabe?"
"In general?"

"About today. About all this."

"When I was a kid, my mother took me to Atlantic City. They wouldn't give us a room at the Marlborough-Blenheim; they didn't take in Jews. I feel the way she must've felt."

"I feel nothing," Maggie said. "I'm not angry. I'm not hopeless. I'm not frightened. I'm disconnected, as though I'd broken my spine."

You said, "I wish. . . ," but whatever your desire may have been, there the invocation ended.

§

A newsphoto of the day fixes the room where the Hearings were held — 518 of the Federal Building — but nothing recalls the building itself, its shape and dimensions, the stone it was made of, and when you explore your mind for such things, all you find is a fifth-floor hallway near the door of 518. The room, remembered even without the photograph, was some forty feet square. The only decoration was a huge flag that was hung flat on a blank wall, its white so like the plaster that you seemed to be looking at a mural of seven red stripes and a blue oblong with forty-eight tears. On a dais below the banner, six chairs, high-backed and forensic, were ranged, and in these sat five members of the House Committee and their interrogating counsel. Dead now, all of them — Clyde Doyle, Francis Walter, John Wood, Donald Jackson, Charles Potter, and Frank Tavenner, inquisitor — dead, but not for you. As they were that day in the flesh, so they are now on a yellowed sheet of newsprint, their looks unimproved by time and oxidation. Before each, as then, is a microphone and a strew of documents, and they're regarding something or someone in the crowd of a hundred behind you, a spectator, it may be, a camera, a disturbance. But you're looking at them, the gentlemen from California, Pennsylvania, Michigan, and Georgia, at faces as interchangeable as the chairs their honors sit in, faces remarkable for nothing, and you think, on this day as on that: Where is the noble feature, the sure bearing, the rare emanation from within. . . ?

Seated with Maggie and her attorney in the front row of benches, you were only an aisle's width from the witness who was testifying, a screenwriter named Michael Wilson.* He was an acquaintance rather than a friend of yours, but you'd known him almost from the time of your coming to the Coast, and you esteemed him for his ability and quite as much for his manner. He was

---

* Winner of an Academy Award for his screenplay *A Place In The Sun,* based on the Dreiser novel *An American Tragedy.*

one who spoke little (Maggie's brother Dan might've said *His tongue ain't slung in the middle*), but you were always struck by the clarity of his thought. Because of his astonishing resemblance to Fitzgerald, you'd call him Scott when you met, not Mike, and in another way also he resembled Fitzgerald: he too was Catholic. There, though, the likeness ended: he lived no life of Crazy Sundays.

On another level, your mind was on the Committee and its counsel, all six lined up against the flag. You studied their faces, their demeanor, their dimensions, and you even took note of the cut of their clothes, and it marveled you that any of them had been sent forth to speak for the many he'd left behind. What qualities had he shown, what set him apart from the ruck, what ring of light crowned his head, and what other auguries had his backers found. . . ?

". . . I lost a son in the Air Force," Congressman Doyle was saying. "You folks that are known Communists, Mr. Wilson, would you give your life for peace?"

And Wilson was saying, "I certainly would. I believe in peaceful existence. . . ."

And still you were trying to descry in the Committee and its Counsel a reason for their elevation. What explained them?, you wondered — what? And now slowly grew the realization that they represented the people because they *were* representative: they'd been chosen not because they were different, but because they were the same. These six, you thought, they'd been put forward by their similars, their fungible selves. Each was any other, the many were as one, and seeking past them through the flag, the wall, the far ranges of fancy, you saw an entire nation of Potters and Doyles and Jacksons, multitudes with their vacancy, their airless minds, their low and lucrative aims. . . .

And Wilson was saying, "But this Committee had defiled peace. . . !"

Calling out from the row behind you, a woman said, "Well, you're one Jew that'll never work again!"

As a bailiff escorted her from the room, Cohn said, "The anti-Semitic bitch!"

"For spectacles like this," Maggie said, "you get spectators like that. It happens Mike Wilson's a Roman Catholic."

"You're kidding me."

"It's true."

"Then, by God, that's a story I spread around New York!"

From the dais, a microphone intensified the sound waves transmitting your name. "John Sanford," someone said. "Is John Sanford in the Hearing Room?"

You raised your hand and said, "He is."

"Please take the stand."

"Good luck, Jabe," Maggie said.

And you said, "*No pasaran,*" as you rose.

§

Beside you now as you write is a transcript of your testimony before the House Committee. Bound in a pale blue cover are three typewritten pages from the day's proceedings as taken down by Noon & Pratt, court reporters of Los Angeles County.

MR. TAVENNER: Have you a lawyer, Mr. Sanford?

MR. SANFORD: I'm a lawyer. They say a lawyer who represents himself has a fool for a client, but I'll take the chance.

MR. TAVENNER: Will you state your full name, please, sir?

MR. SANFORD: John Sanford.

MR. TAVENNER: Have you used a professional name? Different from your own?

MR. SANFORD: John Sanford is a professional name. I was born Julian Shapiro.

MR. TAVENNER: Were you known as Jack Shapiro?

MR. SANFORD: A few people call me Jack. Not many.

Again your mind seemed to be at work on more than one level. While being straight-spoken to Tavenner's questions, you were also, on another plane of perception, dwelling on the nature of his constituency: for whom was he a champion? Words (were they Pope's?) dithered to the surface of memory like aeration—*Whatever is, is right.* Right, of course, for the rich. . . .

MR. TAVENNER: When and where were you born, Mr. Sanford?

MR. SANFORD: In New York City on May 31, 1904.

MR. TAVENNER: What is your occupation?

MR. SANFORD: I am a novelist.

MR. TAVENNER: Where do you reside?

MR. SANFORD: In Encino, California.

It was always right for the rich, you thought, but was it the best of all possible worlds for the rest? By virtue of what were a few set above all others, by what law of nature were the rich the riders and the poor the ridden. . . ?

MR. TAVENNER: How long have you lived in California?

MR. SANFORD: 15 years.

MR. TAVENNER: Prior to that time, where did you live?

MR. SANFORD: In New York City.

MR. TAVENNER: Will you tell the Committee briefly what your educational background has been?

MR. SANFORD: I went to the public and high schools of New York City, and thereafter I attended Lafayette College, Lehigh University, Northwestern, and Fordham.

MR. TAVENNER: Were you then known by the name of Shapiro?

MR. SANFORD: Julian Shapiro.

MR. TAVENNER: Mr. Shapiro, will you—

MR. SANFORD: My name is Sanford.

MR. TAVENNER: Sanford now. . . .

Sanford now, you thought. You bastard! You Jew-baiting bastard! You glanced at the Committee to learn whether it had taken note of Tavenner's slur, but their faces showed nothing, as if nothing improper had been said. What more could've been expected?, you wondered. These were the clerks, the "men of business" of their masters, and they'd been bidden to punish you for siding with the ridden as against the riding. . . .

MR. TAVENNER: Tell the Committee your record of employment since you came to California.

MR. SANFORD: I worked for one year as a screenwriter for Paramount. My only other connection with moving pictures has been a six-month term at Metro-Goldwyn-Mayer in 1941.

MR. TAVENNER: During the time you were associated with the moving picture industry, you should have had knowledge of the existence of an effort to infiltrate the Communist Party. The Committee is conducting an investigation to ascertain the extent of infiltration, the purposes of the Communist Party in organizing the industry, and how it has carried out its projects. The Committee would like for you to tell it all you know of Communism in Hollywood.

Your response must've been almost immediate, for you remember watching the reporter (was it Noon that day, or was it Pratt?) type what you said on his shorthand machine. Still, packed into that tick of time was your life, and every moment of it led to your reply. . . .

MR. SANFORD: Under the Fifth Amendment to the Constitution, no man is compelled to give evidence against himself. I therefore decline to answer the question.

MR. TAVENNER: Are you now a member of the Communist Party?

MR. SANFORD: I decline to answer on the grounds previously stated.

MR. TAVENNER: I have no further questions.

§

289

Leaving the witness-chair, you turned from the faces of the Committee to . . . those in the photo you're poring over now, a blurred and jaundiced gallery encountered for an hour of the past.

As you took your seat beside Maggie, she said, "You did just fine, Jabe."

"Remember," you said. "Watch out for the word *now*—it's one you never use. Tavenner will try to get you to say you're not a Communist *now,* but you don't fall for it. You simply say you're not a Communist, and you stick to it."

Cohn spoke across her, saying, "That stuff about you being known as Jack— what was Tavenner after?"

"I'm not sure, but I think there's a Party functionary named Jack Shapiro. He may have been trying to connect us."

And a voice said, "Is Marguerite Roberts in the Hearing Room?"

You watched her as she went to the witness-table. She had only a short way to go, hardly more than three or four paces, but you could've identified her walk even without seeing it; you'd've known it in the dark or a dream— beautiful her feet with shoes. . . .

MR. WOOD: Let us have order, please. Are you ready to proceed, Counsel?

MR. TAVENNER: Yes, sir.

MR. WOOD: Who will you call?

MR. TAVENNER: Miss Marguerite Roberts.

MR. COHN: May I respectfully request, Mr. Chairman, that there be no television.

MR. WOOD: Who are you, please?

MR. COHN: I am her counsel.

MR. WOOD: I would rather have the witness make her own request. Do you object to testifying before television?

MISS ROBERTS: Yes, I do.

MR. WOOD: Your wishes will be respected. Have a seat.

MR. TAVENNER: Now, what is your full name, please?

MISS ROBERTS: My name is Marguerite Sanford. My professional name is Marguerite Roberts.

MR. TAVENNER: What is your maiden name?

MISS ROBERTS: Smith.

MR. TAVENNER: When and where were you born?

MISS ROBERTS: I was born in Clarks, Nebraska. . . .

She wasn't pressed for her date of birth, which was the 26th of November, 1905, a Sunday, as you'd learned from a Perpetual Calendar, but what now would tell you the time of day or night, the room, the floor if there was more than one? And who would know the weather—mild for winter, was it, or had snow fallen, or had there just been a spell of rain? And what had her mother said when she first laid eyes on her last-born—that she was a plain little thing or, in the family phrase, as pretty as a little red pair of shoes. . . ?

MR. TAVENNER: Now, what is your profession?
MISS ROBERTS: I am a screenwriter.
MR. TAVENNER: How long have you been a screenwriter?
MISS ROBERTS: About 19 years.
MR. TAVENNER: When did you come to Hollywood?
MISS ROBERTS: Late in 1926 or early '27.
MR. TAVENNER: Will you state briefly your educational training?
MISS ROBERTS: I went to grade school in Clarks and high school in Fullerton, Nebraska, and I finished high school in Greeley, Colorado. Then I had about six months at business college, and that's all. . . .

And that's all. She was brought up on the plains, a flat-horizon country smack in the middle of the U.S.A. where nothing much broke the view anywhichway you looked, a barn, maybe, a grain elevator, a stand of trees low down on the sky. And yet sometimes there'd be a long shadow lying on the land, and it would be cast by the very person you were talking to in the road, someone you'd known since 1905, and it would be hard to credit that with *about six months at business college, and that's all,* she was reaching for the mountains she saw only in her mind. . . .

MR. TAVENNER: What has been your record of employment since you came to Hollywood?
MISS ROBERTS: I worked as a secretary for a couple of years, then as a reader in the story department of Fox Film Corporation.
MR. TAVENNER: How long were you employed as a reader?
MISS ROBERTS: About six months. I sold (Fox) a story, and they gave me an opportunity to do the screenplay, and I have been a writer since then.
MR. TAVENNER: What are some of the screen-credits you have received?
MISS ROBERTS: There have been many. I confine myself to twelve and a half years at Metro-Goldwyn-Mayer: ESCAPE, ZIEGFELD GIRL, SOMEWHERE I'LL FIND YOU, DRAGON SEED, SEA OF GRASS, DESIRE ME, IF WINTER COMES, AMBUSH, and they have just finished shooting IVANHOE.*

---

* Unaccountably, Maggie omitted one of her principal credits, HONKY TONK, a film for Clark Gable.

MR. TAVENNER: It is the desire of this Committee to investigate Communist infiltration in Hollywood. You have been prominently identified with the industry over a considerable period of years, and the Committee would very much like for you to tell what you know about infiltration.

(Here witness conferred with her counsel.)*

MISS ROBERTS: I decline to answer on the ground that it violates my rights under the First and Fifth Amendments of the Constitution. However, I am not a member of the Communist Party. I wish to make that clear.

Much more was made clear by the small figure before you. It was as if all at once her person had become a people. She was an album of that people, you thought, and on her pages was the look and the way of their lives, and you thought too of the things of her history, and you saw what she'd seen of the place she'd come from, a one-street town that lay like litter in the round-about wheat, and you saw the Platte, a mile wide, she'd told you, and an inch deep, and you saw gaunt farms and houses that expressed surprise. And now you saw her, one year old and walking with the aid of a spotted dog, and you saw a pet raccoon that slept in her dresser drawer, and you saw her sitting for a camera on a cardboard moon, and wasn't that she in white against the black of a tar-paper shack? She was an American, you thought, the first you'd ever met. . . .

MR. TAVENNER: In testimony here yesterday, Mr. Martin Berkeley stated that you were a member of the Communist Party. (Was he) telling the truth?

MISS ROBERTS: I decline to answer on the grounds stated before.

MR. TAVENNER: I understand you to state that you are not now a member of the Communist Party.

MISS ROBERTS: My exact words were, "I am not a member of the Communist Party."

MR. TAVENNER: You are speaking in the present tense.

MISS ROBERTS: Yes.

MR. TAVENNER: Were you a member on Sunday, the day before the Committee went into session?

MISS ROBERTS: I decline to answer on the grounds stated before.

MR. TAVENNER: Were you a member yesterday?

MISS ROBERTS: I decline on the grounds stated. . . .

The pages turned. They turned to pictures of her on a burro, on a horse, and balanced on the railing of a bridge, to pictures with one or another of

---

* This was done on half a dozen occasions, always for a respite rather than advice.

an endless sequence of dogs, to class pictures, pictures of teams, pictures of a fishing-trip up the Big Thompson. And the pages turned. . . .

> MR. TAVENNER: Is this position that you take, that you are not a member now, merely a cloak for this occasion?
> MISS ROBERTS: Definitely not, sir.
> MR. TAVENNER: When did you cease to be a member?
> MISS ROBERTS: I have given no testimony that I ever (was) a Communist.
> MR. TAVENNER: There is evidence by Mr. Berkeley that you were.
> MISS ROBERTS: I decline to comment on Mr. Berkeley's testimony.
> MR. TAVENNER: I think it is fair that I ask whether you propose to be a member when this Committee has returned to Washington.
> MISS ROBERTS: Definitely not.
> MR. TAVENNER: I have no further questions.
> MR. WALTER (Chairman pro tem): Mr. Doyle, any questions. . . ?

Pictures, you thought, of unpaved places, of ways you'd never known and faces never seen. Pictures of a people who spoke of soil and not, as you did, of dirt. Pictures of a realm where the sun seemed to rise from the earth itself and not, as it had risen for you, from gas-tanks, clothes-lines, and the smoke of burning lives. And from her voice, you knew how the pictures would sound if given speech, not at all as in the reuben turns of the vaudeville stage, but low-toned and, so it struck you, slow to reach the ear; above all, you'd hear no disaccord, it would be as if you were listening to creatures in their stalls, to roosting birds at night. . . .

> MR. DOYLE: You have had a very distinguished and prosperous career in your profession. Have you ever had called to your attention the Federal statute under which this Committee is charged with investigation of subversive conduct?
> MISS ROBERTS: Yes, I understand you are a legally constituted committee.
> MR. DOYLE: I am not asking you that question. Do you know the purposes of this committee?
> MISS ROBERTS: I believe the stated purposes are to show subversive influences in Hollywood.
> MR. DOYLE: That is substantially correct, but not limited, I assure you, to Hollywood.
> MISS ROBERTS: Well, that is the place that touches me. . . .

She was American, you thought, in a way you could never be; as applied to you, the word was largely a designation of the place in which you'd occurred; in her, though, it named the very components of her blood. And yet, here she was being lessoned in matters American by the honorable Clyde Doyle, loyalist from the bayside dump called Long Beach. . . !

MR. DOYLE: We are not undertaking to pick on Hollywood. We investigate un-American propaganda, foreign as well as domestic. Did you ever read the Constitution of the Communist Party?

MISS ROBERTS: No, sir.

MR. DOYLE: Did you ever read the by-laws of the Communist Party?

MISS ROBERTS: No, sir.

MR. DOYLE: Did you ever read in any literature of the Communist Party any pledge of allegiance to the United States?

MISS ROBERTS: I am not familiar with that sort of literature.

MR. DOYLE: I know you must be widely read, because you have had such success in your profession. You claim the benefit of the Fifth Amendment. Our records show that persons that claim that privilege are Communists. Are you in sympathy with any of the objectives of the Communist Party?

MISS ROBERTS: I don't know much about that, I must confess. I am not a political student; I am a writer. . . .

The honorable sucktit from—what was the place? Shorn of office, you thought, he'd've had to beg for permission to lick spit. . . .

MISS ROBERTS (cont'd.): . . . But I have told you that I believe in the Constitution, and if any Communist beliefs run contrary to that, then I would be against them.

MR. DOYLE: Then I take it that you approve of this Committee uncovering subversive attacks against our form of government.

MISS ROBERTS: Well, sir, I think you have done quite a bit of harm to us.

MR. DOYLE: In what way?

MISS ROBERTS: I don't think you really have uncovered any subversive acts. No one has seriously alleged that there has been any Communist propaganda in pictures, and a lot of people have suffered. I honestly think that the bad outweighs the good. That is my personal opinion.

MR. WOOD (resuming as Chairman): My distinguished colleague has violated the rule of five minutes.

MR. DOYLE: I desist further questioning.

MR. WOOD: Mr. Jackson. . . .

294

Distinguished Mr. Doyle, unaware that *desist* required a preposition, managed to desist without one, and Mr. Jackson, equally distinguished, took up at the point of desistance. *Distinguished,* you thought—was this Jackson, who hailed from who knew where, truly *notable for excellence or refinement,* or was he merely another run-of-the-mine wielder of the whip? Was that his excellence, the drawing of blood—and enjoying the sight, was that his refinement? There was no Quaker persuasion here, no friendly wish to share the light; there was only a command will imposed by common soldiers. . . .

MR. JACKSON: You have stated, I believe, that you are not now a member of the Communist Party.

MISS ROBERTS: I have stated that I am not a member of the Communist Party.

MR. JACKSON: But you have declined to answer as to possible previous membership.

MISS ROBERTS: That is true.

MR. JACKSON: I ask if you will be a Communist when you leave this room, or tomorrow?

MISS ROBERTS: No, sir.

MR. JACKSON: Can a believer in the constitutional form (of government) still be a practicing Communist?

MISS ROBERTS: That is a question that puzzles me, because if that were true, Congress would pass a law outlawing the Party, which it has not done.

MR. JACKSON: A great many members of Congress have that in mind.

MISS ROBERTS: They have not yet done it.

MR. JACKSON: You say a lot of people have suffered as a result of this investigation. I submit to you that people have suffered because of their activities on behalf of the Communist Party.

MISS ROBERTS: That is your opinion, sir. It isn't mine.

MR. JACKSON: It is an opinion that is shared by a great many Americans. . . .

By Americans, he meant, like his distinguished self. But what of those for whom there was no inducement great enough to make them share his opinion? Were they less than he, were they Americans of a cheaper grade or a lower class, or, forbid it Heaven!, were they no Americans at all? . . . American, you thought, American—the word was a pervasion, a presence, it was one of the spectators, and in the end it would be a judge of what was happening to the country within the walls of that room. . . .

MR. JACKSON: That is all, Mr. Chairman.

MR. WOOD: Mr. Potter, any questions?

MR. POTTER: Miss Roberts, it is certainly the general conception that the Communist Party is an arm of an international conspiracy dedicated to the overthrow of our government and all governments.

MISS ROBERTS: (The witness made no response.)

MR. POTTER: I regret that you seek not to cooperate with the Committee. I have nothing further, Mr. Chairman.

MR. WOOD: Mr. Counsel, do you have any further questions of this witness?

MR. TAVENNER: Yes. It has been shown through numerous witnesses that hundreds of thousands of dollars have been contributed by persons in your industry to the Communist Party. I would like for you to tell this Committee what you know about the tapping of this great source of wealth.

MISS ROBERTS: I have no knowledge of it.

MR. TAVENNER: I have no further questions.

MR. WOOD: Does any of the Committee?

MR. JACKSON: One short question. (then, to witness) You said this Committee has not uncovered subversion during its investigation. Have you ever heard of Alger Hiss?

MISS ROBERTS: I wasn't referring to any of your activities outside of Hollywood. I know very little about them.

MR. JACKSON: I have no further questions.

MR. WOOD: Is there any reason why the witness shouldn't be excused, Mr. Counsel?

MR. TAVENNER: It's all right to dismiss her.

MR. WOOD: It is so ordered. . . .

§

And then coming toward you was a set of rounds in chocolate brown, and as you rose to greet them, you said, "What can I say?"

And she said, "Did I do all right, Jabe?"

Someone else replied, saying, "You were good, Maggie, very good," and it was Mike Wilson.

A woman approached from the crowd and said, "Didn't I hear you testify you was from Nebraska?"

"Why, yes," Maggie said. "From a little town between Grand Island and Columbus."

"Well, I'm from Nebraska too, and I'm downright ashamed we was born in the same place."

"I'm sorry you feel that way, ma'am."

"I ain't sorry for you, not a bit," the woman said, and she walked away.

"Let's go home and talk to the dogs," you said.

§

From the Civic Center, you took the long route around Griffith Park to the Valley. At that hour, traffic was still light, and you drove with as little thought as if you were watching someone drive. Where were you when at last you spoke, at what stop-light, what street, and how far back was Room 518?

" 'Did I do all right?' you said, and I said nothing. It wasn't because I had nothing to say. It was because I had nothing to say it *with*. We've known each other for a long time, we've been married for a long time, and I've heard you speak of many things. Your talk is like you, like your people—direct, quiet, honest, guileless, always guileless. So when you ask me how you did today, the best I can do is this: if I'd never seen you before, if I'd just happened by and heard you, I'd've asked you to be my wife."
And she said, "Why, Johnny. . . !" and moved herself closer across the seat.

THE COLOR OF THE AIR, XVI

EMMA GOLDMAN—1940
CASTLE-BUILDER IN UNION SQUARE

> *The waving of their outstretched hands was like*
> *the wings of white birds fluttering.*
> —Emma Goldman

At the end, the crowds were only apparitions, the smoke remainder of a stroke at seventy, shades of the furniture in a burned-out brain. And yet, how like they were to the crowds at the start, waiting for her in the Kovno air, there at parturition—the reaching hands, the beating wings! They must've governed her, those auguries, drawn her toward the Square. Mystery codes her: there's no way to construe her choice of roads.

Can we say it was due to her being plain, a five-foot Jew with light brown hair and *pince-nez* worn on a chain? Or that it was because she had t.b. at times. sugar in her urine, an inverted womb, and a tendency to fall? Would such things ravel out a taste for pain, would they gloss her lifelong suicide? Would we know her if we knew of the varicose veins, the broken arches, the throe she had every twenty-eight days? Would it sink in then why nothing swayed her, nothing changed her mind or ways, neither the fines she paid nor her days in jail, not spite and exile, not the poison penned her, the spew from the pulpit, the dead cats we threw — would light be shed and she become clear? Or would she stay a cipher, a disarray of symbols, a lock that lacks a key?

When no one would rent her a room (free lover! anarchist! antichrist! suffragette!), she slept in whorehouses and other public places — streetcars, doorways, toilets in the park — and when horseshit hit her soapbox, she kept on talking and spoke it away. For those she prized — the poor, the put-upon, the ill-used — she went to the stake and lit her own fire. She gave up family, easy money, and the right to come and go, she gave up fashion, honors, nationality, even, and finally the quiet and crayon hours of old age. There's no unriddling that, there's no seeing around the corners of such a heart.

A fat little woman, she grew to be. Her glasses were thicker than before, and she wore them with temples instead of a chain, and she was shorter by an inch or more, and her lungs were scarred, and there was still a trace of sugar in her water, and her legs seemed stuffed with worms. A big-tittied little dame in a dime bandanna and a hand-me-down, a sick old soul, and, damn us all, only yesterday she was stumping for Man out there in the cold! We'll not know why. We'll not know why.

We let her come back to God's country when she died of that punctured artery. We opened the door a crack, about wide enough for a fat little coffin, and she came from the outside world to lie at Waldheim, near those Hunkies we hanged for the Haymarket. We'd rented her a room at last.

SCENE 119

METRO CONFERENCE No. 2 (September 1951)

Typed by Maggie and initialed M.R.S., this entry appears in your record of the period under the date September 21, 1951: *Mr. Mannix telephoned and asked if he could see me at 10:30 on Monday.*

"He called me darling," she said, "and he called me dear."
"Heartwarming," you said.
"You know what I heard about him? That he used to be a bouncer for an amusement park. And now, I'm afraid he's a bouncer for M-G-M."
"They don't call you in to throw you out. If you're out, you stay out,

like that reader who found his stuff in a paper sack on the sidewalk."

"In the long run, it'll be no different for me. I'll be darling and dear with a paper sack."

"Maybe, but right now, your name is still on the door."

"How about on Monday?"

"It'll be there on Monday too."

"Always hopeful, always wrong."

"Nothing's been wrong since the day we met."

"You say good things, and I love to hear them—but Mannix doesn't want to see me to offer me a raise."

"I'll be along," you said. "He'll be seeing *us*. . . ."

The meeting, as you recorded in your three-page summary of it, took place in Mannix's office on the Executive floor of the Thalberg Building. Present with him was Dore Schary, the studio head, and according to your report, *the preliminary greetings and remarks were friendly.* For Mannix's manner and tone, *friendly* may well have been exact, for however common, he was never mean of spirit, never a churl; but even after the assuage of time, the word seems inexact for Schary. Forty-and-some years of age, he was tall, lean, and straight-standing in garments cut to fit. Somehow, though, he failed to fill them, and you thought him ill at ease within their crafted folds. How, then, could he have been *friendly,* a ready-made man in custom-made clothes. . . ?

SCHARY: We'd like it, Maggie, if you elaborated on the testimony
 you gave to the Committee.
MAGGIE: Elaborate? I'm not sure of what you mean.
SCHARY: The Company wants to know where you stand politically.
MAGGIE: I told that to the Committee.
SCHARY: Only just so much of it.
MAGGIE: Then what you're asking, Dore, is that I tell more to
 Metro than I did to Congress. How could I justify that?
MANNIX: Whatever you tell us, it would never get out of this room.
MAGGIE: If you heard my testimony, Mr. Mannix. . . .
SANFORD: May I make a point here?
MANNIX: Sure. Go ahead.
SANFORD: First, a question. Is this conference being taped?
SCHARY: I resent that.
SANFORD: Do you? Well, rest easy: *we're* keeping a record. Our
 last entry was the studio's call to this meeting. The next will be
 what happened here.
SCHARY: You want to make a point, you said.
SANFORD: We'd like it understood that nothing we say here is to
 be taken as an admission that we are or were members of the Com-
 munist Party. Any reference to that will be hypothetical.

SCHARY: What were you saying, Maggie?

MAGGIE: That if Mr. Mannix was listening to me when I was testifying. . . .

MANNIX: A lot of us was listening.

MAGGIE: . . . I think he'd have to allow that I was straightforward and respectful. And if I say so myself, I was honest.

SCHARY: You were all you say, Maggie, but you didn't go far enough. We were hoping for more.

MANNIX: What you said was fifty percent complete, even seventy-five, but the studio was looking for a hundred. You know what I mean—a hundred?

MAGGIE: Yes. You wanted me to be what Martin Berkeley was— an informer.

Informer—to Mannix, the word was a swarm of winged things, unwelcome and annoying, and he waved at it as if to drive it away. Schary, by turning to a window, denied that it was there.

MANNIX: Who's talking about informing?

MAGGIE: You said you were hoping for a hundred percent from me. I couldn't give a hundred percent unless I named names. That's informing, and I want no part of it. I'm sorry if the studio doesn't like what I did, but I simply had to refuse to answer questions about people I may know.

SCHARY: That's what we find it hard to understand. Why did you have to refuse if you're not a Communist?

MAGGIE: Because Martin Berkeley swore that I *was.*

MANNIX: Excuse the language, Maggie, but Martin Berkeley is a son-of-a-bitch.

MAGGIE: Maybe so, but he was the Committee's star witness. If I challenged his testimony, if I said he was lying about me, I'd go broke trying to prove it—and in the end, *I'd* go to jail for perjury, not Berkeley.

SCHARY: Why? It'd be your word against his.

MAGGIE: We're into legal territory. (then, to you) You're the lawyer, John.

SANFORD: Metro doesn't need me to explain the law.

MANNIX: Explain anyway. We can check on it.

SANFORD: Without informers, the Committee couldn't exist; it'd die in a day, like a butterfly. Berkeley gave it a hundred and fifty names, and the whole show out here rests on his testimony. If he falls, it falls, and the Committee falls with it. Do you think the Committee, the government, is going to let Berkeley be proved a liar? Like hell. He'll get their support—a hundred percent.

Schary turned back from the window, where he'd been standing before a third-floor view of sound-stage roofs, of figures passing in a studio street.

SCHARY: Are you implying that the government would knowingly back a perjuror?

SANFORD: Come on, Dore. It would back a snake if the snake bore witness against the Reds. But remember this: Berkeley isn't a perjurer till he's proved to be. And who's going to do that—the people he named? They'd have to prove a negative—that they're *not* Communists. How does a person show that he was *not* at Party meetings, that he did *not* pay dues, that he *never* followed the Party line?

SCHARY: If the people named by Berkeley are innocent. . . .

SANFORD: They're innocent, Dore. It's no crime to be a Communist.

SCHARY: Let's say, then, if the people he named aren't Communists, they owe it to themselves to stand up and call him a liar. That's what we were hoping Maggie would do—that, or admit to prior membership. She did neither.

In the interminable instant before responding, you apprehended your surroundings, the bookcases, the stolid furniture, the faces confronting you and Maggie, the six-sided space you sat in, the almost visible opposition in the air.

SANFORD: You haven't been paying attention, or else you don't care. I told you the dangers of an outright denial, and they're serious dangers, though not for you. As for admitting past membership, once she does that, she's "incriminated herself" within the meaning of the Fifth Amendment, and she can no longer claim its protection.

MANNIX: Why would she need it?

SANFORD: As a defense against being forced to name her associates. If she refused to comply, she'd go to jail for contempt.

MANNIX: But why would she refuse? She could do what Berkeley did.

MAGGIE: Then we'd both be sons-of-bitches.

SCHARY: I'm not asking this question for myself, Maggie; I'm asking it for the main office in New York. Would you be willing to go before the Committee again and take either of the positions I mentioned—denial or admission?

MAGGIE: No.

SCHARY: Suppose we arranged a closed session—no spectators, no reporters, no camera, just you and the Committee.

MAGGIE: I was up before the Committee once—without just cause, to my way of thinking—and I said my say then. Nothing will get me there again.

SCHARY: You're under no compulsion, Maggie. I'm merely trying to find a way to satisfy public opinion.

SANFORD: Has the public expressed an opinion? Or are you talking about the American Legion and the Ku Klux Klan?

MANNIX: Where's the harm in Maggie giving the Committee something to hang their hat on? Nothing much, you understand.

SANFORD: Like what, Mr. Mannix? That her husband taught a class at the Little Red Schoolhouse—and that Dore taught in the room next door?

You knew that Schary was nettled even without seeing his expression; you were watching Mannix, and across his face fled a look of pleasure at the other's pain.

MANNIX: Would you go for something like this, Maggie? A paper saying what you are or what you used to be. A private paper just for the Company, an affidavit.

MAGGIE: I'm sorry, Mr. Mannix, but all I have to say I've already said to the Committee. It's right here in this transcript.

SCHARY: Is that what you're holding—a transcript of your testimony?

MAGGIE: The reporters sent it to me right after the Hearings.

SCHARY: I'd like to give it a careful reading. Could you leave it with me?

MAGGIE: Of course, Dore.

SCHARY: I think we can wind this up for now. Go home, you two, and think things over, the things we've discussed here today. Then we'll talk some more.

The Noon & Pratt transcript was left with Schary, goodbyes were exchanged, and you and Maggie went to the door.

There you turned to say, "What will the studio do if Maggie keeps on refusing?"

And Mannix said, "We'll talk some more," and putting his arms around Maggie, he spoke some words you could not hear.

§

Leaving the Thalberg Building, you crossed the street to the parking-lot and helped Maggie into the car. She looked at you long enough to say, "He called me darling, and he called me dear," and then she began to cry.

SCENE 120

AGAIN, THE CHIEF JUSTICE OF THE ONTRA CAFETERIA
(September 1951)

"Well, Julian," he said, "how did it go?"

You weren't at his usual table, a long one in the rear room where he presided over sessions of the aged to whom he was the law. They were there that day—you could see them through a doorway—but without his restraining presence, they seemed to be unruly, as if they'd already become the children they very nearly were. Without him, you thought, they were ungoverned: it was kindergarten time.

"Well, Julian," he said. . . .

Your table stood against a window, and through it you saw an outside world silenced by a thickness of glass. Cars and people passed, but all you heard was inside sound, a compound of voices, silver on silver, and the flatted tones that china touching china made.

"Only the top brass was there," you said. "Dore Schary, who thinks he's filling Mayer's shoes, and Eddie Mannix, the general manager of the Company and second in command on the Coast. Nobody's above those two except Nick Schenk in New York."

"Why didn't you take Sidney Cohn along?"

"That might've made it a confrontation, and it hasn't gotten that far. We thought I was still enough of a lawyer to handle whatever came up."

"What *did* come up?"

"They sounded Maggie out on going before the Committee again, this time as a friendly witness."

"Meaning. . . ?"

"Denying that she was ever in the Party, or admitting membership and naming names."

His next question was only a look, but you supplied the words and answered them, saying, "And what we said was nix."

This time, he put no question, spoken or otherwise, and you said, "If there's anything you want to know. . . ."

"If I thought you could answer, I'd ask."

"All the same, ask."

"What's going to happen now?"

At the long table in the other room, there was a sudden uprising of voices, and you thought back to childhood affrays over alphabet blocks, over pieces of chalk and wads of colored clay.

"We were told to go home and reconsider, as if what they wanted gave us a choice. There is no choice, papa, not if what you taught me was true."

"I don't recall the particular lesson, kid."

"Sure you do. It was when I wanted to report grandpa's lawyer to the Bar Association for a misuse of funds. You wouldn't let me ruin his career. No son of yours could do that, you said, without falling in your opinion to the ground."

"You give me too much credit. You'd never have turned the man in."

"You think so? If not for you, I'd've had him disbarred."

"Well, it's all past history."

"It's now too. If it was wrong to snitch then, and it was, it's just as wrong today."

At the long table in the adjoining room, another gust of voices rose, a dust-devil of sound, and you wondered about the latest cause of strife, as once it had been a few strands of raffia, a ball, a crayon, a rubber band, or nothing, really, nothing at all.

"Maggie's been at Metro for thirteen years," you said. "She'd never have lasted that long if she hadn't been well-regarded—she delivered for them, and they like her. But it'd be foolish to think that Metro runs on love alone."

"You're wiser than you used to be."

"The wisdom is Maggie's. She knows why they're walking softly. It's because two of her scripts have been shot and are ready for release,* and they don't know what to do about the writing credits."

"I'm in the dark, kid."

"A writer's name must appear among the titles at the beginning of a film. If Metro gets rid of Maggie, can it also get rid of her name?"

"Why should it want to?"

"Because her name is what the Legion is after. If it's on the screen, they may picket the picture."

"What you think, then, is that you have something Metro may have to deal for."

"Yes.

---

* *A Letter To the President,* with Shelley Winters and Ricardo Montalban, and *Ivanhoe,* a far more important production, with Elizabeth Taylor and Robert Taylor.

SCENE 121

METRO CONFERENCE No. 3 (September 1951)

On the day after your conference with Schary and Mannix, Maggie drove to the studio for a script discussion with Armand Deutsch, her producer. When she returned, she told you that very little of her time with him had been devoted to the screenplay.

". . . After only a few minutes, he said it would be foolish not to speak of the Hearings. He'd known about my involvement from the beginning — he's a close friend of Dore's — and now that I'd made an appearance, he wanted to talk about the position I'd taken on the stand."

"He was talking for Dore," you said. "He was making Dore's pitch."

"More than likely. He said I'd gone far in the industry, and I could go even further: people got along with me, and I was a reliable and versatile writer. It'd be a shame, he said, if by refusing to cooperate with the Committee, I lost what I'd gained through high-grade work. Don't be a martyr, he said."

"Just chuck 'em a few names. Nothing much, as Mannix said."

"He implied that I was protecting people who didn't count — nobodies. I was walking the plank for nobodies."

"One of them, I think, was me."

"You or whoever, I got the impression that he thought it was all right to save myself, no matter what the cost. I owed it to my career."

"And what did Maggie say?"

"I said, 'I'm not being a martyr, Armand. I just don't want to feel ashamed to be alive.' "

"Give us a kiss."

SCENE 122

TWO LETTERS (September 1951)

Written after the Hearings, they reached you late in the month — and they were the only ones you received. The first was from Margaret and Albert Maltz, and it read:

Dear Marguerite and John,

I am sorry that the blow had to fall on you also. I want you to know how much we respect you for your principle and courage.

The second, on the letterhead of the Merryman Farm at Moreno on the Riverside road, was from your race-track friends, Ann and Tom Peppers, who said:

Dear Maggie and John:

Sorry to hear of your trouble and we do hope that everything will come out alright. We love you both and want you to know it.

SCENE 123

METRO CONFERENCE, No. 4 (September 1951)

It took place at your request, and it was for the purpose of reporting to the studio the outcome of Maggie's "further deliberations" about a second appearance before the House Committee. Again only Schary and Mannix were present for the Company, and in Maggie's absence, her interests were represented by you and Sidney Cohn.

SANFORD: . . . As you suggested, Dore, Maggie and I talked it over between ourselves, and we did the same with Mr. Cohn. We turned over every stone in sight, and also the stones under the stones. In the end, we'd found nothing to make us change our minds.

SCHARY: That's very disappointing.

SANFORD: Maggie has left it to me to say how sorry she is about having to refuse you. She feels, though, that she didn't deserve to be called before the Committee in the first place, and to appear again would be cruel and unusual punishment for her. In any case, I'd never let her, because she's never done a wrong thing in the forty-six years of her life. She has nothing further to say to the Committee.

MANNIX: Mr. Cohn, you went over this business with Maggie and John. Is there something else, maybe, that you can chip in?

COHN: I think there is. I know about your earlier conferences, of course, particularly about John's explanation of the dangers of trying to refute Berkeley's testimony. John may not know this part of Berkeley's recent history, but the fact is that only a few months back, he himself was named a Communist by the informer Richard Collins. In righteous wrath, he wired the Committee, denying the charge and denouncing Collins as a liar. When he cooled down, he realized what he'd done—he'd challenged a government witness—and bravado not being bravery, he went into panic. Off he rushed to Washington to take it all back, to admit the accusation, and to give the Committee six times as many names as it'd gotten from Collins.

SCHARY: What has that to do with this?

COHN: You surprise me, Mr. Schary.

SCHARY: Indeed.

COHN: The point I was making is this: Berkeley was in the position that Maggie now occupies, a position he could've gotten out of by saying nothing, as Maggie is doing. Instead, he tried to play a lion when he's really only a lap-dog. Maggie has pride; he's contemptible.

SCHARY: Well, all I can say is, this will require further study.

SANFORD: How much further, Dore? Further talk, you said, further deliberation, and now further study. Maggie surely is entitled to know where she stands with the Company.

SCHARY: I wish I could give her an answer.

SCENE 124

METRO CONFERENCE No. 5 (October 1951)

When Maggie came away from the telephone, she said, "That was Deutsch. He wants to see me this morning."

"That's cutting it kind of fine," you said, "calling at breakfast time. Why didn't he call last night?"

"I think you hit it the other day: he speaks for the Brass."

"Then I go along."

"I was hoping you would, Jabe."

§

Maggie introduced you to Deutsch, and after an exchange of pleasantries, you retired to a chair in a corner and remained silent while the script was being discussed. Again, it was not discussed for long before Deutsch turned to the subject of the Hearings.

DEUTSCH: I hear that the studio is arranging for you to make a second appearance before the Committee.

MAGGIE: That's news to me, Armand. I've twice told Dore and Mr.
Mannix that I'd never again have any dealings with the Committee. It's an evil thing, a cruel thing, and I have nothing but scorn
for the dirty work it does.

DEUTSCH: I was only giving you what I heard on the grapevine.
The general feeling upstairs is that you're being a martyr, as I
said once before.

MAGGIE: After going home the other day, I looked up *martyr* in
John's big dictionary, and then I typed the definition on this card:
*one who sacrifices his life, station, or what is of great value, for the sake
of principle.* When I refuse to name names, I suppose that's what
I am, but I don't have any such puffed-up notions of myself. I
just can't go hurting others in order to save myself.

When the meeting ended, you spoke for the first time, saying, "Leave the
card with Mr. Deutsch."

SCENE 125

FRAGMENTS (October 1951)

Sat. Oct. 6—Worked at home on last sequence
Sun. Oct. 7—same
Mon. Oct. 8—same
Tue. Oct. 9—Finished last seq
Wed. Oct. 10—AD called. Meeting tomorrow
Thu. Oct. 11—Meeting at studio. More chges. . . .

§

When she came home, she said, "There's a new nameplate on my door,"
and then she walked past you and into the bedroom.

She was followed closely by Juno, and after a moment, Juno was followed
by you. "Who's in there now?" you said.

"Who's in where?"

"Room 243."

"That's *my* room. *I'm* in there."

"I thought you said. . . ."

308

"Oh. I only meant the *nameplate* was new. It's nice-looking. It's made of brass."

"Mrs. Sanford," you said, "so are you. . . ."

§

Fri.   Oct. 12—Worked at home on chges
Sat.   Oct. 13—same
Sun.   Oct. 14—same
Mon. Oct. 15—Delivd last 15 pges to AD
Tue.   Oct. 16—Meeting on last 15 pges
Wed. Oct. 17—same
Thu.   Oct. 18—same
Fri.   Oct. 19—same. Came home to work. . . .

§

"While you were outside," she said, "I got a call from Steve Ames. He wanted me to know about last night's preview of *A Letter To the President*. It went off fine, he said. Sixty-two favorable cards, five otherwise."

"The usual wisenheimers," you said.

She laughed, saying, "The five, do you mean, or the sixty-two. . . ?"

§

Sat.   Oct. 20—Worked at home
Sun.   Oct. 21—same
Mon. Oct. 22—same
Tue.   Oct. 23—same. Finishd chges on endg
Wed. Oct. 24—Delivd endg to studio typist
Thu.   Oct. 25—To studio for meetg with AD. . . .

§

At midafternoon, she telephoned to say, "I've been in my office waiting for a call from Deutsch, and I just now got it. He said he'd just gotten word from Larry Weingarten that I was off the script, off the assignment."

"Did he give you a reason?"

"I asked, and he said he didn't know."

"Shoot, Maggie, he can do better than that. Why don't you go around and tell him so?"

"I mean to."

"Then come home, and don't talk to anyone else. . . ."

§

"I said, 'Come clean, Armand. I'm no week-to-week writer; I don't get taken off a script with a phone-call. What did Weingarten really say?' He said, 'I give you my word, Maggie—all he said was Roberts was off the script. If I had to guess, though, I'd say it had something to do with the Hearings.' "

"Did he keep a straight face?" you said.

"His usual face is straight."

"How were things left?"

"I had the feeling that he was minded to give me another Company spiel, but if so, he thought the better of it, and out I went."

"Sit tight."

"And do what?"

"Wait. . . ."

§

Fri.   Oct. 26—Waited at home for word from MGM
Sat.   Oct. 27—same
Sun.   Oct. 28—same
Mon. Oct. 29—same. No word. . . .

§

When Maggie came to your room, you were trying to revise a scene in *The Bandage,** but the words, the phrases before you were resistant to change. It was as if, having found their way to the page, they'd established their right to remain there against all comers, all other words.

"Ames just called," she said. "He found out I was off the Deutsch script, and he asked McKenna to assign me to him. You know what McKenna told him? That Schary was reading the script in New York, and I might be needed for further revisions."

"What do you make of all that?" you said.

"What do *you*?"

"That being off the script doesn't mean you're off the lot."

"You think so?"

"Don't you?"

"Frankly, no."

"You always see through a glass, darkly."

"That way, I never see what isn't there. Schary isn't in New York on account of me—I'm not that important—but while he's there, he'll surely consult on the whole Communism-in-Hollywood question. And when he gets back, something's going to happen. I can feel it in my bones. . . ."

---

* Early title of *The Land That Touches Mine.*

310

SCENE 126

METRO CONFERENCE No. 6 (October 1951)

It was a month and more back to the Hearings and twice that long to the service of the subpoenas. Until now, though, neither you nor Maggie was aware of the stress, the strain of the time, nor does your record contain much beyond memoranda of the daily round. On that day, the 31st of October, this note appears: *At 9 o'clock Marguerite Roberts and John Sanford went to Dr. Lipman's office for x-rays on JS.* You have no remembrance of what the x-rays were for, or of the condition, if any, that they eventually revealed: no further reference to them is made in the record. But while at that office, you were reached by Mannix, whose call was transferred from your home: could you, he wanted to know, meet with him during the afternoon. . . ?

MANNIX: I just came back from New York, I was there with Dore, and I put in a lot of time talking to high-up people in the Legion — commanders of this post and that — and, Maggie, I don't have good news for you.

MAGGIE: I don't expect any from that kind.

MANNIX: And Mr. Thau here, he's been talking to Legion people locally, and they all say the same thing.

SANFORD: Which is what, Mr. Mannix?

MANNIX: A while back, they had a convention in Florida — maybe you read about it — and at this convention, they passed a resolution that the Legion (this is in their words) will ferret out and hound anyone suspected of Communism. And it also went on to say they will expose their employers to the public.

SANFORD: What it comes down to, then, is this: will the picture business allow itself to be run by ferrets and hounds?

THAU: This is no laughing matter, John.

SANFORD: If I'm laughing, Mr. Thau, it's a laugh with cold teeth. There's nothing funny about the American Legion. To me, they're German Brown Shirts dressed in blue.

MANNIX: The part where they threaten the employers — you can't blame us for being upset about that. They're going to denounce us, they said. That means boycotting our pictures, picketing theatres, putting articles in the papers. We couldn't stand that kind of a thing.

MAGGIE: If the Legion did all that, Mr. Mannix, it would be just as un-American as the Committee. It would be persecuting you, the same as it did me.

THAU: The Company is in the middle, Maggie.

SANFORD: It isn't, Mr. Thau. It's at one end or the other—our end or the Legion's. The Legion says we have no right to our political beliefs. If you agree, you're on the Legion end.

MANNIX: I don't hold with the Legion. My personal opinion is, the resolution is unfair. But they voted on it, and they're going to act on it, so what can we do?

MAGGIE: If you think it's wrong, oppose it; if you think it's right, fire me.

THAU: Who's talking about firing? All the Company wants is for you to go to the Committee and do more than you did before. Answer their questions. Where's the harm?

MANNIX: Mention people that already been mentioned, people they know about. There's no—what's the word?—stigma to that.

MAGGIE: Judas has been in a hundred films and stool-pigeons in a thousand, and I never saw one who didn't get what he deserved. Naming is naming, whether I do it or Berkeley.

MANNIX: Berkeley is a yellow dog, but what's the good of talking about him? You want the truth, you were on the list long before he come along, and excuse me for saying this, it was account of John here. He's the one you're protecting.

SANFORD: You're wrong about that, Mr. Mannix. I'd never let her go to the wall for me.

THAU: Well, whoever she's protecting, it's a shame she's laying her career on the line for them.

MAGGIE: Is that what all this is about, then—my career depends on whether I fink?

MANNIX: Not so fast, Maggie, not so fast. This is still a friendly discussion.

MAGGIE: I'm beginning to think it's one of those or-else things.

THAU: Nothing of the kind, Maggie.

MANNIX: In fact, I spoke to Dore in New York this morning, and he specially said not to press you. He said you were to go home, like before, and talk it over quietly, no pressure, no threats.

SANFORD: We'll do what you ask, but the decision will rest with Maggie alone, and if I know her at all, there isn't a chance she'll change her mind. . . .

SCENE 127

METRO CONFERENCE No. 7 (November 1951)

Once again, Mannix had sent you home to "talk things over," and once again you'd done as he desired of you. Always in the company of Juno, you'd talked in the house, in one room or another and even as you walked through the hall, and further attended by the blind and near-blind outdoor dogs, you'd talked under the oaks and in the spacing of the orange grove and while pacing between the paddocks and the stalls. You talked long, talked in all four corners of your four-acre freehold, and what in the end had you arrived at, what had you decided to say. . . ?

> *(To this day, the 24th of June, 1988, Maggie insists that the way of the informer was never in view, but you're equally certain that it must've been. All roads began from where you stood, and all but one were marked with the place they led to. Of that one, only the first crooked mile could be seen, and on it went the Judases of your time, impenitent and quite safe still from suicide. It would've been unnatural, it would've been other than human, not to have wondered in that crooked day whether the crooked way was the straight.)*

It was not, but you and Maggie could've known that only after "talking things over" in the mute company of faithful dogs.

§

The conference was brief, "lasting for about 15 minutes," as your record states. In attendance for Metro-Goldwyn-Mayer were Mannix and the studio Comptroller, L. K. Sidney, who may have been present as a witness only, for he did not speak.

SANFORD: . . . We did as you asked, Mr. Mannix. We went home and talked this thing to a fare-thee-well.
MANNIX: And what've you got to tell me?
SANFORD: That we can't do as you want.
MANNIX: I've got to hear that from Maggie.
MAGGIE: John said it, Mr. Mannix. We can't.
MANNIX: For God's sake, Maggie, don't you see where you're heading?

MAGGIE: The studio is asking me to do an impossible thing. I don't mean a difficult thing. I don't mean an unpleasant thing, a thing I'd just as soon avoid. I mean a thing I find impossible.

MANNIX: It was possible for Berkeley, for this Collins fellow, for actresses and actors and other writers. Why should it be impossible for you?

MAGGIE: I don't know the answer to that. All I can say is, some people stick at nothing. Nothing is impossible for the Berkeleys of this world, but I'm not one of them. I'd sooner be dead.

MANNIX: We're getting nowheres, Maggie. All along, I've only been trying to save you from yourself, but it looks like you don't want to be saved.

SANFORD: She's in no danger from herself, Mr. Mannix.

MANNIX: No? Who from, then?

SANFORD: Metro.

MANNIX: How do you figure that?

SANFORD: You're not standing up to the Committee. You're not standing up to the Legion, the Motion Picture Alliance, the fanatics — and that's the danger. You're lying down.

Mannix began to swivel his chair, and you saw him in every aspect of a slow full turn, and then, when facing you again, he brought the chair to a stop.

MANNIX: Well, Dore told me I should try, and I tried. What can I do more? Nothing, so, Maggie and John, with the greatest regret, I've got to put this thing in the hands of our lawyers. . . .

SCENE 128

METRO CONFERENCE No. 8 (November 1951)

Convened by Mannix, it took place as usual in his office, and with his associate Thau in attendance, it *lasted approximately an hour.* No further effort was made to persuade Maggie to reappear before the Committee; instead, the representatives of the Company addressed themselves at once to the settlement of her contract with the studio.

MANNIX: . . . We made it in good faith, and we're honor-bound by it. We're not out to push you into a lawsuit. We don't want to go to court with a person that did well for us for thirteen years.

MAGGIE: The Company has always been fair with me. I wish I could be here for thirteen more.

THAU: I wish it too. I wish John and I could sit down and arrange the terms, like three times we did before.

MANNIX: The pressure groups won't let us keep you. We've been told by the Legion that they're getting up a blacklist, and you know what that means.

SANFORD: We do; it's the studio that doesn't. It means that half-wits are taking over the world.

MANNIX: Well, half-wits or no-wits, they're out for blood, and what they've got over us is this business in Korea—Communists killing American boys in Korea. How you going to beat a thing like that?

THAU: So about your contract, Maggie, which I myself negotiated with John. It's for five years straight at Sixty-five Thousand a year. The Company is asking, what would you accept to cancel it, no hard feelings, goodbye and good luck?

MAGGIE: That would be for a lawyer to say, Mr. Thau—and I certainly don't mean John. I couldn't ask him to dicker for me.

THAU: Why not? He dickered before. He's a stubborn man, but I wouldn't call him stupid. He knows your value.

MAGGIE: For writing your films, yes. But this would be for *not* writing, and my husband will not bargain over that.

MANNIX: She's right, Ben.

THAU: If I said something embarrassing, Maggie, I apologize. Bring this New York guy out, this Sidney Cohn.

SANFORD: We'll call him as soon as we leave.

And you did.

SCENE 129

FOUR DAYS IN ENCINO (November 1951)

They must've been spent in the usual ways, and as they went, you must've touched on the plight you were in, and more than once you must've rued that it was you who'd caused it, and you must've dwelt on her fine behavior, told her how free you found it of begging and boldness—but nothing that was said remains. You must've wandered the house looking at books and pictures, touching pottery, surfaces, things, and you must've gone outdoors at times to walk the paths, to see the tinsel on your citrus trees, and you must've noted the acanthus plant, the tamarisk, the arbutus bush, the flowering eucalyptus near the gate, and with you ever there must've been a dog or two or three—but nothing of that remains. . . .

SCENE 130

A few days earlier, after a year and a half of work, you'd completed *A Walk in the Fire,* Volume 4 of the Autobiography. The manuscript, already more than five hundred pages long, was further expanded by seventeen inserts of historical commentary, each of these addressed to "the color of the air," and the whole was then submitted to Maggie for a first full reading. On finishing, she showed you a list she'd made of your typing errors, your errors of fact and chronology, and, to your chagrin, a spelling error (in your version, the word was *octupus*). You were interested, of course, in her comment on the mechanics of the manuscript, but you were far more concerned with her opinion of its narrative, for in the main it turned on her.

". . . Your subtitle," she said, "is *Scenes from the Life of an American Jew,* but I'm in them as much as you are, even when I'm not actually there. We met, you know, on almost the first page of the previous volume, and ever since then, you've been putting yourself in my shadow. I'm not that good, Jabe, and you're not that bad. You make too much of me and too little of you."

"I've known you for fifty years now, fifty-two," you said, "and on my best day, I was never as good as you. I do stand in your shadow, but even so, the book's about me, not you: it's about a Jew eclipsed."

"There's a word for guys like you—ux-something."

"Uxorious, meaning excessively fond of a wife."

"I'll bet you looked it up."

"Sure I did."

"Well, so did I. It also means submissive. Are you submissive?"

"To my superiors—yes."

"I'm not your superior, Jabez."

"When I first came out from New York, I was one sorry piece of work. If I've made any progress since, it's owing to you, and in these last two books, I'm acknowledging it. What's wrong with that?"

"A reader'll say: He's hugging a bad bargain."

"Reader! Who cares what a reader says? I don't write for readers; I write for you and me. And you're the one who made that possible. I've written eighteen books—sixteen of them are due to you."

"I didn't write them; you did."

"You backed them."

"And if you write them, I'll back sixteen more," she said. "And come to think of it, that's my opinion of *A Walk in the Fire.*"

"And still you say I make too much of you. Why, you're the greatest thing out of Nebraska since Crazy Horse."

She scanned the sheets on which her notes had been made, and you watched her finger tick off the entries—p 177, p 323, p 462—until it came to a stop at a scrawl, a thicket of words that only she could penetrate.

"What does that say?" you said.

"I can hardly read my own writing, but I know what it's about. Three-four times in the book, maybe even more, you speak of older people—your father, my mother—looking off at things that aren't there, or, as you like to put it, things that only they can see. Did you do that deliberately?"

"No."

"Then how do you account for doing it so often?"

"It must have had something to do with the age of the people. I see them as seeing back into their lives."

"To what?"

"I don't say, because I don't know. But what can it be except the color of their air? I'm old too, and all I write about is the color of mine."

She nodded, in approval, you thought. "Eighteen books," she said. "And what'll the nineteenth be?"

"*A Walk in the Fire* ends in 1951. If I go on with the Autobiography, I'll have to cover thirty-seven years before I reach today. I spent all those years writing books. Volume 5 would only be a book about the writing of books."

"And of course, nothing else happened—you wrote books, and the world stood still. Do you remember what you said when the Nazis surrendered in 1945? *There's nothing left to write about.*"

"Christ, did I say that?"

"You did, college-boy, and you said it to me."

"I didn't go to enough colleges."

"You went to too many," she said. "There'll always be something write about. As long as two people are left on the planet, one of them'll be skinning the other, coloring the air. . . ."

SCENE 131

METRO CONFERENCE No. 9 (November 1951)

With Mannix for the first time were the Company attorneys Maurice Benjamin and Saul Rittenberg, of the law firm of Loeb & Loeb. Maggie was represented by Sidney Cohn and you, but she stayed away, refusing to be present at what she regarded as a sale of merchandise. During the early part of the discussion, however, the talk was far afield.

MANNIX: . . . So when I say I'm all mixed up by this situation, I'm telling you the God's honest truth. Here you got a girl with an established name and the best part of her career still ahead of her. This is her home, Metro, this is where she belongs, and if not for this Committee thing, this is where she'd stay. But in her mind, she's got—what do you call it?—scruples about going back on her friends. . . .

SANFORD: How would you feel, Mr. Mannix, if one of those friends was you?

MANNIX: I wouldn't be in that position. And the people who are have no claim on her to give up her career for them. In this world, it's everybody for himself.

SANFORD: That's not a very good argument for this world.

MANNIX: It's the one we got.

COHN: Where is this leading? Maggie has said time and again that the stand she took at the Hearings is the only one she'll ever take. If she were going to cave in, she'd've done so for a Committee of Congress, not for a paycheck. If this has truly been her home for thirteen years, it's precisely because in behaving with honor, she honors the Company. . . .

BENJAMIN: Counselor, you're getting pretty high-flown about a client whose distinction, as I see it, is her defiance of Congress.

SANFORD: You've been hostile from the start, Mr. Benjamin, and that's what you're paid for. But if you speak of my wife again in that tone, you'll be sorry you were born.

MANNIX: What is this—a street-fight? We're here to settle a contract. Let's settle.

COHN: Would the Company care to make us an offer?

BENJAMIN: Why should we make an offer?

COHN: Because Miss Roberts has a valid contract, and the Company wants to break it.

BENJAMIN: You're forgetting the Morals Clause. Where would you be if the Company elected to invoke it?

COHN: Oh, come off it, Mr. Benjamin. Morals means morals, not politics, and if you try to equate the two, you're in for serious trouble.

MANNIX: We're not talking Morals Clause. We're talking settlement. That means paying out money. . . .

BENJAMIN: . . . that the Company might not owe.

MANNIX: We owe it. The question is, how much?

BENJAMIN: If the Company paid in full, it would come to Three Hundred and Twenty-five Thousand Dollars. I propose that sum as a ceiling and One Dollar as a floor.

COHN: I'll accept that as a starting-place. Before any numbers are mentioned, though, I'd like to remind the Company of what Miss Roberts is being asked to value in dollars. A distinguished career, which the Committee itself has recognized; a high salary over a five-year period; credits on films completed but not yet released; additions to her pension—and most important of all, a position among the best in her profession.

BENJAMIN: I think we're all aware of those things, Mr. Cohn.

MANNIX: What remains, then, is we get in touch with New York and find out how far we can go.

SANFORD: Maggie asked me to say this, Mr. Mannix. If a settlement is reached, she'll be receiving pay without working for it. She offers to render services, either here or abroad, for whatever sum the settlement calls for. It would be a private arrangement.

MANNIX: We appreciate her good will, John—tell her that. But it couldn't be kept private, and when it got noised around that Metro didn't really settle the contract, instead it was still using her, where would we be? Suppose it got in the column of that bastard Westbrook Pegler—we'd never live it down.

SANFORD: Well, she wanted me to say it, and I'll report that I said it.

MANNIX: Report this too: she's a high-grade person and a high-grade writer, and I hate to see her go.

COHN: Please give John a call when you've heard from New York. . . .

SCENE 132

MAGGIE, AS MERCHANDISE (November 1951)

On returning from the studio, you reported the course of the conference to her, and thereafter, for the day's remainder, your ways were lines that rarely crossed. Though usually within hearing of each other, you recall nothing that she said to you, nor whether in fact she spoke at all. You were in separate rooms, you thought, and you were breathing different air, wherefore you could not have known the weight of her sadness, nor could she have weighed yours.

For much of the afternoon, you stayed out-of-doors, and you were still there as the sun began to splinter through the trees, and the shadow of tall things grew from the smallest, even from a blade of grass. But all the while, in the light and the shade, you thought only of the impending trade of what Maggie valued for what she did not. On the morrow, an offer of money would be made for her career, and though she would not be there to hear the numbers, she'd know, wherever she was, that other numbers would oppose them — and that somewhere in between, a mean would be reached and a bargain struck. In that instant, as hands were being shaken, a life she loved would be taken away, and you knew of nothing that would requite her, surely not you. Dark within, you remained outside till it was dark there too. . . .

SCENE 133

METRO CONFERENCE No. 10 (November 1951)

In your record, you listed the names of those who were there, taking care this time with the spelling, but do they matter now, and did they then, the four you faced in the room that day, and with whom does it count that it was *Morris* Benjamin, and not Maurice? The record of the meeting is in narrative form, little more than the memorandum of a skirmish, and from it no sounds of engagement rise, no shots, no cries, no smash of things, and no smoke rolls across the page. It's quiet these days, that field, and its markers and monuments exist only in your mind, and only you can tell where the affrays occurred, and only you know what fell there. A certain number of dollars were offered.

A certain number of dollars. . . .

SCENE 134

METRO CONFERENCE No. 11 (November 1951)

It was held at the offices of the Company attorneys, and then and there was the bargain of the day before rendered in the crackjaw jargon of the law. At that time and that place, a paper was drawn, and, called *Agreement of*

320

Termination and Release, it provided that *Loew's Incorporated, a Delaware corporation (hereinafter referred to as Loew's), and Marguerite Roberts (hereinafter referred to as Roberts)*. . . , and from that beginning, in an onrush of bonebreaking syllables, the document went on to its stated end — the termination of *Roberts* and the release of *Loew's.*

To be paid at certain times and in a certain manner, valuable considerations were to pass from the *Delaware corporation* to *Roberts* (both hereinbefore mentioned), in return for which *Roberts* was to hold harmless forever *Loew's* and/or its associates, successors, and assigns — and save for signatures and handshakes (goodbye and good luck, no hard feelings), all was over between the party of the first part and the party of the second.

SCENE 135

NOT WITH A BANG NOT WITH A WHIMPER (November 21, 1951)

Later in the day, when the two-page instrument had been subscribed by *Loew's* and *Roberts,* farewells were taken of Ben Thau, who embraced Maggie and kissed her face, and Ed Mannix, who said something to her that you failed to hear, and then the two of you went downstairs to the floor below, where, in Room 243, you retrieved a pair of porcelain figurines, and then, after one last straightening of the Manet print, you descended to the street-level and walked toward the door.

"What did Mannix say?" you said.
"He called me darling again, and he called me dear."

This time, though, she did not cry.

THE COLOR OF THE AIR, XVII

House UnAmerican Activities Committee (HUAC) — 1951
ON REFUSING TO ANSWER

> *What do you think you are — a martyr?*
> *I think you're a God damn fool!*
> —a friend, 1951

You had dangerous thoughts, they said: in the round of your head swirled the smoke of subversion. It dwelt, they found, in the aqueduct of Sylvius and the fissures of Rolando, it spanned the twain of hemispheres, it tainted too the cells of Purkinje, and when they put you on the stand, they'd find proof of what they knew in the membranes and meninges of your mind. There in those gyri, those gray and white meanders, the vapors of revolution rolled. Behind your teeth and eyes, they claimed, deep in the fosses of your brain, plans were being framed for an alien order, one that put the top dogs at the bottom and the bottom at the top. You were a danger, therefore, to them that bought and sold in the temples and them that trafficked in doves.

When made to appear before them, you knew that you stood among the priests and the Pharisees, that soon you'd be tendered silver for the mention of a name. And though so it was, they didn't demand a Jesus from the garden beyond Kidron—they'd settle for less than a Savior, they said, a cheaper brand of merchandise, a smaller size would do. Give us, they adjured you, the equivalent of the thieves; surrender, they suggested, some unimportant lives, the faceless, the unheard-of; arraign the put-upon, the sodden rejectamenta, the dreamer, the dejected; cast blame upon those that none will ever miss. We'll doom the sons-of-bitches—all you do is spell out whom.

It struck you as strange, their offer of absolution: we'll wash you, they said, of the deep-dyed sin, the doing-in of your brother; we'll relieve you of guilt, we'll speak to your God, tell Him how you anguished, say it was we who constrained you, we who turned the screw. Come, they said, how hard can it be to peach on a nobody, a nix or two, a pair of treys? What stays you, the stares of those whose nights are long? What gives you pause, what debt do you owe to drawers of water, to the ruck that sits below the salt, what writs run that you dare not scorn?

You gave them nothing, and they paid in kind. There were no badges of honor for you, no cordons, ribbons, wreaths of laurel. From then on, you were without a country, a wanderer within it, an internal outcast. You'd worked yourself loose, like some minor component of a giant machine, a shim, a grommet, a superfluous spring, and ground by its shaking, you made a small sound for a while and then fell silent, as if you'd worn away. *What do you think you are—a martyr?*, you heard your friend say.

How could he have thought you'd so suppose when you'd never felt the thorn, never endured the nail? He knew, as you did, that you'd merely chanced on your hill of skulls and pondered on the purpose of the pyre. How, a martyr, when you were your own victim?—you'd chosen the stake, you'd lit the fire. *I think you're a God damn fool!*, he said, and in the ways of the world, you were, but did he deeply believe his words, or did he simply say them, having found them in his mouth? Why his anger?, you sometimes wondered, what harm had you done him in giving none but yourself away? What made him mock you? What did he note in a Simple Simon, what could he not bear to see and hear? Or was he seeing and hearing himself, was he on the stand instead of you, was he giving you away?

Printed March 1989 in Santa Barbara & Ann Arbor
for the Black Sparrow Press by Graham Mackintosh &
Edwards Brothers Inc. Design by Barbara Martin.
This edition is published in paper wrappers; there
are 300 cloth trade copies; 150 hardcover copies
have been numbered & signed by the author; & 26
copies handbound in boards by Earle Gray have been
lettered & signed by the author.

JOHN SANFORD is the name of the principal character in *The Water Wheel*, a first novel by Julian Shapiro published in 1933. Adopting it as a pseudonym, the writer has used it ever since. Born in the Harlem section of New York on 31 May 1904, he attended the public schools of that city, Lafayette College, and finally Fordham University, where he earned a degree in Law. He was admitted to the Bar in 1929, and at about the same time, influenced by his friend Nathanael West, he too began to write. Published at the outset in vanguard magazines of the period—*The New Review, Tambour, Pagany, Contact*—he soon abandoned the legal profession and produced through the years a series of eight novels. Concerned always with the course of American history, he interspersed his fiction with critical commentaries on the national life from the Left-Liberal point-of-view. As a result of such dissent, he was summoned before the House Committee on Un-American Activities, and for refusing to cooperate with it, he was blacklisted. In spite of difficulty in obtaining publication, he continued to write in his chosen vein, ultimately stripping his work down to its historical content only. During the last several years, he has written four books of creative interpretations of the Land of the Free: *A More Goodly Country, View from This Wilderness, To Feed Their Hopes,* and *The Winters of That Country,* all four titles deriving from a single passage in William Bradford's *History of Plymouth Plantation.* John Sanford has been married to the writer Marguerite Roberts since 1938; they are long-time residents of Santa Barbara, California.